The Peripheral Centre

JAPANESE SOCIETY SERIES

General Editor: Yoshio Sugimoto

Lives of Young Koreans in Japan
Yasunori Fukuoka

Globalization and Social Change in Contemporary Japan
J.S. Eades Tom Gill Harumi Befu

Coming Out in Japan: The Story of Satoru and Ryuta
Satoru Ito and Ryuta Yanase

Japan and Its Others:
Globalization, Difference and the Critique of Modernity
John Clammer

Hegemony of Homogeneity:
An Anthropological Analysis of *Nihonjinron*
Harumi Befu

Foreign Migrants in Contemporary Japan
Hiroshi Komai

A Social History of Science and Technology in
Contempory Japan, Volume 1
Shigeru Nakayama

Farewell to Nippon: Japanese Lifestyle Migrants in Australia
Machiko Sato

The Peripheral Centre:
Essays on Japanese History and Civilization
Johann P. Arnason

The Peripheral Centre

Essays on Japanese History and Civilization

Johann P. Arnason

Trans Pacific Press
Melbourne

First published in 2002 by
Trans Pacific Press, PO Box 120, Rosanna, Melbourne, Victoria 3084, Australia
Telephone: +61 3 9459 3021 Fax: +61 3 9457 5923
E-mail: enquiries@transpacificpress.com
Website: http://www.transpacificpress.com

Copyright © Trans Pacific Press 2001

Designed and set by digital environs Melbourne. enquiries@digitalenvirons.com

Printed in Australia by McPherson's Printing Group, Maryborough, Victoria

Distributors

Australia
Bushbooks
PO Box 1958, Gosford, NSW 2250
Telephone: (02) 4323-3274
Fax: (02) 9212-2468
Email: bushbook@ozemail.com.au

USA and Canada
International Specialized Book Services (ISBS)
5824 N. E. Hassalo Street
Portland, Oregon 97213-3644
USA
Telephone: (800) 944-6190
Fax: (503) 280-8832
Email: orders@isbs.com
Web: http://www.isbs.com

Japan
Kyoto University Press
Kyodai Kaikan
15-9 Yoshida Kawara-cho
Sakyo-ku, Kyoto 606-8305
Telephone: (075) 761-6182
Fax: (075) 761-6190
Email: sales@kyoto-up.gr.jp
Web: http://www.kyoto-up.gr.jp

UK and Europe
Drake International Services
PO Box 733, Cardiff CF14 2YX
UK
Telephone: (0292) 056-0343
Fax: (0292) 056-1631
Email: info@drakeint.co.uk
Web: http://www.drakeint.co.uk

All rights reserved. No production of any part of this book may take place without the written permission of Trans Pacific Press.

The publishers gratefully acknowledge the assistance of the Japan Foundation in the publication of this volume.

ISSN 1443–9670 (Japanese Society Series)
ISBN 1–8768–43 95–0 (Hardback)
ISBN 1–8768–43 07–1 (Paperback)

National Library of Australia Cataloging in Publication Data

Arnason, Johann P., 1940–.
  The peripheral centre : essays on Japanese history and civilization.
  Bibliography.
  Includes index.
  ISBN 1 876843 07 1 (pbk.).
  ISBN 1 876843 95 0.
  1. Japan - Civilization. 2. Japan - Social conditions.
  3. Japan - Civilization - East Asian influences. 4. Japan –
  Civilization – Western influences. 5. East and West.
  I. Title. (Series : Japanese society series).

Contents

Preface	vii
Acknowledgements	ix
1 Introduction: The Peripheral Centre and Its Transformations	1
2 East Asian Approaches: Region, History and Civilization	24
3 Comparing Japan: The Return to Asia	41
4 Is Japan a Civilization *Sui Generis?*	66
5 State Formation in Japan and the West	92
6 Elias in Japan: State Formation, Military Elites and Organized Violence	117
7 Multiple Modernities and Civilizational Contexts: Reflections on the Japanese Experience	132
8 Miracles and Mirages: Comparative Perspectives on Japanese Capitalism	158
Notes	203
Index	225

Preface

The papers collected in this book are offshoots of a larger project. The oldest one, 'State formation in Japan and the West', was written in connection with work on an earlier book; the others reflect more recent attempts to develop ideas adumbrated in the book.

To write on Japanese history without using Japanese-language sources (which I cannot read) is a very risky venture. But the standard excuse is as valid as ever: Japan is simply so important for comparative historical sociology that non-specialists will always be tempted to enter the field, and their work should be judged by its results. Comparative perspectives, with particular reference to Europe on the one hand and East Asia on the other, are central to all arguments developed in the book. Some fundamental themes – civilization, state formation, and the multiple forms of modernity – reappear more frequently than others, but I do not think that the discussion has become unduly repetitive.

Theoretical premises, explicit or unstated, are indispensable to comparative studies. No systematic theoretical statement is to be found in this book, but some of the papers raise theoretical questions in connection with specific approaches to Japan. The most extensive discussions of that kind deal with problems of civilizational theory; this is, despite recent signs of growing interest, still an underdeveloped branch of social theory, and it seems particularly likely to benefit from closer contact with the Japanese experience.

The last, longest and most recent paper discusses various aspects of Japanese capitalism. Triumphalist visions of the capitalist order as a revealed truth of history have been characteristic of the last decade, and are not about to disappear, but more balanced views on capitalism as a complex social and historical phenomenon – not as an economic machine – seem to be gaining ground. The tribulations of the Japanese economy during the last fifteen years have overshadowed a long historical experience which ought to be central to any debate on different paths of capitalist development. This paper should be read as an exploratory overview of themes and issues; the topic is too important to be left out of the present inquiry, but I hope that some of the questions will be taken up by writers with more expertise in the field.

Acknowledgements

Thanks are due, first and foremost, to Yoshio Sugimoto for his abiding interest in my search for holes in the *kanji* curtain; to the Japan Foundation, for financial assistance, and to Irmela Hijiya-Kirschnereit and Shmuel N. Eisenstadt for their support in that connection.

The more recent parts of the book – both new papers and revised versions of old ones – owe much to my stay at the Swedish Collegium for Advanced Studies in the Social Sciences, Uppsala, during the academic year 1999–2000. I am grateful for this opportunity to work in an exceptionally hospitable and stimulating environment, and the results can be expected to extend beyond this book.

My attempts to understand Japan have benefited from conversations with many people. A complete list would be too long to be included here, but in addition to those mentioned above, the following should be noted: Augustin Berque, Christoph Deutschmann, Greg and Toshiko Ellis, Andrew Feenberg, Chalmers and Sheila Johnson, Katō Tetsurō, Kawamura Nozomu, Mishima Ken'ichi, Herman Ooms, Ian Reader, Wolfgang Seifert and Richard Tanter. Maria and Jan have shared my interest and reinforced it by developing their own versions of the Japanese connection.

I am indebted to office staff in the School of Social Sciences, La Trobe University, for help with the production of the book. Bronwyn Bardsley solved technical problems which were altogether beyond my comprehension; Merle Parker and Elaine Young typed large parts of the manuscript.

Some of the papers have been published elsewhere. The second and the fifth appeared in *Thesis Eleven*, no. 57 (1999), and *Theory, Culture and Society*, vol. 12, no. 3 (1996); the third was first published in *Japanstudien,* vol. 10, 1998. They are reprinted here with the permission of the original publishers, Sage Publications and iudicium verlag. An earlier version of the essay on multiple modernities was presented to an international conference on 'Japan in comparative perspective' at the International Research Center for Japanese Studies in Kyoto in January 1998, and published in the proceedings (International Symposium no. 10, 1998). I am grateful to the International Research Center for the invitation, and for the permission to publish the revised and expanded version here. Earlier drafts of the fourth and sixth paper were presented to a conference on 'Japan in the social sciences' at the German Institute for Japanese Studies in Tokyo in September 1997, and to the Norbert Elias Centenary Conference in Amsterdam in December 1997. Thanks are due to the organizers of both events.

1 Introduction: The Peripheral Centre and Its Transformations

Historical outlines

The following essays were written at different times, and although they link up with earlier work, the variety of themes and contexts may be more visible than the underlying connections. A retrospective survey may help to clarify the overall direction of a project which has been pursued in somewhat unsystematic ways. The Japanese experience is, as I would like to show, of singular but still not fully understood importance for social theory and comparative history; the particular aspects explored here are perhaps best understood in relation to a basic conceptual distinction which has proved difficult to integrate into more established modes of theorizing, but continues to signal uncharted regions between theory and history. Notions of centre and periphery are most easily applicable in geographical and geopolitical contexts, and have most recently gained currency in the 'world system' version of geo-economics (the preference for 'core' rather than 'centre' in the latter school of thought is immaterial to the issue: core states or societies are those which benefit from central positions). A more ambitious proposal to use them as key categories of social ontology raises questions of the most fundamental kind. Within the framework of a brief introduction, links to the problems discussed below cannot be substantiated in detail. But we can at least note some major points of contact.

A brief glance at the Japanese trajectory is enough to set the course for further debate. On the one hand, the *longue durée* of Japanese history is characterized by unusually self-contained patterns. On the other hand, the geopolitical setting has undeniably played a crucial role; its effects have been both enabling and constraining, and the balance between the two aspects has shifted at critical junctures. The Japanese case thus invites reflection on links between the two levels – the geographical and the sociological – of the problematic of centre and periphery. But more specific connections are implicit in familiar features and standard accounts of the Japanese tradition. A whole series of paradoxes concerning the relationship between centre and periphery has been noted by observers and historians whose insights can be taken as starting-points for a more theoretical analysis. In several regards and successive phases, the key distinction seems to take a self-relativizing turn: structures, traditions or institutions derive their centrality from peripheral contexts, but at the same time, the perceived disparity between central status and peripheral condition becomes a source of more or less sustained aspirations to change.

This pattern is, to begin with, evident in the history of Japan's relations with the rest of the East Asian region. During the early imperial phase of Chinese history, the Japanese islands were a remote periphery, increasingly open to cultural influence but outside the orbit of political or military expansion; the subsequent creation of an autonomous Japanese centre took a much more original turn. It was preceded by a transitional phase which lasted from the early third to the late sixth century AD. After the disintegration of the first Chinese empire, successor dynasties and Inner Asian conquerors disputed the territory which it had controlled, while a cluster of more or less consolidated states emerged on both sides of the Korea Strait. A peripheral state system thus developed alongside a permanently unstable central one. When the Sui and T'ang dynasties rebuilt the Chinese empire on an enlarged scale, the insular part of the peripheral system was integrated into a state which had probably set out to achieve more ambitious goals. The Yamato kingdom thus mutated into imperial Japan. This new centre made extensive use of Chinese models and remained open to selective borrowing, but drew on adapted indigenous traditions to claim a divine origin which made it more than equal to the Chinese counterpart. The refusal of incorporation into the Chinese world order did not lead to imperial rivalry (apart from a Mongol invasion of Japan, launched from China, and an abortive confrontation in Korea at the end of the sixteenth century, there was no Sino-Japanese conflict between the seventh-century demarcation and the nineteenth-century Western disruption of the regional order). Rather, it kept open a cultural space for re-combinations of Chinese and Japanese sources. China remained central to the Japanese imaginary, often in ways which had more to do with visions from afar than with historical realities, but the indigenous centre was – throughout the transformations to be discussed below – strong enough to sustain a permanent counter-current. The interaction of the two trends could lead to mutual reinvigoration: during the last largely self-contained phase of East Asian history, the Tokugawa regime combined strictly limited economic contacts and complete political isolation from China with a more intensive ideological use of the Confucian tradition. In response to this simultaneous affirmation of autonomy and dependence, new interpretations of nativist themes developed into a more radical vision of Japan as a superior and pre-eminently sacred centre. The ideological legacy of this epoch was of major importance when Japan's place and role in the region had to be redefined after 1868. In particular, the cultural legitimacy claimed by the Japanese empire at its most expansionistic – a mission to master and transform the East Asian region as a whole, through methods which ranged from assimilation in Korea to informal control in China – drew on both sides of the bipolar tradition. Invocations of Japanese uniqueness and appeals to a broader civilizational identity could be balanced in different ways as circumstances changed.

More figurative notions of centre and periphery have been used to describe developments within Japan after the seventh-century transformation. The imperial centre, constructed as a symbol of mimetic rivalry with the older and more advanced Chinese one, underwent a long-drawn-out process of decomposition and lost power to a military state whose core institutions had taken shape in the margin of the traditional regime. Relations between the two foci of state formation changed over time, and internal shifts occurred on both sides; spatial separation was important at crucial moments, but less so at other stages, and one version of the military state relocated its headquarters to the imperial capital. In the present context, the long-term redistribution of central and peripheral roles is more relevant than the changing patterns of coexistence. After an initial phase of power sharing and an unsuccessful counter-offensive, the imperial institution was confined to the periphery of the power structure. But although it clearly lost some of its symbolic authority when its material resources were at their lowest ebb (in the late fifteenth and early sixteenth centuries), it was never openly denied a central place in the symbolic order of the Japanese tradition, and the regime which completed the transfer of power to a unified military state was also intent on restoring and instrumentalizing imperial prestige. On the other hand, the military state rose to become an effective and uncontested centre of power, and there were significant attempts to translate its victory into an appropriate ideological language, but the ultimate failure to sever symbolic links to the imperial centre left the military rulers in an incongruous position. In that sense, their strategy of centre-building had a peripheral character.

The Meiji transition to advanced modernity began with a restructuring of state power and a fusion of the previously separate parts of the political order. But as historians of modern Japan have often noted, the integration of the imperial institution into a bureaucratic, developmentalist and expansionist nation-state gave rise to new structural problems. Direct imperial rule was never meant to be more than an ideological construct; when it was adapted to the principle of constitutional government, the sacred authority ascribed to the *tennō* became an obstacle to the exercise of political leadership. The sovereign was too detached from the political process to become an effective ruler, but his prerogatives were exorbitant enough to hamper the workings of the governmental system. Rival factions within the ruling elite sought to legitimize their strategies through direct access to the emperor or imaginary union with the 'imperial will', and the regime as a whole was vulnerable to protest in the name of a restorationist project which professed loyalty to the imperial centre. In short, the Meiji pattern of politics was characterized by unstable distinctions and unsolved problems of coordination between central and peripheral parts of the regime. In the final phase, these inbuilt tensions became acute on an imperial scale.

Finally, the distinction between centre and periphery has some bearing on Japan's postwar history. To cut a complicated story short, a strategic reorientation gave first priority to economic development, set strict limits to independent political action in the global arena, and ruled out the option of re-militarization. Economic affairs thus became more central to interstate competition, and the traditional concerns of power politics correspondingly less so; this shift prompted some observers to argue that post-imperial Japan was a society with an 'empty centre' or that it lacked a state in the full and proper sense. If we describe the new constellation as another redefinition of central and peripheral aspects of social life, we are obviously stretching the figurative meaning of the twin terms even further than in the above context of cultural and political patterns. A closer look at the underlying assumptions is therefore in order.

Theorizing centres and peripheries

These introductory observations do not go beyond the basics of accepted facts about Japanese history. More controversial questions will arise if we pause to reflect on the concepts of centre and periphery, and on the theoretical connotations of their use in social and historical inquiry. This detour will, in due course, open up new perspectives on the Japanese experience; but we must begin at the level of elementary issues.

The distinction between centre and periphery is not a commonplace of social theory. The two terms – understood as sociological concepts – were introduced by Edward Shils, and S. N. Eisenstadt has incorporated them into a framework for the comparative analysis of civilizations, but apart from these pioneering efforts, there has been very little discussion of the subject (although a more or less consciously metaphorical use of the distinction is not at all uncommon). Affinities with other debates will, however, be easier to establish if we reconstruct the broader background to Shils's argument. His case for analyzing societies in terms of centres and peripheries states some aspects of the problematic much more clearly than others, and some clarification of the less explicit points is needed to redress the balance. As Shils developed his ideas, he became more and more aware of disagreements with the structural-functionalist mainstream; definitions suitable for our purposes are therefore more easily found in his retrospective reflections than in the text where he first spoke of central and peripheral zones in social life. The following summary seems particularly instructive: 'The center exercises authority and power; it also espouses and embodies beliefs about things thought, by itself and by other centers and by their peripheries, to be of transcendent importance, that is, "serious". "Serious" things are things thought to be fundamental, that is, which affect the fate of human beings on earth, in life and in death...Being a center means designating the proper objects of attention, both by command or recommendation, or by embodiment.'[1] Other formulations in a similar vein serve to round off the statement: 'What is important is that certain social actions and functions are concentrated rather than dispersed...The point of concentration of those functions is a collectivity or a part of a collectivity or it is an institution or institutions around which a collectivity is formed; the part of the collectivity which is around the center is the periphery or the peripheries.'[2]

A centre is, in other words, a complex constellation whose focal point can shift from one part to another. It may be seen as a cluster of meanings, a collectivity or a set of institutions. As for the periphery, it is obviously a more derivative category, but Shils argues that it should not be treated as a residual one. Although his positive descriptions of the periphery are much less conclusive than those of the centre, their implications can perhaps be summed up in three points. The first defining feature is a certain *distance* from the centre: no periphery is completely controlled or permeated by a centre, and no centre is fully accessible from a periphery. On that basis, a more or less extensive *autonomy* of peripheral actors, institutions or cultures may be achieved, and this can in turn lead to active *contestation* of the centre. Here the argument seems to trail off. Shils does not pursue the question of differences between peripheral rejections of the centre, demands for inclusion and visions of unity transcending the distinction as such. But his emphasis on pluralism on both sides strengthens the case for a non-residual conception of the periphery. He stresses that 'the concept of center does not imply the singularity or internal unity of a center...; there is probably no center without competing centers within the same society.'[3] The plurality and heterogeneity of peripheral sectors is even more obvious, and it is less closely linked to rivalry. Peripheries are, by definition, more dispersed and mutually isolated than centers. There is, however, another side to peripheral diversity: 'Some sectors of the periphery may perform central functions for other peripheries; they might do so as agents of the center, or they do so against the center, or they might be a center of a part of the periphery which is relatively isolated from the center.'[4] If central zones can emerge within the periphery, we can by implication speak of peripherality or peripheralization with regard to parts of the centre, or to some centres in relation to others. The distinction can, in other words, be redrawn on each side of the original border, and there seems to be no a priori answer to the question whether this multiplication leaves a main dividing line intact.

Although Shils makes no explicit reference to hermeneutics, his interpretation of centre and periphery is hermeneutical in the sense that it is meant to articulate and deepen the self-understanding of both sides. As he notes, the mutual orientations of centres and peripheries are subjective states; but the specifics of these states depend on cultural contexts and vary with the transformations of overall cultural patterns. A common denominator is, however, inherent in the distinction as such. If the concepts of centre and periphery are to be understood as translations of mutual perceptions, the metaphorical spatial figuration which they indicate is by the same token constitutive of the social relations between the two sectors, and it can be expected to result in a spatial demarcation of the centre. Shils admits that the centre 'almost always has a definite location within the bounded territory in which the society lives'[5], and that this amounts to more than the spatial location which is a defining feature of all social action. But a comparative analysis of such spatial configurations is not on his agenda; he is much more interested in theorizing the non-spatial essence of centrality.

It remains to consider the reasons for attempting to re-conceptualize societies in terms of centres and peripheries. In retrospect (and in light of debates unfolding across the spectrum of social theory), Shils's model can be seen as an early response to a series of central questions and compared to other views of the same problematic. The most fundamental issue has to do with social integration. Shils was dissatisfied with the notion of integration through shared values and norms, and claimed that those who defended it – especially Talcott Parsons – had never been able to spell out an intelligible meaning. This criticism prefigures later objections to an over-integrated image of society. Arguments in that vein, mostly advanced by authors whose ideas and sensibilities were otherwise vastly different from Shils's (including Alain Touraine, Michael Mann and Anthony Giddens), led to critical reappraisals of the whole sociological tradition. Shils did not develop this theme in detail, but some obvious implications of his distinction between centre and periphery may be noted. It highlights the incomplete, uneven and asymmetric character of integration; in a somewhat more oblique fashion, it points to the role of the imagination in integrative patterns (the spatial metaphor is an order-building and identity-maintaining image).

Other aspects of Shils's analysis relate to the problematic of integration in more indirect ways. His most extensive discussion of the classical legacy and its shortcomings links the concept of centre to Weber's concept of charisma. As he argues, Weber's account of the charismatic phenomenon was inadequate in that it identified high intensity of meaning with exceptional qualities and eruptive forces outside the domain of ordered social life. By contrast, the concept of centre serves to underline the omnipresence and permanence of the charismatic dimension – the contact with foundational meaning – in social formations, as well as the unequal distribution of charismatic authority. This revised version of a key Weberian theme could be combined with another line of criticism, absent from Shils's work but in part concerned wit the same set of questions. If Weber's interpretation of charisma reflects – in a displaced and unbalanced way – an underlying but undeveloped conception of culture as a meaningful articulation of the world, Shils's search for what he calls a more comprehensive understanding is a significant step towards a thematization of this background.[6] A more explicit grasp of culture and its world-constitutive capacities would add another layer to Shils's problematic: the cultural modes of world articulation and the patterns of social integration intertwine with each other, and their interrelations vary from one civilizational setting to another. These connections and differences have been obscured by the dominant and uniform models of integration through norms and values. If the world-related cultural context is taken into account, one of Shils's most provocative statements can be interpreted in more nuanced terms. As he puts it in his first formulation of the idea of centre, the aim is to spell out the permanently valid core of the principle *cuius regio, eius religio.* In light of his more detailed analyses, this is best understood as a variation on a theme of comparative civilizational studies: the widely shared view that cultural frameworks of power are reducible to legitimizing devices is grounded in an uncritical generalization of specific European traditions (not the European tradition as a whole), and it fails to account for the more direct input of cultural orientations into the definition and constitution of power structures.[7] The concept of centre is clearly intended to capture this closer involvement (in contrast to the more external relation suggested by the concept of legitimation). Although Shils undertook no comparative analysis, his reflections on centres and their relations to the rest of society are easily linked to the insights of other authors who have stressed the cultural variations to the meaning of power, as well as the equally variable ways of representing it in a public arena.[8] The cultural plasticity and polymorphous character of power are in large measure due to its embeddedness in patterns of articulation. This cultural context is relevant to another theme which Shils touches only in passing: the ambiguity of social conflict. As he notes, the attitude of radical – even revolutionary – leaders and movements to existing centres is often hard to define in unequivocal terms. Demands for recognition and strategies of appropriation intermingle with visions of more radical antagonism. Other theorists – notably Alain Touraine – have taken a more sustained interest in this problem and shown that antagonistic social forces can invoke alternative versions of shared cultural models.

To conclude our summary of Shils's ideas, two additional topics should be mentioned. Empires and civilizations have been notoriously marginal to sociological discourse; significant attempts to theorize both subjects did not develop into more continuous inquiry. Shils's concepts of centre and periphery apply to imperial as well as civilizational formations. According to his own testimony, the explicit idea of centre – foreshadowed by several converging lines of argument – grew out of his study of relationships between India and the British empire. More generally speaking, empires are structured around centres of a particularly prominent and authoritative kind; at least in the most important cases, they combine concentrated power with formative cultural models. There is, in other words, a civilizational side to the imperial phenomenon, but since civilizations do not always crystallize into empires, the two categories must be kept apart. For Shils, 'a civilization is a constellation of societies, sharing certain features.'[9] This definition is in line with the classics of the French sociological tradition, but Shils adds that 'a civilization is marked by the centrality of one or several particular societies'[10], and that 'centers rise and wane within a particular civilization.' Civilizational unity and identity are thus predicated on more or less convergent relations between centres and peripheries. Comparative analysis could begin with the difference between monocentric and polycentric civilizations, but the composition of centres operative at a civilizational level is another obvious variable. Spatial, cultural, institutional and collective aspects can combine in different ways.

As we have seen, a closer look at the concepts of centre and periphery opens up far-reaching theoretical perspectives. But the only systematic attempt to expand Shils's frame of reference was made by S. N. Eisenstadt. His adaptation of Shils's categories begins within the domain of political sociology and continues in the broader context of civilizational theory; in the latter connection, his analysis of the Japanese historical experience – the most detailed of his civilizational case studies – is particularly interesting. He accepts Shils's distinction between centre and periphery as a key to important yet widely misunderstood dimensions of societal differentiation, but adds a specific reference to the political sphere: it 'has a special, although not exclusive relation to…centrality.'[11] This privilege of the political, due to its key role in integrating power and meaning, is most evident when asserted on an imperial scale: 'It is in…empires that we find the fullest differentiation, specification and crystallization of centers in general and of political centers in particular as autonomous, structurally and symbolically distinct entities.'[12] But alongside the particular emphasis on political centres, Eisenstadt gives another twist to Shils's problematic, less visible at first but increasingly important to his later work. Centres are salient and authoritative foci of collective identity. A strong tendency to neglect the question of collective identity – or conflate it with other issues – was inherent in basic assumptions of the sociological tradition: an over-integrated image of society lent itself to identification with a macro-subject (or with the more implicit notion of subjectivity built into the idea of the social system). The constitution of society could thus be theorized in ways more or less directly suggestive of the formation of collective subjectivity. When social integration is reinterpreted from a less pre-programmed angle (as in Shils's analysis of centres and peripheries), its multifocal and multi-dimensional character becomes clearer and the patterns of collective identity are more easily distinguishable from the cultural, institutional and organizational structures of social formations. Shils's concept of centre is designed to aid new approaches on all these levels of analysis, but it was left to Eisenstadt to spell out specific implications for the question of collective identity, and to analyze civilizational variations to their connections with social structures.

The perspectives outlined above are central to Eisenstadt's work on Japanese civilization. The details of his interpretation of Japan, as well as of contrasts and parallels with other civilizations, are beyond the scope of the present discussion; here I will only deal with the arguments most directly related to the problematic of centre and periphery. Eisenstadt's relatively brief comments on this aspect of the Japanese experience begin with an emphatic acknowledgement of eventful history: 'Changes in the structure of regional and urban centers continually developed, especially during the monarchical and feudal ages, with the relative strength and fortunes of the various centers changing greatly over time – some even disappearing or becoming incorporated into others. These fluctuations were often closely related to the construction of strong regional identities.'[13] But this variety of contending and successive centres stands in stark contrast to stability at another level: 'The various centers were continuously embedded and incorporated within the broad framework of the Japanese collectivity and its central symbols, often epitomized in the symbolism of the emperor.'[14] Eisenstadt thus distinguishes between two levels of centrality. One of them has to do with strong and enduring symbols, grounded in comprehensive cultural visions of the world and embodied in core institutions. But the reference to the imperial institution serves as a reminder that the symbolic centre has a political content. Practical effects on the exercise of power varied from one historical phase to another: The earlier history of the imperial institution included phases of direct rule, followed by a lasting separation from power structures which nevertheless continued to derive prestige and legitimacy from links to the imperial centre. The imaginary institution of imperial rule after 1868 differed from both these traditional alternatives. Imperial sovereignty became a more operative principle, but did not translate into an effective reunion of authority and power. At the same time, the nation-state that inherited and incorporated the imperial institution drew on the legacy of recurrent centre formation at the second level. Eisenstadt's description of the changing forms and fortunes of secondary centres implies that the history of the military state – from Kamakura to Edo – should be interpreted in this context, rather than as a series of attempts to construct complementary or alternative centres at the first level. But as he is careful to note, the exclusive primacy of the imperial institution did not immunize it against history: the uses and applications of the central symbolism reflected changing constellations of social forces. It is all the more noteworthy that these successive reorientations could be accommodated within a framework which retained both a cultural and an institutional identity.

When it comes to comparisons with other civilizations, the difference between two levels of centre formation is – as such – not a distinctive feature. More or less similar hierarchies develop within every configuration of multiple centres. The significant contrasts have to do with the internal constitution of centres, as well as the patterns of their interrelations. The dynamics of conflict and change, and even more so the level and content of ideological projects associated with them, vary from one civilizational context to another. To cut a long story short, Eisenstadt's comparative framework focuses on the characteristics which mark Japan as a non-Axial civilization and set it apart from the Axial ones (principally Europe, India and China).[15] For present purposes, a summary definition of Axial traditions is enough: they originate in cultural breakthroughs which open up new horizons of meaning and – as a result – new perspectives for the ideological interpretations of power as well as protest. These parallel historical experiences do not lead to uniform relations between centres and peripheries, but they are reflected in similarly high-powered fusions of ideological projects with the formations and transformations of social power. European civilization was, as Eisenstadt sees it, characterized by a particularly overt, conflict-ridden and ideologed pluralism of centres; the structural and institutional affinities between medieval Europe and medieval Japan – often noted by historians – are beyond dispute, but the broader contexts were very different. Indian civilization was less polycentric and its core cultural orientations less conducive to acute ideological conflict, but the deeply ambiguous relationship between Brahmins and kings blocked the formation of a unified centre. China's exceptionally durable imperial order may seem most similar to the Japanese patterns, and the lasting influence of Chinese culture on Japan strengthens this impression, but Eisenstadt argues that the underlying civilizational structures differ in fundamental ways. The cultural model of the Chinese imperial centre was derived from Axial sources (even if the transcendental and universal thrust was more muted than in other Axial civilizations), and the ideological dynamic due to that background also found expression in tensions within the core power structure; there was no Japanese parallel to the recurrent conflict between Confucian reformism and the despotic tendencies inherent in imperial rule. The Japanese centre maintained unbroken links to a particularistic collective identity, capable of extension to a broader social basis at a later stage, and it preserved basic elements of an archaic cultural tradition (with a strong emphasis on the mutual embeddedness of natural, cultural and sacred orders) which limited the impact of borrowings from other civilizations.

Deep structures and historical dynamics

The tradition which Eisenstadt describes as an enduring non-Axial pattern can be traced back to the beginnings of the Japanese imperial state and to the most formative phase of interaction with Chinese civilization; in more precise terms, the seventh century AD stands out as a historical watershed. All conjectures about more remote origins are on much more uncertain ground. If we accept that the result of Japan's encounter with the restored Chinese empire was an original civilizational contellation, rather than an imitative construct with residual indigenous trappings (the image of Japan as a 'satellite civilization' should be laid to rest), there are two possible interpretations to be considered. We can either posit a set of pre-given cultural premises, anterior to the encounter and resilient enough to remain operative throughout later phases; or stress the creative synthesis which took place in a specific historical setting and gave rise to a framework for further interaction between indigenous and imported traditions. For the sake of convenience (and without any claim to conformity with other uses of both terms), the first approach may be described as culturalist and the second as historicist. Any attempt to theorize the Japanese experience as a distinctive historical world must opt for one view or the other, but in either case, the evidence is too fragmentary and ambiguous for conclusive proof to be possible. Assuming that both positions will remain in debate, we can nevertheless try to justify a preference for one or the other in terms of relative strength.

The culturalist view can only be defended on the basis of evidence for entrenched and pervasive modes of thought or visions of the world. Eisenstadt's account of the Japanese cultural tradition and its inbuilt interpretive schemes is therefore crucial to his overall culturalist line of argument. The permanence of specific cultural premises throughout a long history of structural and institutional change, as well as their manifest affinity with archaic cultures in other settings, lend support to the idea of a non-Axial continuum. A critique of this claim need not contest the existence of certain strikingly persistent cultural traits: the question is rather how they fit into a broader context, and from that point of view, a strong case can be made for the historicist approach. As I have argued elsewhere, a historicist analysis of the seventh-century transformation seems justified for a number of reasons.[16] The encounter with China was only the beginning of a complex process which transformed both the borrowed models and the domestic background; a radical and comprehensive restructuring of institutions was accompanied by a reconstruction of cultural frameworks; religious traditions were combined and rearticulated in a way which left no native substratum intact. The details of the argument will not be recapitulated here. But a brief sketch of the long-term results – with particular reference to the configurations of centres and peripheries – may help to clarify the historicist perspective.

The interpretation to be discussed here lays a strong emphasis on creativity. There are two sides to such claims: on the one hand, they stress the discontinuity and novelty of emergent patterns, but on the other hand, the same patterns appear as long-term formative frameworks for subsequent historical developments. Creative innovations become traditional paradigms. Major examples of this dialectic (in the strict sense of a unity of opposites) are easily found, and they show that it can take very different forms. One of the most prominent cases is the creation of the Chinese imperial model (in two stages of unequal duration and different character, represented by the Qin and Han dynasties): it gave rise to an exceptionally enduring tradition, not immune to breakdowns but capable of survival in imagined versions and re-embodiment under new circumstances. Another empire merged at roughly the same time on the western margin of the Eurasian continent, but it did not create a comparable paradigm of imperial rule. When the Roman realm finally mutated into a Christian empire, the new model could not provide more than a temporary solution to growing structural problems, and although it was to leave multiple imprints on later history, its mode of survival was less clear-cut than the Chinese one.

These two examples of macro-historical paradigms, directly or indirectly operative on a very large scale, contrast sharply with the case to be considered here. The core structures of the Japanese tradition proved eminently suitable for the adaptive containment of historical change, but they were also markedly 'incapable of travelling', to invert the phrase which Durkheim and Mauss used to describe the diffusion of civilizational models. Spatial confinement was, in this case, the other side of historical continuity. The persistence of this pattern is all the more remarkable in view of the fact that it took shape through interaction with one of the imperial traditions mentioned above. It seems convenient to refer to the crucial phase of this process as the 'seventh-century transformation', but the period in question was at least a long seventh century (the *Cambridge History of Japan* dates the 'century of reform' from 587 to 710), and a case could be made for the two hundred years from the introduction of Buddhism to the death of Emperor Shōmu (756). This was, in other words, a long-drawn-out development, and the overall convergence of efforts and purposes did not exclude shifts or readjustments of strategic goals.

The first and most fundamental aspect to note is the sustained adaptation of the Chinese imperial paradigm to the Japanese context. As Joan Piggott puts it, the model imposed by the Yamato architects of reform was 'an insular version of "all under heaven."'[17] We might add that it was based on a genealogized version of the mandate of heaven, and linked to a territorialized version of the way of heaven (the Chinese notion of the way – *dao* – was fused with indigenous religious traditions in a flexible framework which allowed for further local variations). The geopolitical construct of imperial rule on an insular scale was thus matched by the geocultural tailoring of universalistic visions to a particularistic frame of reference. Multiple components were involved on both sides. Piggott's analysis highlights the importance of martial as well as sacred kingship in the Yamato tradition. As for the Chinese model, its seventh-century version was particularly pluralistic and this enhanced the scope for autonomous choice on the part of its insular interpreters. The fully developed form of Japanese kingship, as defined during Shōmu's reign, was more emphatically centred on Buddhist doctrine and imagery than any phase of Chinese imperial rule: the image of the *tennō* as a 'servant of the Buddha', and therefore a 'saviour lord' in his own right, combined with the Chinese notion of heavenly rulership to produce 'the most extravagant claim to universal sovereignty ever lodged by a Japanese monarch.'[18] Strong claims to Buddhist legitimacy had been made by the Sui dynasty (the first to rule a reunified Chinese empire from 589 onwards), but in the Japanese context, the relative weight of the Buddhist connection was much greater. Japanese perceptions and uses of the Confucian tradition focused on its institutional forms, which became an integral part of the state apparatus established during the reform period. Confucian statecraft thus helped to lay the foundations for a self-contained Japanese polity. But since no corresponding effort was made to appropriate Confucian ideas and texts, the religious hegemony of Buddhism became much more complete than in China (the imperial connection to indigenous cults was crucial for the new regime, but the accompanying mythology could not play the role of a doctrinal counterweight).[19]

Piggott suggests that the state-building process which culminated in the middle of the eight century may have resulted in a 'pathology of over-centring'.[20] This idea is presented as a working hypothesis, based on widely accepted views of developments during the following Heian period but in need of more detailed analysis of that whole phase of Japanese history (794–1192). It seems worthwhile to consider some implications of the argument. First and foremost, Piggott's thesis should not be confused with the more traditional view that the *ritsuryō* state-builders imported a Chinese model incompatible with underlying realities, and that the gradual but irresistible disintegration of this superstructure was the dominant trend of the Heian period. Such explanations were put forward – in different versions – by Kan'ichi Asakawa, George Sansom and John W. Hall. The idea of indigenous over-centring differs from their models in that it portrays the ascendant phase of state-building as a more original synthesis of multiple sources, and the aftermath appears as an interplay of active forces, rather than a unilinear readaptation to Japanese conditions. The recurrent and multilateral devolution of power (beginning with aristocratic influence at court and culminating in the joint rule of court, temples and warriors in the twelfth and thirteenth centuries) may be seen as a response to over-centring. But the dynamic of centre formation did not simply go into reverse: attempts to establish direct imperial rule, in more or less autocratic form, were made at successive junctures and had major effects on the power structure, even if there was no lasting success. Some of the seventh- and eighth-century emperors were effective rulers, and the transfer of the capital to Kyoto in 794 was followed by a significant episode of direct rule. At a much later stage (from the eleventh to the twelfth century), the imperial dynasty invented a curious strategy of compensation for the progressive loss of power: intrafamilial authority was vested in retired sovereigns who sought to reassert control outside the formal framework of the imperial institution. Finally, the last and most spectacular bid to revive imperial authority and power (the short-lived Kenmu restoration from 1333 to 1336) ended in a defeat which left no chance for a comeback; but at the same time, the failed project reflected the ability of a shrunken centre to counter-attack with heightened awareness of new conditions and possibilities, and the legacy of this last episode of overcentring imposed constraints on the victors.

The intermittent efforts that came to an end in 1336 can perhaps be described as examples of internal imperial overstretch. The obverse of over-centring was an unquestioned strategy of detachment from continental affairs. In virtue of its location on the periphery of the East Asian region, the Japanese state could build a centre whose ambitions exceeded long-term capacities, and derive prestige from mimetic rivalry with the Chinese empire, without any risk of involvement in more material forms of interstate competition. But the isolation which at first aided overcentring was also – in the longer run – conducive to a particularly sustained process of de-centring. A series of counter-states, constructed and dominated by military elites, claimed a growing share of power at the expense of the imperial institution. In the end, the original centre was reduced to a peripheral part of the power structure. But its uncontestable claims to status, prestige and legitimizing authority continued to limit the autonomy of the new centres. This enduring dependence on a pre-structured framework left its mark on all versions of the counter-state. In view of the background and the main power basis, we can speak of military regimes or states, but these terms must be used with caution: historical research has disproved earlier notions of a continuous progress of military power. The successive shogunates were neither stages in a self-contained process of state formation, nor instruments of a uniform and cohesive warrior class. Their inescapable entanglement with the pre-existing imperial model was reflected in strategic constraints, as well as in tensions and conflicts within the warrior stratum (alienated military factions played a key role in the Kenmu restoration), and as a result of periodic crises, the power structure had to be rebuilt in new circumstances. In general terms, two ways of adapting to the imperial legacy were characteristic of all military regimes: they tried to harness the legitimizing potential of the imperial institution to their own purposes, and they imitated imperial patterns of centre-building. But these complementary strategies could be combined in different proportions, and their specific directions varied from case to case.

In this context, the record of the second military regime is of particular interest. Recent work on the Muromachi shogunate

(1338–1573) has changed the received picture; although the evidence is in many respects inconclusive and the ultimate aims of the Muromachi rulers can only be guessed at, the most plausible interpretation is that they envisioned a new, integrated and exclusive centre (if this strategy had been fully implemented, it would probably have led to the dethronement of the imperial dynasty and perhaps to a redefinition of the relationship with China). Their ambition was, on this view, to move beyond both imitation and instrumentalization – towards a complete absorption of the imperial institution and its symbolism. It seems that this aspiration to undivided rule took shape in response to the failed but unmistakably radical project of imperial restoration. However, the power basis of the new regime was too fragile to sustain such policies, and the various measures taken to extend control provoked centrifugal reactions. The Muromachi power structure began to disintegrate during the first half of the fifteenth century. But the point of no return was reached in 1467, when the internal conflicts of the regime exploded into a ten years' civil war in the capital. This breakdown of the centre triggered a countrywide, multi-focal and century-long struggle for power, known as the *sengoku* period (often dated from 1467 to 1568, or less precisely from the 1480s to the 1570s).

It would be difficult to find a comparable case of abrupt and all-round reversal of the relations between centres and peripheries. The term *gekokujō,* referring to an apparent turning upside down of the whole social order, is sometimes extended to a pre-1467 phase of the crisis, but the most massive upheaval coincided with the *sengoku* period. Pierre Souyri sums up the dynamic of this process: 'From the end of the fifteenth century to the 1570s, Japanese society is thus transformed by two contradictory trends: the fragmentation of power, as well as the quest for autonomy by popular strata in central Japan, contrast with the building of regional states in pursuit of hegemony…'.[21] The upstart states, more peripheral in geographical terms but more effective as new centres of power, proved stronger than the popular movements. When the most successful state-builders had eliminated their rivals and re-established social control, they went on to reactivate a traditional framework for the new order, and the imperial institution came to play a key role in that context. But at the beginning of the *sengoku* transformation, the strategies of the warlords had little to do with any traditional entitlements. As

Souyri puts it, 'their legitimacy was not derived from any form of legal power. They prevail by force, and their authority over vassals and subjects depends on their ability to maintain peace and prosperity in their realm.'[22] The most articulate regional state-builders presented their projects as combinations of brute force, personal ability and strategic reason. *Mutatis mutandis,* the same would seem to apply to the movements: both states and movements were radically peripheral in the sense that they bypassed the issue of their relationship to the traditional centre. It is true that there was no overt rejection of the imperial institution, but this was probably in large part due to its obvious marginality. It had been relegated to another kind of periphery by the rival centre which imploded in 1467; the very weakness of its claims to central status made it easier to survive the *sengoku* phase and re-emerge after unification.

In view of all this, the Ōnin war (1467–77) can be described as the beginning of the transition from traditional to early modern Japan. This thesis was first put forward by Naitō Konan in the 1920s, and some recent works by Western historians have drawn similar conclusions.[23] By the same token, the notion of a separate medieval period becomes untenable, and the traditional phase is best defined as extending from the seventh-century transformation to the late fifteenth-century breakdown: the Ōnin war and its sequel represent a much more momentous break than the twelfth-century re-distribution of power. Early Japanese modernity (or protomodernity – the choice may be left open) begins with a radical disjunction of centre and periphery. In some ways, this change came closer to a new beginning than any developments in Europe during the corresponding historical period. Paradoxically, the dynamic of unconstrained peripheral power led to a reconstitution of central rule in ways more resistant to further innovation than in Europe.

As suggested at the beginning, changing constellations of centres and peripheries are particularly important to the long-term patterns of Japanese history, and the detour through theoretical debates has brought out some further implications of this point. Here I cannot discuss the modern transformations which affected both central and peripheral parts of society. But to conclude, a few words should be said about the relevance of this problematic to the question of Japanese nationalism and its historical sources. Allowing for a wide spectrum of opinions on ethnicity in earlier phases of Japanese history, most analysts would probably agree that if we use Anthony Smith's typology of ethnic collectivities, premodern Japan belongs in the lateral category rather than the vertical one (the ethnic bond was, in other words, more a matter of shared aristocratic culture and identity than of strong roots in popular traditions). This leaves open the question of the specific impact of the imperial institution (and its symbolic framework) on the Japanese version of ethnicity, and on the historical process of inclusion that culminated in the Japanese nation-state. The point at issue is not simply the relative strength or the social spread of these core symbols at successive stages of premodern history.[24] We must also take into account the indirect effects due to containment of other foci of integration or identity, and the long-term potential inherent in constellations of meaning. With reference to the distinction between lateral and vertical types of ethnic identity, it may be suggested that some versions of the lateral pattern are more predisposed to verticalization than others, and the imaginary framework of the Japanese imperial institution seems to be a striking case of that kind.

Critics of traditional historiography argue that the seventh-century construction of a Japanese state gave rise to a myth of uniformity which has been perpetuated in more sophisticated forms, and that a methodical deconstruction of this model is essential to a better understanding of premodern Japan. Advocates of this view – notably Amino Yoshihiko[25] – have broken new ground in research on Japanese history between the seventh and the fifteenth centuries: regional and social diversity was obviously more significant than the traditional self-image would have it. But there is another side to the picture. Although the structural problems of a state exposed to centrifugal regional forces were obviously of major importance for political developments during the Heian period, conflicts and divisions at the decisive level of the power structure do not seem to have been directly linked to regional particularisms. The first serious challenge to the Heian rulers was the rebellion of Taira Masakado in 926; it drew on a regional power basis in eastern Honshū, but there is no evidence of any appeal to regional identity. On the most radical interpretation, Masakado was using his genealogical connection to the imperial dynasty to stake a claim to rule as a 'new emperor', without specifying whether the old line should be replaced or forced to share authority. Later bids for partial or unofficial power were more successful but less openly disruptive of the imperial order, and they resulted in redistribution among competing but interdependent elites, rather than fragmentation along regional lines. The dyarchy of court and *bakufu* (from 1185 to 1333) has been extensively analyzed by Japanese and Western scholars; more recently, attention has been drawn to a third power bloc, made up of the major temples and shrines. The religious elites lost ground when the Muromachi shogunate set out to restructure central power, but even during the Kamakura period, they had suffered from an institutional drawback. Mikael S. Adolphson's analysis of the 'shared rulership' of monks, courtiers and warriors highlights this point: 'Although the warriors and nobles both had their own governments and sociopolitical hierarchies, the religious establishment lacked that degree of unity and coherence.'[26] But this weakness of the religious elites reflects an enduring strength of another claimant to power. The role of a supreme sacred centre had been pre-empted by the imperial institution, in its capacity as a dynastic embodiment of both political and religious authority, as well as of the unity of Buddhism and indigenous cults. No separate religious institution could rival this set of claims.

In short, the resilience of the Heian power structure – despite the decomposing trends evident from the outset – and the stabilization of shared rulership during the Kamakura period suggest that ethnic unity of the lateral kind had been successfully imposed on the multiple regions of the archipelago. When it comes to the more specific question of images, symbols and ideological contents that might have lent particular force to this ethnogenetic process and foreshadowed a later phase of nation formation, the conception of Japan as *shinkoku* (land of the *kami)* is the most obviously relevant part of a more complex story. It is the main link between traditional ethnic particularism and modern nationalism. Kuroda Toshio's analysis of its development during the late medieval phase seems especially pertinent to our present concerns.[27] As he shows, a '*shinkoku* discourse' emerges from the eleventh century onwards (although the term as such can be traced back to the early eighth century), and it is closely related to other religious and ideological trends. Kuroda's view – now widely accepted – was that Japanese religion during the late Heian and Kamakura periods was best understood as a flexible synthesis of exoteric and esoteric Buddhism (he coined the term *kenmitsu taisei* for this combination), and that indigenous religious traditions had become an integral but subordinate part of that pattern. The late medieval resurgence of Shintō cults and beliefs was a new twist to the *kenmitsu* constellation, rather than a return in strength of a separate but previously marginalized tradition. As for the *shinkoku* discourse, it was not simply a by-product of growing emphasis on Shintō elements within the syncretic tradition. As Kuroda saw it (this thesis is more controversial than his general interpretation of the *kenmitsu* system), it was also a response to the innovations of Kamakura Buddhism. Earlier historians of Japanese religion had mostly seen the new sects of the Kamakura period as expressions of a new religiosity, and sometimes as exponents of a reformation with some affinities to trends in more transcendental religious traditions. According to Kuroda, the new movements were heterodox offshoots of the *kenmitsu* tradition, and their distinctive features – a reaction against polytheism and a stronger appeal to a popular audience – were linked to social struggles. Conversely, the established power structure – the shared rule of courtiers, warriors and temples – was reaffirmed by countercurrents within the *kenmitsu* framework. From that point of view, *shinkoku* discourse was a conservative reaction to subversive challenges. But its long-term impact can only be understood in light of its content.

The *shinkoku* ideology was – to use a theoretical language different from Kuroda's but not incompatible with his insights – based on a complex of imaginary significations. Four main components may be distinguished. An emphatic territorialization of the sacred was fundamental to everything else: as the 'land of the *kami*', Japan enjoyed a privileged relationship to the multiple deities of a composite tradition. This special status set Japan apart form other countries; when India, China and Japan were singled out as 'three countries' (*sangoku*), defined in terms of their respective religious claims to distinction, a separate identity was affirmed in the broadest possible context – extending beyond the East Asian region – and with more or less explicit connotations of ultimate superiority. The divinity of the realm was inseparable from the divine origin of the dynasty which reigned – and sometimes aspired to rule – over it. Last but not least, the divine ancestry of the ethnic collectivity was interpreted in a way which did not restrict it to the ruling elite, even if the explicit inclusion of the whole population was not fully accepted until much later.[28]

The importance of this background to modern processes of state and nation formation should be obvious. The details of that part of the story cannot be discussed here. But it seems appropriate to conclude with a few comments on the imperial institution. Although it was never the only centre, nor a wholly self-contained one (its centrality depended on a broader constellation of meaning, and other forces were always involved), it was always a very central part of the civilizational pattern. Critical historians have often been reluctant to recognize it as such. There is, however, no convincing reason why its role in Japanese history should not be analyzed as dispassionately – and with as much awareness of the ambiguities and paradoxes of history – as the part which monarchies played in the formation of European states and nations. This aspect of the Western European trajectory (and of East Central European history before the rise of the early modern empires) is no longer an ideological apple of discord. In comparison with European cases, the Japanese imperial institution has a longer history and its role has varied more significantly from phase to phase; it was a key component of the framework which demarcated Japan from the surrounding civilizational domain, and after it ceased to take a direct part in power struggles, it became an indispensable complement to more transient sources of authority. A record of this calibre and complexity calls for careful analysis, rather than grand gestures of deconstruction.

2 East Asian Approaches: Region, History and Civilization

Traditions and transformations

Contrary to some recent trends, the following reflections on the East Asian region will be based on a narrow definition of its boundaries and identity. From a historical point of view, it includes three countries – China, Korea and Japan – whose destinies have been interconnected in complex and changing ways. But in contemporary geopolitical terms, we are dealing with five states: Japan, the two Koreas and the two Chinas (i.e. the imperial mainland polity and Taiwan). This constellation has remained unchanged during the second half of the 20th century and outlasted the Cold War; there are good reasons to expect changes, but no plausible ways of predicting their course. Although the unification of Korea would be a return to historical normalcy and a logical result of international developments, incalculable factors on all sides are important enough to allow for a variety of possible outcomes. As for a future rapprochement of Taiwan and mainland China, it is not unlikely to come about in one way or another, but there the range of imaginable options is even wider. If East Asia is defined in the above sense, its unity is grounded in three successive layers of historical experience. Prior to the 19th-century intrusion of Western powers, enduring geopolitical and geocultural patterns – the predominance of the Chinese imperial centre, even when taken over by conquerors from Inner Asia, and the broader influence of Chinese cultural models – had been characteristic of the region. In the very long-term process of Chinese expansion towards the south, empire-building and cultural assimilation had gone hand in hand, although not without some significant divergences. By contrast, the inclusion of Korea and Japan in a Sinocentric world was based on cultural superimposition without imperial control, but the two countries developed very different versions of this pattern. An abortive attempt to conquer the Korean kingdoms at the height of Chinese imperial expansion (in the seventh century) hastened the consolidation of an independent unified state; the autonomous Korean polity then went on to combine symbolic recognition of Chinese sovereignty and orthodox elaboration of Chinese ideological paradigms with power structures notably different from those that prevailed in China. In Japan, the seventh century also marks a turning point, but here a perceived Chinese threat was enough to inspire a more original strategy of state-centred transformation and a more complex cross-adaptation of Chinese and native traditions; the Japanese state opted out of the symbolic world order centred on China, and the appropriation of Chinese culture took a reflexive turn which proved compatible with extensive reinterpretations and nativist self-rediscoveries.[1]

There are, of course, significant differences between successive stages of East Asian regional history before the final onset of Western expansion, most obviously in regard to the form and degree of Chinese predominance; but for present purposes, the next phase to be considered is the century between the beginning of the Opium War in 1840 and the defeat of Japan in 1945, marked by the presence of superior Western power and the development of regional responses to it. Simplistic notions of global Westernization – now more popular among critics than among defenders of the West – are still too common for it to be widely understood how unique the East Asian reactions were. Each part of the regional triangle was affected in particular ways, but one of them became most central to historical events during the century in question. In Japan, the mid-nineteenth century encounter with the West triggered an upheaval which transformed this most peripheral state of the region into the most expansive and actively modernizing one. Japan was the only modern imperial power that set out to colonize or at least dominate a geopolitical and civilizational area within which it had previously played a marginal role. This project dominated East Asian geopolitics for the better part of a century, and it had a more decisive impact on the regional dynamic of modernization than any direct Western influences. Its history can, in retrospect, be divided into four stages. The Japanese bid for hegemony began with a unilateral change in the relationship to China: the rules of the old regional order were replaced by a strategy modelled on Western forms of interstate competition and more in line with the modernizing lead already taken by Japan. The second stage was marked by military conquest and colonization. Japan annexed the most outlying Chinese province (Taiwan), thwarted Chinese attempts to transform a traditional symbolic authority over Korea into more modern mechanisms of control, and went on to incorporate Korea into its own emerging empire. During the interwar years, inconclusive attempts to expand an informal empire in China took a new turn with the creation of a client state in Manchuria, through which Japan became a contender in the multipolar struggle between aspiring successors to the defunct Chinese empire. But this third phase quickly shaded off into the last one, an all-out war of conquest against China. The results were catastrophic for the Japanese empire, but the global repercussions were far more significant than previous effects of Japanese expansion: the Pacific War not only brought the American superpower into East Asian geopolitics, but also played a major role in pushing the Chinese revolution towards a Communist takeover.

This last point brings us to the question of Chinese responses to the Western inroads that became irresistible after 1840. It has become increasingly common to speak of the Chinese revolution as a long-term process which began with the Taiping rebellion – the bloodiest and most destructive conflict of the nineteenth century – in 1850, did not finish in 1949, and is still going through a transitional stage. The transformative dynamic set in motion by the joint impact of internal crises and external defeats is the most salient non-European counterpart to the great revolutions of the West (nothing remotely comparable occurred in other major Asian civilizational spheres), but also the most instructive counter-example to theoretical models which tend to over-generalize the European pattern. Analogies between historical landmarks in China and the West have proved difficult to sustain. What occurred in 1911 was neither a bourgeois nor a democratic revolution (the old order fell apart, but no new power elite, social force or institutional set-up was ready to replace it), and 1949 differed from other Communist takeovers in that it was preceded by a phase of rivalry between alternative foci of imperial reconstruction, during which Chinese Communism began to develop some of the distinctive characteristics which were to pit it against the Soviet centre and prevent it from stabilizing along Soviet lines. But more detailed comparative analyses of the different relationships between revolutionary episodes and long-term power restructuring, as well as between structural dynamics and social actors, have yet to be undertaken.

The Chinese response was thus very different from the Japanese one, but no less original and important for comparative history. As for the Korean experience during this historical period, it stands in stark contrast to both the other parts of the triangle. No other country with a comparable cultural legacy, historical continuity and strength of ethnic identity was as abruptly transformed into a battleground for imperial rivalry. After the enforced end of Korean isolation, the internal attempts at change – ambiguous and limited in any case – were overshadowed by the three-cornered contest between Russia, China and Japan; Japan's victory over the two other powers led to outright colonization and finally to a drive for cultural assimilation which has few if any parallels in the recent history of imperial power; finally, the collapse of the Japanese empire and the consolidation of two global blocs led to the division of Korea into two states whose separate survival was assured by external forces. There was, however, another side to this sequence of disasters from without: the experience of colonial rule gave rise to a particularly tenacious and pervasive cultural nationalism (reflected, among other things, in one of the most nationalistic offshoots of the communist movement). This factor was to prove crucial to the strategy and outlook of the two post-war Korean regimes.

The third and most familiar defining phase of East Asian history is the late twentieth-century record of exceptional economic growth. It began with the 'Japanese miracle', increasingly visible from the early 1960s onwards, and continued with the rise of South Korea and Taiwan as economic power-houses; the most recent stage is the post-Communist take-off of the mainland Chinese economy. It is generally accepted that these successive breakthroughs add up to a regional trajectory, based on the legacy of the Japanese empire as well as on lessons drawn from the Japanese experience of post-imperial development, but more specific connections are a matter of debate.[2] Here we can only note the geopolitical background to economic changes. The post-war emphasis on growth and development reflects a regional shift from military to economic power. Most importantly, the Japanese developmental state revised its project and gave first priority to economic strength; the retreat from imperial visions did not mean an end to global strategy, but the reorientation was more radical than any measures taken since 1868. The two Korean states remained much more overtly militarized than Japan, but the protracted stalemate after 1953 forced them to engage in economic competition as war by other means. In the Chinese case, the overwhelming strength of one side made all comparative assets of the rival regimes less relevant than the global causes of division; it is, however, beyond doubt that the Taiwanese version of the developmental state took shape as part of a strategy for long-term political survival. As for mainland China, the paradox of post-Communist economic policies accompanying the reconsolidation of party dictatorship can only be explained in terms of strategic readjustment: Maoist-style political and ideological mobilization had failed to produce the expected self-strengthening results, and economic modernization was seen as a more promising alternative.

These successive conversions to developmentalism were in large measure due to changes in the global context of regional history. The partial imposition of American hegemony after the Second World War put an end to intra-regional imperialism and resulted in the internationalization of two civil wars, albeit in different conditions and with different consequences. The post-imperial Japanese state was not created by American reformers (in that sense, the comparison of the occupation with the Meiji Restoration and the seventh-century Taika Reform seems misguided[3]), but it was the outcome of innovative adaptation to new rules set by a victorious power. The Japanese model was, in other words, transformed in response to an American input, whereas the two other countries were divided between allies and adversaries of the American order. In China, the civil war was internationalized in its very last phase (with the official inclusion of Taiwan in the American zone of strategic interest) and as a result of more direct intervention elsewhere, and the geopolitical effects were therefore limited. The only lasting outcome was the insulation of a province which had been a late addition to the Chinese empire and then part of the Japanese one for half a century; it now became a sanctuary for the non-Communist version of Chinese nationalism and its experiment in self-reinvention. By contrast, the Korean conflict was internationalized in an early phase and with momentous results for both sides. Although war broke out between separate states in 1950, the two regimes drew support from antagonistic social forces, aspired to unify the country and rejected division as incompatible with national sovereignty; it is therefore appropriate to speak of civil war.[4] Intervention from abroad stabilized the rival states and put an end to outright war, but the subsequent pattern of competition differed from other divided countries. For a long time, the contest between the two Koreas was much more open than in Germany or Vietnam; both states could effectively claim nationalist legitimacy; and the strong nationalistic stance helps to explain the unusual ability of both sides to pursue autonomous policies despite structural dependence on stronger powers.

The Confucian image: renaissance, reformation or reinvention?

Definitions of East Asia as a region often go beyond the above set of historical traits and postulate a more self-contained cultural identity. The most familiar construct of that kind is the idea of a Confucian tradition, region or civilization. Such claims have been made from inside as well as from outside the East Asian world; here we are, to begin with, mainly concerned with the insiders. The overtly Confucian turn in East Asian definitions of identity is of recent origin, and its impact within the region varies widely. In the early 1980s, official use of – or allegiance to – Confucian principles was most characteristic of states marginal to the contest for hegemony, especially Taiwan (then less prominent as a developmental showcase than it has now come to seem) and Singapore (a partially East Asian enclave within Southeast Asia). Confucian themes were much less central to Japanese ideology-building, because of the enduring concern with uniqueness and the adaptability of nationalist attitudes; in Korea, general awareness of Confucianism's key role in the old order went together with doubts and disagreements about its role in modernity. But the most important shift towards an official reinstatement of Confucianism began in mainland China after the demise of Maoism and became more visible as the regime moved further away from the ideological commitments of the Cold War era. Confucianism has not formally replaced Marxism-Leninism, but the reorientation is marked enough for some observers to speculate on the possibility of 'national Confucianism' as a new orthodoxy.[5] The Confucian turn has thus unmistakably progressed from the periphery to a more central part of the region.

The idea of a Confucian world is best understood in relation to the historical experience recapitulated above. Confucianism appears as a guarantee of continuity throughout the modern vicissitudes of the region; it has, on this view, survived the derailment of East Asian history by Western expansion, resisted the ideological inroads of rival Western models and reasserted itself through the more autonomous and distinctive developmental strategies of recent decades. A temporarily submerged tradition is thus credited with a renaissance which has reactivated its core values as well as a reformation which has brought them into more effective contact with the modern world. The Confucian legacy is, furthermore, expected to aid a reunification of the region across barriers created by Cold War geopolitics. Last but not least, the appeal to Confucian sources and foundations helps to give more than a purely geographical meaning to the claim that a previously ascendant region is now re-emerging as a potential successor to Western hegemony.

The obvious connection between resurgent power and revalued traditions has led some observers to describe the Confucian revival as a reinvention, grounded in contemporary trends rather than in a genuine return to the sources. One of the most uncompromising diagnoses in this vein dismisses the new Confucianism as a product of 'global capitalism' in search of ideological models for new growth areas, and at the same time as a strategy of 'intellectuals …who serve as brokers of power within the new configuration of capitalism'.[6] Here the illusion of regional autonomy is put on a par with the self-projection of ideological superstructures, and both are reduced to window-dressing of a capitalist world economy. But to the best of my knowledge, no convincing attempt has ever been made to explain the specifics of post-war East Asian growth in terms of world-systemic mechanisms. As for the somewhat less obviously untenable equation of Confucianism with ideology, the first objection that comes to mind is that the ideological discourses in question have drawn on a broader and more open-ended set of debates. There is no denying that active shapers, more or less official spokesmen and participant observers of East Asian modernizing regimes have become interested in the ideological potential of Confucianism, but this does not entail a uniform use of it. More importantly, the debates that unfolded against this background were accompanied and to some degree influenced by two other developments. On the one hand, received views of Chinese history in general and Confucianism in particular, widely accepted within the sociology of modernization and development, were challenged by historians who presented a more multi-dimensional image of the old order as well as theorists in search of a more adequate comparative framework, often through a critical dialogue with Weber.[7] In both cases, more nuanced interpretations of the Confucian tradition drew attention to critical and transformative trends, incompatible with the Weberian account of Confucianism as an ethic of adaptation. On the other hand, Confucian thought had been overshadowed but not eliminated by the rival ideologies of Westernization and revolution; the question of its continuing presence in the Chinese world and beyond became more relevant as Chinese Communism lost its appeal and other versions of Chinese modernity began to take shape.

The 'new Confucianism', as its adherents called it (an intentional twist to the Western term 'Neo-Confucianism', originally applied to much earlier developments in Chinese thought) was neither tied to the old order nor aligned with any particular contender for revolutionary leadership; after 1949, it could more easily survive in Hong Kong and Taiwan than under the Communist regime, although some important figures stayed on the mainland. The most ambitious thinkers of this school combined a 'meta-moral ontology'[8] with more Western-style techniques of argumentation and system building. As for their views on China and the West, a programmatic text written before the self-destabilizing turn of Chinese communism is of particular interest.[9] To begin with, the authors criticize two contradictory but often combined Western misunderstandings of China. Overdrawn parallels with materialist and rationalist philosophies of the Enlightenment have obscured the religious aspect of Confucianism; on the other hand (and often at the same time), the culture dominated by Confucian ideas and values has been seen as conducive to closure and stagnation. But if – as the authors argue – the Confucian vision of humanity and its place in the cosmos has a religious core, different in form and content from the religious systems more familiar to Western thought, a culture based on such foundations is by the same token capable of an active quest for permanence, rather than the inert continuity perceived by Western observers. It is not being suggested that the spiritual dimension and the creative potential of Chinese civilization were equally evident at all times: the philosophical thought of the Song and Ming periods (i.e. roughly speaking, from the eleventh to the mid-seventeenth century) is presented as the most authentic part of the Confucian legacy.

This reassessment of the past throws new light on the question of learning from the West. China's earlier technological achievements are cited to prove that Chinese culture is by no means alien to the spirit of modern science, but it is admitted that to catch up with the West, a clearer grasp of the autonomy and legitimacy of intellectual – as distinct from moral – inquiry is needed. Similarly, the Chinese tradition is credited with a proto-democratic conception of popular support as essential to legitimacy, unique among traditional regimes, but this falls short of the modern Western idea of constitutional democracy. In short, the need to appropriate the results of Western breakthroughs in the cognitive as well as the political dimension is acknowledged; at the same time, the authors insist on indigenous preconditions for an autonomous strategy. Finally, Chinese Communism is – 10 years before the cultural revolution – dismissed as a failure on both counts. Its alienation from the Chinese tradition, together with its fundamental misunderstanding of the West, make it incapable of solving China's problems and therefore unfit for survival.

Towards a comparative framework

It should be clear from the above summary that meaningful questions about Confucianism and its relationship to modernity were being raised well before the emergence of 'industrial East Asia', and that they were posed in a way which did not fit into any ready-made ideological strategies. With this background in mind, we should now return to the problematic of Confucianism and modernization and explore some ways of linking it to comparative perspectives. The discussion will begin with some reflections on the putative links between Confucian tradition and capitalist development (1) and move on to consider the case for Confucian values as social and cultural counterweights to the dynamic of capitalism (2), as well as the more far-reaching visions of a Confucian civilizational framework that might serve to re-embed a fragmented and disoriented modernity (3). All these issues are, in the first instance, related to the Chinese context.[10]

(1) Those who would like to show that the Confucian ethic made a positive contribution to the spirit of capitalism do not always focus on the same factors. It may even be difficult to distinguish clear-cut positions: for example, one author stresses first 'the devotion to education and the emphasis on savings' and then 'an affective model

of economic development, which emphasizes human emotional bonds, group orientation, and harmony'.[11] But the theme that comes closest to a common denominator is probably the rationalizing and mobilizing potential of meritocratic hierarchy. Confucianism – at least in its more action- and reform-oriented mode – is supposedly conducive to loyal acceptance of committed and knowledgeable authority, and such attitudes help to reorient society towards sustained growth, even if that was not their original rationale. Since this argument seems to reverse Weber's well-known verdict on Confucianism in a very abrupt way, sceptical commentators have seen the about-turn as a reason to cast doubt on both the traditional and the revised view: interpretations of cultural traditions seem to be adaptable to the changing facts of economic life. But the claims made in relation to a Confucian ethic differ from the *Protestant Ethic* thesis in at least four fundamental ways (these contrasts seem to have been neglected by both sides to the debate). First, the point of contact between Confucian mentality and modern capitalism is located on the level of inter-human relations, not – as in the other case – within the horizon of human relations to the world. For Weber, the breakthrough due to the Protestant ethic is inseparable from the 'rationalism of world domination', i.e. the interpretive and practical attitude that turns the world into an object of control through calculation. No such interpretation of Confucianism can be imagined; more generally speaking, there are no episodes in its history that can be understood as radical transformations of a traditional world view. Second, the goals of gainful work and self-perpetuating accumulation are less internal to the Confucian ethic than they were – in Weber's view – to the Protestant one. Weber's analysis of this point is notoriously ambiguous, but it is at least clear that he wanted to derive a new cultural definition of economic activity from the encounter of religious reform with a changing social context. By contrast, the theorists of the Confucian ethic have in mind the adaptation to and incorporation of a goal coming from outside the tradition and first encountered in conjunction with other aspects of a rival cultural model. Opinions vary on how far the subtradition of 'merchant Confucianism' may have gone in legitimizing commercial activity, but the perceived novelty and otherness of Western-style capitalist accumulation is not in dispute. This line of argument links up with a hypothesis suggested but never developed by Weber: he hinted at the possibility that the constellation which had blocked a capitalist breakthrough in China might be less resistant to the import of capitalism from elsewhere, and that some aspects of Chinese culture might even be conducive to such a response. Third, the distinctively paradoxical character of the Weberian connection between Protestantism and capitalism has no parallel in the Confucian case. As Weber saw it, a radicalization of religious ethics had paved the way for a self-sustaining systemic process – capitalist growth – which in the long run undermined not only all religious claims to authority over economic life, but also the very possibility of inner-directed conduct in the economic domain. No such self-destructive turn is ascribed to or predicted for the Confucian ethic: the economic virtues attributed to it are defined in terms which suggest at least the possibility of a durable and mutually reinforcing symbiosis with capitalism. Finally, the Confucian contribution to capitalist development is at the same time seen as a cultural matrix for a particular type of capitalism. The Confucian primacy of relations (linked to a strong emphasis on the family as a social microcosm and in some cases to the defence of a more specific family-based communitarian model) serves to explain the network-based rather than entrepreneurial character of East Asian capitalism, and thus to provide a background to facts noted by many observers of the region.

(2) If the unfolding argument about Confucian sources of modern East Asian capitalism is in some ways comparable but far from identical with the debate sparked by Weber's *Protestant Ethic*, it may be useful to consider affinities between the broader perspectives that have in both cases been opened up beyond the question of economic change. S. N. Eisenstadt redefined the problematic of the *Protestant Ethic* in terms of a general 'transformative potential' (i.e. a capacity to initiate, articulate and legitimize institutional innovations) rather than an exclusive link to the ethos of capitalist pioneers.[12] The most obvious field to examine from this angle is the whole complex of political transformations which marked the road to modernity; given that the East Asian region was, on the whole, less receptive to the political aspects of Western modernity than to the economic ones, any corresponding extension of the Confucian problematic must take a different course. So far, two main themes seem to have emerged. On the one hand, the conspicuous role of the developmental state in East Asian modernization, and its ability to adapt political and economic strategies to each other, has prompted some analysts to look for traditional sources of its strength. Nobody

would think of postulating a complete Confucian model of the developmental state, but attempts have been made to show that aspects of the Confucian tradition lend themselves to reorientation in a new global context, and thus could help to rationalize and legitimize the developmental state. Léon Vandermeersch argues that a functionalist conception of statecraft was built into the Confucian mode of thought: the state was part of a socio-cosmic order and its practical tasks within that framework were defined in administrative rather than political terms.[13] This premodern version of functionalism left an adaptable legacy which facilitated the building of a modern bureaucratic state, insulated from political conflicts and committed to developmental goals. Vandermeersch's thesis reflects the condition of the mid-1980s: developmental states on the erstwhile East Asian periphery had proved their viability and mainland China was visibly moving in the same direction after a revolutionary crisis which had – as Vandermeersch saw it – been all the more prolonged because of the fundamentally anti-revolutionary patterns of Chinese society. A more cautious and qualified line was taken by Thomas Metzger, whose analysis of the Taiwanese experience stresses the necessity as well as the difficulty of far-reaching revisions of the Confucian legacy.[14] For Metzger, the developmental state is crucial to Chinese modernization, and it can draw on Confucian sources, but its success presupposes a thoroughly non-Confucian conversion to instrumental rationality, as well as more contingent favourable conditions, and the dangers inherent in the Confucian mindset are exemplified not only by the later imperial mirage of an intact tradition annexing Western rationality as a purely technical device, but also by the disastrous Maoist phantasm of a complete fusion of wisdom and rulership.

On the other hand, political changes in Taiwan and South Korea, as well as the much less successful demands for democratic reform in mainland China, have raised questions about the relevance of Confucian traditions to modern democracy. Here the connection must – if it can at all be claimed – be more tenuous than in the case of the developmental state. No critical analysts deny that ideological and institutional obstacles to modern democracy were integral to the Confucian tradition; the case for more positive influences can only be made in indirect terms, i.e. on the basis of established or potential links between Confucianism and the constitution of civil society. Such affinities might then be seen as contributing causes of democratization. The debate on this issue has so far been very inconclusive, not least because of the notoriously unfocused use of the concept of civil society (it tends, here as elsewhere, to shift without warning from minimalist and descriptive claims to strong and normative ones), but we can at least note some markedly different approaches. At one end of the spectrum, Edward Shils's speculations on Confucianism and civil society centre on the intellectual content of classical sources; neither the differences between Confucius and Confucianism nor the interaction between Confucian traditions and Chinese society are taken into account. The upshot of Shils's argument is that the Confucian paradigm has no place for the institutions of civil society (in particular, there is no notion of citizenship or the rule of law, and the public sphere is as absent as the problem of conflicting interests), but some bearing on the virtues most needed in civil society, especially those that can be subsumed under the notion of 'civility' in the sense of concern for the common good. The 'obligation of the highly educated to serve society' [15] is crucial.

The wholly ahistorical stance of this interpretation casts doubt on its value, and the same can be said about its dependence on an idealized Western model (civil society is, in the end, equated with 'liberal democratic national society'). At the opposite extreme, Metzger's reflections on the Taiwanese experience throw light on a very specific situation but do not lead to strong generalizations. In Taiwan, a differentiated Confucian culture was integrated into a pluralistic 'mix of ideologies'[16] which also included liberalism and statist nationalism; in this context, Confucian orientations could reinforce the demand for moral consensus and economic justice as indispensable complements to modernization, and thus help to strengthen societal counterweights to state-centred development.

The most promising way to broaden the terms of this debate would be to link it to recent controversies about the rise of civil society and a corresponding public sphere in imperial China, not only during the late imperial phase which preceded the collision with the West, but (in a less continuous fashion) over the much longer period of time that began with the eleventh-century shift to a more commercial, less aristocratic and at the same time less directly state-controlled society. Some of the most interesting recent work in comparative history has been devoted to this problematic; but although new perspectives have certainly been opened up, the need to rethink basic concepts and avoid over-generalizations of European patterns is not always recognized. The most original (and to my mind most convincing) models proposed to make sense of the Chinese constellation are those of the 'stretched empire'[17] and the 'third realm between state and society'.[18] The former refers to the more flexible and diversified patterns of imperial control which evolved in response to growing social complexity. Power was delegated, elites were co-opted, and interests as well as identities accommodated in various ways, but within a framework which allowed no question of the centre or of its cosmological symbolism. A ritual, rather than formal-legal, mode of regulation served to integrate the diverse components of the power structure. At the same time, a wide range of unofficial, i.e. formally uncodified, arrangements and practices was tolerated, but effectively prevented from coalescing into an alternative social sphere. The latter model highlights a specific aspect of the former: the 'third realm' was a complex of judicial, administrative and other public activities, delegated to local elites in an informal and often improvised fashion, without ever – during the imperial phase – becoming a field of confrontation between state and society. Both lines of argument are directed against the thesis, put forward by various historians, that an endogenous development of civil society and the public sphere, in a more or less European sense, was taking place in late imperial China before the encounter with the West. There is no denying the significance of socioeconomic changes during the phase in question, but as Chevrier and Huang argue, the imperial mechanisms of containment, including the cultural ones, were too resilient and comprehensive for the sociopolitical impact to measure up to models derived from a more transformative process.

Intellectual and social history still tend to progress on separate tracks, and these debates have therefore not been closely linked to new perspectives on the Confucian tradition (work in that field has drawn attention to distinctive metaphysical approaches, shifts towards a stronger emphasis on the self as a source of insight and initiative, and changing attitudes to textual foundations). But some recent contributions[19] suggest that reorientations of Confucian thought were related to changing relations between imperial power, officialdom and local elites.

(3) These ramifications of the Confucian problematic raise a more general question: to what extent can we think of Confucianism

as a comprehensive civilizational pattern and how relevant is that viewpoint to the East Asian ways of mixing tradition and modernity? There are, at first sight, some good reasons for a sceptical answer. As Mark Elvin notes, comparison with world religions leads to a clear-cut conclusion: 'of all the great pre-modern systems of belief, Confucianism is the only one that has to all intents and purposes disappeared'[20], at least in the sense that its canonical texts have – in contrast to the sacred books of surviving religious traditions – lost their scriptural status. On the other hand, Vandermeersch argues that the very obsolescence of Confucianism as a belief system makes it more mobilizable as a cultural resource: 'to fertilize change, tradition had to transform itself into a wholly devitalized humus'.[21] This claim is, however, based on tacit assumptions about prior trends at work within the traditional order. The metaphor of the 'humus' makes no sense if it does not refer to cultural orientations and behavioural patterns which survived the collapse of their original text-based framework and can be adapted to a new context.

The two diagnoses can be construed as complementary rather than opposed (Elvin speaks of a 'psychological momentum', left behind by the defunct doctrine and all the more difficult to assess or measure because of its free-floating condition; this post-traditional residue would seem comparable to Vandermeersch's notion of operative remnants). Contemporary attempts to re-formulate the Confucian paradigm take issue with both aspects of the argument. For those who seek to reconstruct a philosophical and/or *sui generis* religious core of the tradition, the texts remain open to more detached readings after the demise of the social order that they served to defend, and the cultural potential of the Confucian ethos is not exhausted by its contribution to the material infrastructures of development. On this view, the distinctively Confucian conception of the relationship between humanity and the cosmos has some mutually instructive affinities with organic paradigms in modern and contemporary Western thought; the corresponding vision of the social world acquires new meaning in context of the search for communitarian alternatives. The writings of Tu Wei-ming are perhaps the most representative works in this vein.[22]

Further discussion of the prospects and credentials of neo-Confucian thought is beyond the competence of the present writer. But to conclude, we should briefly return to the question of comparative perspectives; divergent views on the legacy and afterlife of the Confucian tradition often seem to reflect an unstated disagreement or uncertainty on its civilizational status, and that issue must be seen in a broader context. Here we can do no more than indicate the most relevant classical source and the most promising contemporary project in the field. Max Weber's interpretation of China cannot be left out of account, and although it has been subjected to more telling criticism than most other parts of Weber's work, its core idea is still a useful foil for alternative views. Weber's cardinal error was to equate the absence of Indian or Western-style 'religious rejection of the world' from Chinese culture with a cognitive as well as a moral failure to move beyond the magic universe; as a result, he vastly underestimated the role of scientific inquiry, ethical reflection and political protest in the history of Chinese civilization. Eisenstadt's theory of the 'Axial transformation' is designed to incorporate Weber's insights while avoiding his fixation on particular religious traditions as well as his dismissive treatment of cultures which took a different course. For Eisenstadt, the Chinese pattern reflects a specific response to problems posed by landmark developments in major cultural centres during – roughly speaking – the second third of the last millennium BC (the other exemplary cases are India, ancient Greece and ancient Israel). The structural similarity of these new constellations is no less striking than the chronological parallels: the shared 'Axial' experience may be described as a previously unknown rupture and problematization of order, and the uniform core of the interpretive answers consists of a distinction between transcendental and mundane order. Cultural models built on this basis have far-reaching consequences for the legitimation of power, the articulation of social conflicts and the institutionalization of dissent. The otherworldly orientation which Weber described as a religious rejection of the world can then be seen as one variant among others within this framework; for Eisenstadt, China represents another distinctive type, characterized by a strong this-worldly vision of order achieved through social and cosmic harmony, a uniquely privileged role of the political centre in implementing this model, and – as a result – a 'far-reaching fusion of the cultural and the political'.[23] There is no doubt that both the general idea of the Axial transformation and the specific interpretation of China need further debate and more detailed analyses of changing configurations. Critical responses to Eisenstadt's work have raised questions about the adequacy of the idea of transcendental order, as well as about the complex and contested relationship between the imperial centre and other sociocultural forces; they have also emphasized counterweights to the official alliance of culture and politics.[24] The Axial model is thus a far cry from scholarly consensus, but it is hitherto unrivalled in its capacity to relate the key questions of Chinese history to more general problems of civilizational theory.

3 Comparing Japan: The Return to Asia

Japan has, for obvious reasons, been a particularly attractive field for comparative research in history and sociology. But some comparative approaches have been more sensitive to Japanese realities than others, and the results are correspondingly uneven. In general terms, it is safe to say that Western historians have done more justice to the Japanese experience than Western theorists. Apart from such persistent imbalances, major shifts of focus and context have occurred in response to changing historical trends. A recent and familiar example is the growing interest in Japan as an integral but distinctive part of the East Asian region, rather than a case of quasi-Western development in an Asian setting. This new (or renewed) comparative perspective will be central to the following reflections. But its bearing on theoretical questions inherited from an earlier frame of reference is one of the themes that can only be outlined with a view to further discussion.

The widely accepted image of Japan as an exceptional counterpart to the West within the non-Western world was based on present evidence and a more conjectural reading of the past. Japan's unique record of Westernizing on its own terms raised questions about indigenous preconditions and suggested long-term historical parallels which have to some extent been confirmed by research. Similarly, the shift towards more emphasis on Japan's affinities and connections with other East Asian countries is founded on observable fact. The emergence of new developmental states in the region (Korea and Taiwan, followed – albeit with some qualifications – by mainland China) has cast doubt on earlier constructs of Japanese exceptionalism and drawn attention to more broadly shared patterns of modernization. It is the whole 'Sinified new world'[1], i.e. a cluster of countries with a common heritage of Chinese origin, rather than Japan alone, which is now seen as the non-Western modernizer par excellence. The apparent spread of similar models of growth to Southeast Asia has prompted some analysts to subsume that region under an expanded idea of East Asia.[2] However, though the tendency to disregard historical and cultural boundaries may well be strengthened by the current 'Asian crisis', this line will not be taken here. Within a more circumscribed context, the recent ascendancy of East Asia has served to remind comparative historians of the very distinctive regional responses to Western expansion and hegemony, as well as of a well-established identity and prominent place in history prior to the encounter with the West. The early modern phase of East Asian history is of particular interest. This may not be the only non-Western region that can be said to have 'entered the modern age as a mature but still vigorously productive civilization',[3] but such judgments are more obviously applicable to it than to any other part of the world outside Europe. There is, in short, a whole series of reasons to reflect on the interpretive problems inherent in theorizing the East Asian experience – and the Japanese part of it – from a comparative angle.

The view from Europe

To grasp the implications of the turn from Western to East Asian starting-points for comparative analysis, it may be useful to recapitulate some aspects of the earlier approach. The East Asian connection is not only important for its own sake, but also as a necessary background to any further comparison across regional or civilizational boundaries, and it may be relevant to problems first posed in a European perspective.

Interpretations of Japan by Western historians and social scientists are rooted in broader but less articulate ways of relating one cultural universe to another. If we begin with these underlying views, the notion of Japan as a particularly distant and enigmatic 'other' is too familiar to need references. It may be less widely understood that this idea has coexisted with strong claims about parallels or convergences between Japan and Europe. A fundamentally alien identity seems compatible with inbuilt affinities of a more specific kind. Arguments in that vein range from sixteenth-century views of the Japanese as the most perfect natural Christians to recent presentations of Japan as a pioneer or model of postmodernity. In between, we may note Marx's reference to Japan as a museum of European institutions and the later image of Japan as 'the essential modernizer'[4], i.e. as more directly predisposed to modernizing change than the original Western cases in point. In short, it seems evident that Western visions of Japan have tended to highlight a paradoxical combination of essential difference and contingent similarity.

It may be possible to spell out the underlying logic of this dual image. On the one hand, the exceptionally pronounced otherness of Japan has to do with a pattern of collective identity that is less dependent on universalist models and therefore less open to interpretation along their lines than are the cultural models linked to world religions or to civilizations shaped by them. Radical particularism is more resistant to a fusion of horizons than the rival universalism of non-Western traditions. On the other hand, the attitudes seen as conducive to change or comparable to Western sources of dynamism are not unrelated to the particularist background. The very self-defining distance inherent in the latter makes it possible to pursue a course of adaptive learning and transformation without loss of identity. The particularist core is constructed in terms of self-contained variability, rather than firmly defined contents, and it is compatible with practices which observers can interpret in terms of pragmatism, relativism or eclecticism; whether such dispositions are treated as modern or post-modern may depend on the conceptual framework.

There are thus some grounds for arguing that a pre-theoretical conception of contrasts and similarities between Japan and Europe (more generally between Japan and the West) has long been operative, and that it prefigures the theoretical task of accounting for a very peculiar case of structural convergences across a cultural divide. But this pre-comprehension is not easily translatable into a more analytical language. More systematic versions of comparative historical inquiry entail a one-sided focus on social structures, by definition easier to thematize from a comparative angle, and lead to overstated analogies at that level, in contrast to a cultural domain of residual and under-theorized otherness. The far-reaching conclusions drawn from problematic parallels between European and Japanese feudalism are perhaps the best-known claims in this vein.[5]

When it comes to sociological analysis in the more restricted disciplinary sense, the account of contrasts and affinities is even less balanced. A strong tendency to transfigure Western developments into general trends leaves little scope for specific parallels with the Japanese case. Similarities can at best be seen as accelerating or facilitating factors, relative to uniform patterns of change, and the most exceptional aspects of the Japanese experience can in that context only play a limiting role. This way of thinking culminated in the rival models of orthodox Marxism and mainstream modernization theory during the first postwar decades. But if we want to reconstruct the history of Western sociological approaches to Japan in somewhat greater detail, three phases may be distinguished. For the classics, Japan was a very marginal theme, but intriguing enough to inspire some speculation about its particular importance to comparative sociology. Arguments along these lines are, however, prone to exaggerate the affinities between Japanese and Western history, sometimes to the point of contradicting their own underlying assumptions. Durkheim used the work of a Japanese sociologist to construct a very comprehensive model of parallel development (presented as a prelude to, rather than an application of general theory), including – even then – manifestly untenable claims about the role of urban communities and a rising bourgeoisie in Japanese history. Weber compared the divisions of medieval Japanese Buddhism to those of the European Reformation, but this seems incompatible with his simultaneous attempt to show that there was no specific religious background to Japanese economic and political modernity, as a religious *tabula rasa* would not allow any meaningful comparison with Protestantism.

Constructions of this kind had been discredited when the later theorists of modernization began to develop a more systematic framework for comparison. Their strong commitment to universalist readings of Western experience led them to minimize the autonomous development of Japan as well as of other societies outside the original home of modernity. The only comparative perspective that could be developed on this basis had to do with Japan's pioneering role and privileged place among non-Western latecomers. Modernization theory was thus left with an ambiguous model which could highlight either Japan's exceptional success or the essential similarity of choices imposed by global constraints in spite of cultural diversity, and stress either the early dynamism of Meiji Japan or the persistent imbalances of its legacy.[6] Finally, the most recent developments in Western sociological theory are ambiguous in another sense: on the one hand, the major protagonists of conceptual innovation are markedly uninterested in lessons from the Japanese experience, but on the other hand, there are significant – albeit still very atypical – attempts to rethink central theoretical problems with particular reference to Japan. Eisenstadt's work on Japanese civilization is the most representative project of the latter kind.

Reconstructing a region

The above-mentioned approaches have one thing in common: they consistently sidestep the question of Japan's belonging to the East Asian region and the implications of that context for comparative analysis. Recent interest in the East Asian connection has more to do with historical changes than with theoretical reflection, and if it is to be shown that the regional perspective has some bearing on broader issues, we must begin with a brief survey of past and present constellations.

Cultural patterns and historical trends

It should, first of all, be noted that we are referring to East Asia in the narrow sense, i.e. distinguishing it, on cultural and historical grounds, from Southeast Asia. If the region is defined in this way, its core consists of China (not including the Central Asian territories now ruled by the Chinese state), Korea and Japan. Its contemporary profile has been significantly affected by the separate development of two offshoots of China (Taiwan and Hong Kong). From a long-term perspective, it is perhaps more important that successive waves of Chinese migration to Southeast Asia projected East Asian patterns of organization and development beyond the borders of the region; Singapore is the only independent political embodiment of that trend.

Some further details might be added to the historical picture. The maritime and commercial polity of the Ryukyu Islands was an interesting and anomalous part of the regional state system, but did not survive the transition to advanced modernity and tougher interstate competition. Finally, there are important overlaps with other regions. Vietnam is often seen as a part of the Chinese cultural sphere, but it seems more appropriate to treat it as a historical mixture of East and Southeast Asian elements. The profound and durable influence of the Chinese model was counterbalanced by older patterns of Southeast Asian origin, as well as by the dynamics of interaction with neighboring Indianized states. At the opposite side of the Chinese heartland, Manchuria is best described as a shifting borderland between two regions. For most of premodern history, it was a peripheral part of the Inner Asian zone of imperial counter-formation.[7] In the seventeenth century, it became the launching pad for the last Inner Asian conquest of China, and as a result, it was more thoroughly assimilated into the Chinese world than other external arenas. In the twentieth century, it became a decisive battleground for three different visions of China's future, namely Japanese hegemony, Nationalist state-building and the Communist revolution.

These comments should suffice to show that East Asia was, historically speaking, a very complex configuration of central, peripheral and external parts. In some ways, Japan combines central and peripheral characteristics, and the latter aspect suggests some interesting lines of comparison. The interplay of Chinese and indigenous traditions in Japan and Vietnam took very different directions, but some analogies can be found. Comparison with the Ryukyu Islands may serve to highlight aspects which were submerged or marginalized by the development and later decomposition of the Japanese imperial state. In general terms, the interplay of foreign conquest and counter-expansion is absent from Japanese history before 1868 (apart from an unsuccessful invasion in the thirteenth century and an abortive bid for a mainland empire at the end of the sixteenth century), and this record can be contrasted with other parts of the region. But here we must limit the discussion to more central themes. The focus will be on Japan as one of the three core countries mentioned above. After a brief survey of basic common characteristics, some questions relating to Japan and each of the two other countries in particular will be considered.

The East Asian region is, as has often been pointed out, characterized by a particularly tangible source of cultural unity: the Chinese writing system. This conspicuously distinctive feature becomes even more significant if we accept that it is not a case of an archaic technique failing to follow the mainstream pattern of evolution towards alphabetic writing, but rather of a written language achieving a unique degree of autonomy and self-rationalizing capacity vis-a-vis the spoken one.[8] The independence and durability of ideographic writing can, in turn, only be understood in the light of cultural foundations and connotations: it depends on a 'shared conceptual language of textual precedent'.[9] In the Japanese case, the cultural background to the Chinese writing system stands out in particularly clear relief because of its encounter with a native but eminently receptive tradition. The relationship between imported and indigenous elements remains controversial, but some basic facts are beyond doubt. An imported writing system could not have been imposed on an alien language without backing by a comprehensive and superior cultural model.[10] Conversely, the tensions and dissonances created at this most elementary level of discourse were bound to affect the whole cultural context, however difficult it may have been be to reduce their ramifications to a general formula. From the present perspective, this intercultural constellation may be seen as an exceptionally acute variant of the regional pattern which maximizes the distance between a culturally charged and standardized written language on one side and oral, local or subaltern discourses on the other.

To complement and counterbalance this strong *prima facie* case for cultural identity, some aspects of regional political history should be noted. The East Asian zone has never been united within one imperial formation. The only serious premodern attempt to achieve that goal was made by conquerors coming from elsewhere (the Mongols), and symbolic sovereignty without imperial control (the Chinese 'tributary system') was a more regular and codified part of the traditional order than anywhere else. But the existence and predominance of a uniquely permanent imperial centre was nevertheless crucial to the cultural unity of the region. The prestige and legitimizing potential of the Chinese cultural model was more durably dependent on imperial power than any other comparable civilizational framework (in the case of Islam, the initial connection to an imperial project was more direct, but also much more short-lived). Cultural influence goes beyond imperial control, most obviously in the case of Japan, but it reflects imperial presence of an unusually massive kind.

We are thus faced with a distinctive pattern of interrelations between culture and power, characteristic of the region for a long time and constitutive of the identity that makes it one of the more clearly demarcated long-term geocultural and geopolitical arenas of world history. But this configuration is also reflected in a historical trend which became more pronounced after a temporary shift in the other direction. The East Asian region has mostly been less actively involved in world affairs and global developments than its relative strength and internal dynamism would have seemed to warrant. More specifically, East Asia has – in contrast to some other major civilizational areas – not given birth to universal religions with a missionary thrust, and the power dynamics of the region were not very conducive to projects of imperial expansion beyond cultural boundaries. The prevalent pattern was, in short, characterized by a mutual closeness of culture and power which set specific limits to developments on both sides. The vision of cosmic order and the model of imperial order that took shape together during the formative phase of the Chinese tradition did not wholly exclude deviant modes of thought, but they were confined to marginal roles and derivative themes. The original Chinese combination could be reproduced on a peripheral scale with more or less significant modifications and simultaneous reconstructions of native traditions (Japan and Korea represent two very different variants of that pattern), but no rival center or alternative claimant to hegemony could develop alongside China. The relationship between the interpretive framework and the imperial paradigm could be redefined in a more or less far-reaching fashion, but the dominant way of doing so centred on the reappropriation of classical sources.

Although the smaller-scale replication of the Chinese model within the region did not lead to the intra-civilizational power struggle that developed in other major regions, it could be translated into strategies of isolation, designed to minimize direct contact despite ongoing or even intensified cultural borrowing. The ambitions and effects of such policies varied greatly in the course of East Asian history. But from our point of view, it is of particular interest that both the overall detachment of the region from the global arena and the pattern of interstate seclusion within the region became more pronounced with the transition to early modernity, i.e. at the very historical juncture when the first wave of Western expansion was gathering momentum. The efforts of East Asia, in particular by China, to 'be a world on its own and…to remain so'[11], despite growing involvement in an international economy and increased visibility in the global arena, cannot be explained as a defensive response to Western initiatives. The most plausible view is that the logic of cultural orientations favoured a more inward-looking strategy than the wealth and power of the region might have suggested. Analogously, the isolationist stance of the two smaller countries in question cannot be seen as a purely strategic position; the measures taken went far beyond any situational constraints and are in both cases linked to cultural legitimation, be it through exclusivist claims to particular perfection of the Chinese model (Korea) or constructs of an imaginary alternative to the Chinese world order (Japan).

These aspects of early modernity in East Asia seem particularly striking when contrasted with the exceptional dynamism of the region after the nineteenth-century breakdown of the old order. East Asian responses to Western expansion in its culminating phase, exemplified in different ways by the long-drawn-out revolutionary upheaval in China and the sustained state-guided transformation of Japan, have been more momentous than those of any other non-Western societies. The relationship between early modern strategies of containment and advanced modern patterns of change is an intriguing and still underdeveloped theme for comparative history.

China, Japan and Korea

To complete this survey of the region from a historical point of view, a few relevant aspects of Japan's relationship to the two other core countries should be noted. As for China, the traditional view is that premodern and early modern Japan was a cultural satellite of China (this leaves room for debate on the relative importance and authenticity of surviving native traditions, and also on the question of continuous trends or separate waves of signification). However, this very condition and the attitudes it had fostered made it possible to shift the focus of learning and borrowing to the Western powers which displaced the Chinese empire. It was therefore – in conjunction with other factors – instrumental in setting the Japanese modernizing process apart from the much more protracted Chinese one. The civilizational shift from Chinese to Western models was, moreover, accompanied by an attempt to restructure the regional order along Western lines, re-centre it around Japan and reduce the former centre a to peripheral status. While this interpretation is not fundamentally wrong, it must be integrated into a more balanced picture which has gradually emerged from historical research.

First and foremost, the traditional relationship between Japan and China should be analyzed from both sides. As Marius Jansen has argued, China's role in relation to Japan was unique: it was a 'cultural colossus which endured', combining – in European terms

– the characteristics of ancient Greece, the Roman Empire, Renaissance Italy and eighteenth-century France.[12] But Japan's position with regard to China was no less peculiar in that it combined features which elsewhere tend to diverge. Cultural assimilation on a scale usually linked to foreign conquest or control was in this case counterbalanced by political segregation to a degree normally incompatible with cultural unity. This constellation gave rise to further distinctive developments. Political autonomy enabled the Japanese importers and interpreters of Chinese culture to construct and reconstruct a model of the latter on their own terms, to pursue strategies of selective appropriation with changing priorities and to keep the synthesis of the Chinese and native traditions open to new combinations. Cultural borrowing made it possible to reinforce the authority of the Japanese state within a particularist framework and without entering into an open contest with the Chinese centre, whose symbolic resources were thus put to independent but not antagonistic use. In brief, it may be suggested that these interconnected aspects of the Japanese tradition resulted in the constitution of a virtual regional centre alongside the real and formative one. As far as I can judge, there was no comparable development within any other civilizational complex. The modern transformation of East Asia can then be seen as a radical – but still inconclusive – restructuring of the relationship between the two centres.

With regard to the more specific mechanisms and pathways of the modernizing process, changing perspectives have brought the Chinese and Japanese variants closer to each other. The decay of Chinese Communism has effaced the apparent contrast between two incompatible and equally systematic models of modernity. On the Chinese side, affinities between the late imperial projects of self-strengthening statecraft and the post-Communist search for a strategy of development are becoming more visible.[13] This continuity can at the same time be seen as a much weaker parallel to the progress of the Japanese developmental state. In other words, it now seems less plausible to interpret the last century of Chinese history in terms of an alternative path to modernity, and it may make more sense to see it as a series of interrupted moves in a direction prefigured by Japan, but obstructed by the Chinese imperial legacy and its revolutionary mutant. This does not mean that we can reduce the role of Chinese Marxism to a disturbing factor which did not operate in Japan. As recent comparative research has shown, the strikingly different destiny of Marxism in the two countries should not obscure the fact that its rise and decline was in both cases linked to processes of state-building and formation of national identity.[14] Japanese Marxism was a theoretical alternative as well as an elusive but not unimportant contributor to the nationalist strategy of the developmental state, and Chinese Marxism served to legitimize the most effective among rival strategies of state-building during the twentieth-century post-imperial crisis, although it also played a role in the self-destructive turn taken after a phase of consolidation.

Comparisons of Japan and Korea face a very different task as they must begin with the closely – and one-sidedly – linked trajectories of the two countries after the nineteenth-century turning-point in East Asian history. *The prima facie* case for a crucial Japanese input into the Korean modernizing process is obvious, not only with regard to the Japanese colonial state (and the economic policies implemented as part of its buildup for further expansion), but also in the sense that Korean strategies of development from the 1960s onwards drew on Japanese precedents. Evidence of Korean originality can, on the other hand, be found in distinctive features of the developmental state and its nationalist ideology, but this side of the argument has been less focused, and its most forceful versions tend to stress indigenous obstacles rather than impulses.[15] There has been less debate on the long-term historical background, i.e. the specific and enduring structural differences that might to some extent account for the very different Japanese and Korean responses to the end of East Asian isolation. The traditional and still widely held view is that Korea took the common condition of cultural dependence on China much further than Japan, combined the symbolic acceptance of Chinese sovereignty with a self-image centred on small-scale reproduction and conservation of the Chinese model, and was therefore much less capable of the ideological and political mobilization of indigenous traditions against the old order. It may be possible to restate the valid part of this claim in terms which make it more amenable to qualifications.

It seems clear that there was a very significant difference between the ways of combining Chinese and native traditions in Japan and Korea: in the Korean case, there was no parallel to the construction of Shintō, i.e. no ongoing refashioning of a pre-existing religious culture with the aid of inputs from elsewhere but for the purpose of maintaining an ostensibly separate source of identity. And by the same token, there was no equivalent to the Japanese imperial institution as an extensively Sinified but artificially archaized version of sacred kingship. These contrasts are obviously important, but they do not exclude other differences which might have to do with more original Korean variations on the Chinese pattern. Drawing on the work of James B. Palais, it may be suggested that such divergences can be located on the level of power structures, and that they open up new perspectives for comparing Korea and Japan. On this view, the two countries were characterized by significantly different ways of maintaining a more aristocratic social structure than their common model civilization had done, and this was in both cases achieved through reconstruction in response to change, rather than simply by virtue of entrenched traditions.[16]

In Korea, as in Japan, we can distinguish successive waves of Sinification; the fourteenth-century wave led to a much more thoroughgoing Confucianization of Korean thought and culture than ever happened in Japan, but this process was – paradoxically – accompanied by the consolidation of an institutional framework markedly different from the one that had already taken shape in China. The dominant element of the new order was the *yangban* aristocracy. Its virtual monopoly of access to bureaucratic office contrasts with the 'real' Chinese model, but the fusion of aristocratic and bureaucratic power can, as Palais argues, be seen as an authentic institutional expression of the ambiguities inherent in the Confucian vision of authority. On this view, the Korean social regime embodied and sustained a balancing act which proved impossible in China and was never attempted in Japan. But on the other hand, the Confucian-bureaucratic nexus was only one aspect of a more complex aristocratic power structure which differed markedly from Chinese principles and practices. Palais notes the persistence of large-scale slavery (unique in the East Asian context), the institutionalized limits to strong monarchy, and the permanent struggle between hereditary factions who strove to control the centre, rather than to decentralize power.

The *yangban,* the dominant class at the centre of this configuration, was a hereditary elite, but of a peculiarly elusive and potentially unstable kind: it was based on a shifting combination of property, power and prestige. Here a comparison with Japan would seem particularly relevant. Both the court aristocracy of the early Japanese imperial state and the samurai of the early modern epoch were more strictly defined and more clearly demarcated hereditary elites than the *yangban*. However, in between, Japanese society went through a prolonged phase of relatively fluid and contested hierarchy which has no parallel in Korea (the *yangban* regime can perhaps be seen as a more limited loosening of earlier and stricter rules). We cannot pursue this topic further, but a general conclusion can be drawn: when discussing the transformations of the Chinese model in the East Asian context, the question of aristocratic limits to bureaucratic rationality and Confucian ethics cannot be posed in simple terms. The character and meaning of aristocratic elements depends on the historical context, and the forces that block certain Confucian potentialities may favor others.

Confucian traditions and civilizational traits

So far, we have outlined the historical contours of the East Asian region and briefly explored the most obvious lines of comparison. The next step will involve more theoretical issues: the problems of conceptualizing the identity and trajectory of the region must be confronted, with particular reference to Japan's place within it and with a view to integrating other perspectives on the Japanese experience.

Traditions in context

Historical formations of the type and dimensions to be discussed here have traditionally been a key theme of civilizational theory. The conceptual foundations are notoriously uncertain. For our purposes, it will be enough to note a strong tendency to equate civilizational spheres with major religious traditions. This is evident in the conventional notions of the Christian, Islamic or Hindu civilization. If we try to approach the East Asian area from this angle, we face a dilemma. On the one hand, Buddhism, the regional tradition that can most convincingly claim the status of a world religion, was imported from elsewhere long after the emergence of a distinctive regional macroculture. It suffered major setbacks during later phases (although not everywhere to the same extent), and could never – even temporarily – achieve the exclusive primacy which other versions of it enjoyed in some other parts of Asia. On the other hand, Confucianism, the tradition most closely identified with regional identity, seems to lack some of the features usually regarded as essential to a religious belief system.

Among Western interpreters, its status as a religion has therefore been permanently contested, all the more so since this religious underdevelopment appears to explain its failure to resist the uniquely peaceful spread of Buddhism in the region. If we go on to consider the Japanese case, the difficulties are compounded with regard to both traditions. They did not simply interact and mix with indigenous sources – which is not exceptional – but rather, they became parts of a much more uncommon pattern which allowed for an ongoing recombination of traditions without mutual absorption or concluding synthesis. And if we add to this the fact that Japan later proved exceptionally receptive to Western civilization without any significant opening to its dominant religion (the absence of large-scale Christian inroads after 1868 is all the more remarkable because of the contrast with a short-lived early modern success), it is tempting to conclude – as Max Weber suggested in his brief excursus on Japan – that Japan represents a case of religious under-determination.

Notwithstanding the problems noted above, the idea of a Confucian region, tradition or civilization is still the interpretive key most frequently used to theorize the East Asian experience, and most favoured by those who try to situate Japan within that context (the notion of a more broadly defined Buddhist civilization has proved much less viable). This line of argument is often based on more or less explicit attempts to present the apparent weaknesses of Confucianism as underlying strengths. The absence of fully-fledged orthodoxy in the style of universal religions is taken to mean that Confucian ways of thought could prevail in a more flexible fashion and constitute a common frame of reference without a frontal assault on other traditions. By the same token, Confucian hegemony was less dependent on codified doctrine and more a matter of strategic institutions, such as the family, the examination system and the imperial bureaucracy. The emphasis on institutional practices can, moreover, be seen as a secularizing bent which prefigures more systematic shifts in the course of modernization. Confucianism would, in this regard, seem to have been more predisposed to a modern reorientation than the otherworldly traditions sometimes credited with that capacity. Let us note in passing that these considerations are not easily applicable to Japan. In the Japanese tradition, Confucian elements could not claim the central and formative role which they played in China; key institutions and official rituals were never adopted, and the most emphatic invocations of Confucian ethics after the transition to advanced modernity were linked to an explicit resacralization of authority.

Another obvious but answerable objection to the idea of a Confucian civilization has to do with the ambiguity of basic premises. It is a matter of ongoing debate whether the notions of 'heaven' and 'will of heaven' refer to a sacred dimension of reality, and how thoroughly it has been de-personalized. The Confucian ideal of a 'gentleman' can be interpreted as a proposal to humanize and moralize a pre-established aristocratic regime, or as a more radical meritocratic model. And the well-known emphasis on the family as a paradigm of order is similarly double-edged: it reflects a vision of social integration through family solidarity, as well as a prior adjustment of family organization to political imperatives, and the relative weight of the two orientations remains controversial. All these points cast further doubt on notions of Confucian orthodoxy, but the civilizational perspective can be articulated in a way which puts them to more constructive use. The ambiguities in question – as well as others – can be seen as starting-points for different lines of interpretation, and the Confucian universe of discourse and practice will then appear as a cluster of interrelated but not mutually integrated traditions. This redefinition of the Confucian framework, with a stronger emphasis on its internal differentiation, is doubly relevant to the countries which borrowed Confucian ideas at a later stage. Here the different components of the original configuration could be appropriated in a more selective fashion and adapted to the demands of a milieu which did not share the whole history of the Confucian complex.

Confucianisms compared: A rejoinder to Rozman

With these considerations in mind, we should now take a closer look at the Japanese case. Gilbert Rozman's essay on Confucian values in China and Japan will be a convenient starting-point for further discussion.[17] It is, if I am not mistaken, the most systematic attempt to show that traditional constellations and modern developments in China and Japan can be analyzed as variants of a common Confucian pattern (there is no reference to Korea, but as the above comments suggest, comparison with the particular features and directions of Korean Confucianism might open up interesting perspectives). Rozman's account of Japan's place within the Confucian world is, moreover, designed to explain the very characteristics which could, from a more one-sided point of view, be seen as symptoms of Japanese exceptionalism and reasons for suggesting analogies with the West.

The case for approaching the problematic of East Asian identity and development from a Confucian angle can be summed up very briefly. In the light of past and present achievements, it seems appropriate 'to view this region as an imposing sociological phenomenon in which human relations have been moulded to maximize collective action'.[18] During earlier historical periods, this mobilizing and organizing capacity was most evident in unusually sustained dynamics of state formation. In the advanced modern phase, the same underlying logic leads to a new emphasis on economic development as a collective goal, with a strategic role reserved for the state. The grounds for assuming a distinctively Confucian contribution to this historical record have to do with persistent attitudes rather than any doctrinal contents. The commitment to education, the mutual reinforcement of families and larger collectivities, and the combination of hierarchy and mobility did not *ipso facto* subvert the traditional order, but after a modernizing turn in response to external pressures, they could be harnessed to developmental goals.

Apart from these preliminary observations, for our purposes, Rozman's argument can be recapitulated in two steps. He first distinguishes five traditions within the Confucian complex. As he sees it, they all existed in Japan as well as in China, even if some of them differ in significant ways and the overall configuration does not take the same form. The beliefs and rituals most closely associated with central political authority can be described as *imperial Confucianism;* in Japan, this was 'less central and more detachable from other parts of the tradition'[19] than in China. *Reform Confucianism,* persistently underestimated by those who see the whole tradition as conformist or adaptive, represented a counterweight and corrective to imperial rule, in that it gave voice to demands for a moral upgrading of authority, but it could be co-opted by rulers intent on improving their public image as well as their techniques of control. As Rozman points out, the latter trend was stronger in Tokugawa Japan than in late imperial China, and it can to some extent be seen as a precursor to later governmental activism. *Elite Confucianism* was the set of cultural orientations and codes of conduct essential to the collective identity of a dominant group. Here the contrast between China and Japan is perhaps most pronounced, because of the differences between the scholar-officials and the samurai. *Merchant-house Confucianism* represents an attempt by an officially downgraded group to codify its own version of 'loyal service to an organization that modeled itself on the family'[20]. Finally, Rozman's last category, *mass Confucianism,* is residual in that it refers to changing, but on the whole increasing, results of the diffusion of Confucian notions among the peasantry.

In short, Rozman's account of Chinese and Japanese Confucianism leads to the conclusion that the latter was more flexibly structured, and therefore more easily recomposed and reoriented. But at a more general level, his interpretive framework is still Sinocentric and inadequate to the Japanese context. The claim that 'the values are largely the same, although Japanese tradition gave greater weight to some'[21] is fundamentally misleading. It would be more appropriate to say that Japanese ways of combining Confucian values with others differed from the Chinese model and changed the relationship between various Confucian traditions. The difference is perhaps most obvious with regard to the symbolic centre of the tradition. Although the imperial institution drew on Confucian language and imagery in varying ways at different junctures in its history, the charter myth of a descent from heaven, instead of a mandate of heaven, must be seen as an unequivocal invalidation of Confucian principles. There was, strictly speaking, no tradition of imperial Confucianism, only a selective use of Confucian resources to dignify and consolidate an institution whose core had been immunized against the rationalizing and transformative potential of Confucianism, and because reform Confucianism was ultimately dependent on the same frame of reference as its imperial counterpart, the relativization of the latter affected the whole character of the former. The reformist version of the Japanese imperial imaginary was a restorationist stance, often reinforced by Confucian ideas but retaining its distinctive link to the dynastic myth. Although its ideological expressions and political implications varied in the course of Japanese history, the continuity of underlying orientations set it apart from other components of the tradition. As for the category of elite Confucianism which Rozman distinguishes from the traditions of rulers and reformers, it is perhaps even less applicable to Japan than the others. The history of samurai responses to Confucian culture is long and complex, and it includes episodes of intensive appropriation as well as emphatic distance. But as recent work on samurai ethos and identity has shown, a highly developed honor culture with strong ideological connotations predetermined the possible uses of implanted traditions, including Confucian ones.[22] A Confucian collective identity can be attributed to the Chinese scholar-officials, but not to the samurai. Finally, it seems unnecessary to discuss the two last categories – merchant house and mass Confucianism – in this context. Rozman sees them as derivative and subaltern in relation to the three dominant ones, and if the latter are less homogeneous than he claims, that must also apply to their secondary offshoots.

We can thus speak of different social forces and cultural currents involved in the Japanese reception of Confucianism, but in each case, the Confucian elements become parts of traditions with notably non-Confucian roots. On the other hand, the unifying aspects of Chinese Confucianism – canonized texts central to the educational system, a discursive framework built around those texts, and a corresponding set of cultural institutions – were absent from the Japanese version. It is therefore impossible to treat the two cases as comparably distinct and coherent variants of the same model. In more general terms, we cannot understand the Japanese adoption of the Chinese model as the transfer of a dominant tradition, even if we allow for some internal elasticity. Japanese transformations of the Chinese tradition changed the relative weight of its components and the relations between them. Chinese and indigenous sources interacted in a way which left them open to ongoing inputs from each other as well as to the possibility of re-polarization. Because of both these factors, the internal pluralism of the Japanese tradition took a distinctive form, different from the Chinese one. But it seems equally implausible to treat this outcome as a result of subsumption under preexisting native patterns. Such claims do not do justice to the historicity and originality of the successive constellations created in the course of Japan's engagement with China. The relationship between these two unequal centres of the East Asian region can thus serve to clarify a general point about civilizational theory: its field of inquiry cannot be limited to enduring and encompassing cultural patterns; rather, its frame of reference must be defined in such a way that it allows for the formation and reconstruction of such patterns, in and through interaction with other forces.

The most important of those other forces may be easier to identify if we return briefly to the other part of Rozman's argument. His analysis of the Confucian legacy as a cluster of traditions paves the way for an understanding of the Confucian imprint on modernity as a new tradition in the making, perhaps best described as developmental state Confucianism. Rozman does not use this term, but the idea seems implicit in his account of the modern fate of Confucianism in the two countries. As he sees it (or saw it at the beginning of the 1990s), phases of decline and rejection have in both cases alternated with those of partial reactivation, but in China, the phases of decline have been longer, the counter-trends more explicitly rejectionist, and the revivals much less effective. Most importantly, the Japanese search for a stable synthesis of Confucian attitudes and modern practices has gone far beyond anything attempted in China. This argument is obviously not about a self-perpetuating or spontaneously mutating tradition. Rather, aspects or elements of the Confucian complex are mobilized or marginalized as parts of a more comprehensive strategy. The mere fact that the relative role of Confucian elements varies conspicuously from phase to phase suggests that the decisive factors are to be found elsewhere, and Rozman's concrete analysis makes it clear that they are primarily political. The consolidating phases of the Meiji state and the postwar developmental state after the Occupation reforms were characterized by the most extensive and effective use of Confucian traditions. In China, both the ineffective Nationalist state between the wars and the inconclusive reforms after the anti-traditionalist paroxysm of the Cultural Revolution fell far short of Japanese achievements in this field. The link to more or less successful strategies of state-building does not mean that the Confucian framework is a purely ideological construct; it should rather be seen as a cultural resource which helps to articulate, embed and justify the projects of the developmental state.

But if the modern vicissitudes of Confucianism are thus related to the more or less successful strategies of the developmental state, it might seem appropriate to shift the line of argument towards the latter. Rozman's own analysis reaches a point where the continuing relevance of Confucian values as such appears less important than their progressive adaptation to historical innovations in the economic and political sphere. And in view of the stark contrasts between Chinese and Japanese achievements in that regard, it is tempting to link the changed perspective to a corresponding view of regional history. The focus on state-centred modernization goes together with a strong emphasis on Japan's central role in the modern transformation of East Asia. On this view, the transition to advanced modernity coincides with an abrupt transfer of primacy and initiative from one centre to another, and a Japanocentric approach to recent history is therefore no less justified than the Sinocentric one in earlier phases. It can then be argued that the more or less far-reaching direct or indirect impact of Japanese growth and expansion on the other countries in question is the key factor in the political and economic dynamics of the region.[23]

Long-term perspectives

There is, of course, no denying that Japan was – after 1868 – the main regional catalyst of change, and that this role continued in less conspicuous ways after the retreat from expansionism. But this is not the only point highlighted by the above argument. A brief outline of other implications may serve to suggest a more balanced view of regional interconnections. It would do more justice to the autonomy of the Japanese trajectory within the traditional framework as well as to the plurality of developmental patterns during the last century. The key to that perspective is a more long-term approach to the prehistory of the developmental state. Although we cannot go into details, it seems safe to say that recent work on the Tokugawa period has opened up new possibilities of linking the Japanese case to more developed accounts of long-term state formation in other parts of the world, without losing sight of the specific features which set it apart. This does not entail any strong constructions of continuity: no historian has ever suggested that the Tokugawa regime could be described as a developmental state, and growing insight into the Meiji origins of the latter is related to better understanding of the whole Meiji constellation as a particularly innovative phase. Rather, the most striking aspect of the transition from Tokugawa to Meiji is a paradox. Control, containment and isolation had been the unconditional priorities of the Tokugawa state, imposed in an exceptionally methodical fashion; but this very regime then proved to have created essential preconditions for conversion to developmental goals. Some of the underlying and unintended connections that help to explain this have been explored by historians. The particular characteristics of the Tokugawa power structure (the division of authority between center and domains) gave rise to unusually intensive forms of bureaucratic administration. At the same time, the structural logic of the regime transformed its social basis – the samurai class – in ways which proved conducive to a more activist version of the bureaucratic ethos. The 'global' strategy of the Tokugawa (best understood in terms of the vision of an imaginary world order centred on Japan, not to be confused with isolationism pure and simple) fostered a more radical kind of particularism, not identical with, but eminently adaptable to modern nationalism; other factors could be added to the list.

It would be instructive to compare China and Japan from this angle. As noted above, observers have recently become more aware of similarities between the nineteenth-century beginnings and the present phase of Chinese modernization, and of the crucial role of statecraft in both cases. The imperial legacy inherited by the Chinese pioneers of state-controlled opening was very different from the Japanese one, and so was the configuration of social forces which shaped the setting of Chinese history after the terminal crisis of the empire. A closer analysis of these background contrasts would throw new light on both sides.

On the other hand, the distinctive course of state formation in Japan did not begin with unification under Tokugawa rule. The power structure established after 1600 was the outcome of a long process with major turning-points, changing overall patterns and more or less visibly foreshadowed alternative lines of development. For the purposes of comparative analysis, it is essential to integrate this aspect of the Japanese historical experience into the framework of civilizational theory. This task reflects a more general theoretical issue: so far, the most seminal analysis of state formation in a long-term perspective – the work of Norbert Elias – has done more to generate a separate strand of civilizational theory than to enrich a broader agenda. Its theoretical and historical results have yet to be synthesized with those of the more widely pursued study of civilizations from a culturalist angle. The implications of such a conceptual fusion for the Japanese case are obvious: to analyze the dynamics of state formation is to give a more concrete historical content to the political autonomy which we have already noted as an important aspect of the civilizational relationship between China and Japan, and to specify the context in which the ongoing adaptation of the Chinese model took place. To reduce the imported Chinese traditions to mere instruments of state-building would be no less misleading than to explain political history in terms of a cultural program. But the focus on the interactions and interrelations of cultural patterns and power structures sets the course for a civilizational theory without inbuilt reductionist assumptions or one-sided explanatory models.

To conclude these reflections, a few words should be said about the implications of our civilizational and regional perspectives for the questions raised at the beginning. As suggested above, the rediscovery of Japan's East Asian roots might provide a new context for discussing the problems left pending by inconclusive comparisons of Japan and the West. Conversely, the significance of the East Asian connection can only be fully spelt out if we relate it to broader horizons. Our analysis of Japan's civilizational setting suggests a comparative perspective which may prove useful in both respects. Briefly, it seems possible to identify some interesting contrasts and parallels between Japan's relationship to China and that of Western civilization to its sources. This theme has not been completely absent from earlier discussions. For example, the two pioneering statements on feudalism in Europe and Japan – those of Marc Bloch and Otto Hintze – linked the rise of feudal institutions to the failure of attempts to revive or imitate imperial models, namely the Roman Empire in the West and the Chinese Empire in the East. Given the strong civilizational connotations of both models, this can be read as a pointer towards civilizational theory. But there is no explicit recognition of the need for it, and when civilizational points of view appear in later work on Japan and the West, they are mostly unrelated to the issue which interests us here.

A recent book by Rémi Brague contains a particularly interesting discussion of one of the paradoxes of European civilization: its derivative character as a source of originality. If we trace the history of European cultural and historical formations from Greek and Jewish beginnings to the modern globalizing turn, each stage is characterized by a constitutive relationship to earlier sources and paradigmatic precedents, but this background is integrated at a distance and identified with a past that has ceased to play a directly formative role.[24] The result of this specific relationship to an anterior 'significant other' (Brague uses the term *secondarité*) *is* an open-ended and pluralistic cultural identity, open to universalistic traditions and at the same time capable of questioning the orthodoxies that grow out of them. The most provocative part of Brague's thesis is that Roman attitudes to Greece marked the decisive step in this direction. This question is beyond the scope of the present paper, but its more general context may have some bearing on our understanding of Japan.

To elaborate on this point, let us briefly return to Jansen's comments on China and Japan. If the Chinese source differed from those of European traditions in that it combined the roles of successive historical strata and continued to exist as a dominant cultural and political centre, the Japanese relationship to it had to be correspondingly different from European constructions of origins and legacies. It can, however, be argued that this was also a case of derivative originality. If we can speak of a distinctive 'Japanese synthesis of China' (to use David Pollack's term), it must be added that China's continuing and overwhelming presence affected the character of this synthesis. Also, the maintenance of a separate identity alongside the internalized great tradition had to be based on an appropriately reinforced and reconstructed particularism, rather than a simple perpetuation of preexisting traditions. No stationary archaism could have sustained the ongoing and active encounter with China. Similarly, the preservation of political autonomy on the periphery of an imperial power was, in historical terms, bound up with an unusually self-contained process of state formation. But the long-term dynamics of that process were co-determined by lessons learnt from the regional environment in general and Chinese experience in particular.

From both points of view – the cultural and the political – the contrasts between Japanese and European patterns are obvious, but the background parallels seem strong enough to make comparison possible and relevant. Further details cannot be discussed here; suffice it to reiterate that the civilizational perspectives outlined above link up with the initial questions about Japan seen from the West, and confirm that they can more easily be answered from an East Asian angle.

Postscript: Empires and commonwealths

If the rediscovery of the East Asian region has opened up new comparative perspectives on Japan, a further question may be suggested: can we compare Japan's position within the East Asian constellation with similar situations elsewhere? The first point to be noted is that the core component of the East Asian complex – an enduring imperial formation at the centre of a larger civilizational zone – is a very rare phenomenon. In fact, there seems to be only one comparable case: the Roman-Byzantine empire and its civilizational setting. I use the term 'Roman-Byzantine' to avoid controversies about periodization. Although there are, in my opinion, good reasons to see the seventh century AD as a transition from the Late Roman to the Byzantine empire, many historians prefer the fourth century, and the argument to be considered here takes that line. The concept of the 'Byzantine Commonwealth' was first proposed by Dimitri Obolensky, with particular reference to the period between the ninth and the thirteenth centuries; more recently, Garth Fowden has argued that a 'First Byzantine Commonwealth' emerged between the fourth and the seventh centuries, but disintegrated under the impact of Islamic expansion.[25] The term 'commonwealth' refers to peripheral states which accepted Christianity and were more or less profoundly influenced by Byzantine culture, but did not come under direct imperial domination. At various historical junctures, this category included independent states in the Balkans, Russia and the Christian states in the Caucasus. In very general terms, this constellation resembles the East Asian one. But there are some obvious contrasts. The Byzantine pattern was more fluid and variegated (there is no parallel to the stability of the Sino-Korean-Japanese triangle), and the two successive versions of the commonwealth differ in important respects. On the other hand, Fowden argues that monotheism played a decisive role: 'The invention of commonwealth was an unintended result of Constantine's adoption of monotheism as a suitable creed for empire.'[26] Monotheism as a cultural and implicitly political model was not containable within the boundaries of the empire, and at the same time, its spread beyond them led to the multiplication of heterodoxy. The non-monotheistic model of the East Asian empire followed a different logic.

These questions have yet to be tackled in a systematic fashion. But they can perhaps be linked to one of the more intriguing recent exercises in comparative history. Donald Levine argues that parallels between Japanese and Ethiopian history are more extensive and significant than historians have hitherto noticed (late nineteenth- and twentieth-century Ethiopian aspirations to empire-building and modernization have occasionally been compared to the much more successful Japanese project, but without any discussion of similarities in the traditional backgrounds).[27] His argument is too complex and detailed to be recapitulated here. But it may be suggested that the Roman-Byzantine connection is not irrelevant. The Aksumite kingdom (the ancestor of the later Ethiopian state) was the most remote, least controllable and most ambitious member of the 'First Byzantine Commonwealth', and it does not seem too far-fetched to compare its relationship to Byzantium with the Japanese relationship to China. Levine mentions the conversions to Christianity and Buddhism as early turning-points in Ethiopian and Japanese history, but does not refer to the Byzantine Commonwealth. In any case, this problematic merits further discussion.

4 Is Japan a Civilization *Sui Generis*?

The reference to a civilization *sui generis* should be taken as a twofold claim: it suggests a civilization in its own right and on a par with others, but also a case which constitutes a civilization of a particular kind and in an atypical sense. The concept of civilization would, in other words, not be applicable without more or less significant twists to its mainstream meaning. If we accept this qualifying clause, the above question can – as I will argue – be answered with a cautious and conditional yes. There are valid reasons to interpret the Japanese experience in terms of civilizational theory, but the analytical framework will have to be adapted to the specific case. The civilizational identity that can be attributed to Japan is best understood as a self-singularizing pattern, constructed in relation and in contrast to pre-existing paradigms; it took shape in and through historical processes and remained open to further historical shifts; and its formative role must be analyzed in the context of a complex interaction between internal and external factors, rather than in the meta-historical perspective too often associated with civilizational theory. But before developing these points in more concrete terms, we should take a closer look at the conceptual backgrounds, so as to distinguish the present approach to civilizational theory from other uses of the same language.

Basic concepts and contested perspectives

The long and complex history of the notion of civilization (largely shared with the idea of culture) has given rise to multiple meanings, and debates about civilizational theory are often marred by a confused picture of this background. In the present context, suffice it to say that we will take our bearings from questions and controversies within the sociological tradition: here the concept of civilization emerges as a complement and corrective to a dominant image of society. This critical thrust – an effort to open up perspectives blocked by restrictive models – is evident in the Durkheimian contributions to civilizational theory, as well as in later attempts to turn this neglected aspect of the Durkheimian legacy against the structural- functionalist line of development.[1] In brief, the concept of civilization serves to highlight large-scale units and long-term processes which cannot be adequately accounted for within the self-limiting conceptual framework of conventional sociology. The concept of society, based on an idealized vision of normative integration and later translated into more abstract systemic models, tends to align the analytical perspective with inbuilt but illusory claims to closure (more precisely, as critics have argued, those of the nation-state). It is also conducive to another reductionist move: the bias in favour of social and/or systemic integration facilitated the 'retreat of sociology into the present' (Norbert Elias). The one-sided emphasis on a self-contained identity made the historical dimension of the social world seem less important.

By contrast, the concept of civilization – as defined and introduced by Durkheim and Mauss – is explicitly related to historical units made up of a plurality of societies. To speak of a civilization is to speak of a civilizational zone or area, and the unity of the latter is cultural rather than political (not that political unification of civilizational complexes is impossible, but it is obviously regarded as the exception rather than the rule). But civilizations also have a longer historical life span than the societies which they encompass, and there is a close connection between spatial and temporal aspects of this expanded field of sociological inquiry. The distinctive features and developmental potentials of large-scale units are revealed in long-term processes; conversely, the dynamics of the latter can only be understood in relation to a correspondingly broad context. On this view, analysis of 'determinate social organisms' (Durkheim and Mauss use this term to describe societal units in contrast to civilizational complexes) is doubly insufficient: it lacks the geocultural and macrohistorical horizons that are essential to the understanding of social life.

If we follow Mauss's most detailed outline of civilizational theory, four main themes may be distinguished.[2] The analysis of civilizations must begin with the elements of which they are composed; they are, as Mauss puts it, 'capable of travelling' across societal boundaries, and cultural patterns are the most obvious cases in point, although models of economic and political organization can also be included. Civilizational forms – the unifying principles of civilizational complexes – are based on distinctive combinations of such elements. In concrete historical terms, civilizational forms give shape to separate areas or regions. Finally, the interactions and interconnections of societies within a civilizational area vary – at least in part – with the civilizational form; for Mauss, a civilization is a 'family of societies', but it may be added that its form determines the specific content of the familial relationship.

This concept of civilization is obviously tailored to the cultural traditions that shape the history of whole geographical regions, such as the Islamic, Indian or Chinese worlds. Before going further, we should note the obvious problems in applying it to Japan. To speak of a separate civilization would, in this case, run counter to the main criteria invoked by Mauss: a Japanese civilization, defined apart from – and in contrast to – the China-centred East Asian complex, has to be constructed without reference to a regional mobility of socio-cultural patterns. The fact that the Japanese tradition has shown a markedly limited 'ability to travel' makes the argument all the more counter-intuitive. As I will try to show, it can nevertheless be sustained; at this point, suffice it to say that the question of Japan's civilizational identity cannot be settled without close analysis of the structural and self-interpretive relationship to the regional context. Other problems emerge when we consider the historical dimension. If Japanese history is in some ways unusually self-contained, that has more to do with political continuity (a long-term process of state formation, undisturbed by external forces) than with the cultural context; the latter is characterized by markedly varying levels of openness to external models, and at two crucial junctures (in relation to China and the West), heightened receptivity led to exceptionally radical realignments of the socio-cultural order. An underlying cultural continuity – one of the defining features of civilization in the Maussian sense – is thus anything but self-evident, and the case for an enduring civilizational identity or framework cannot be made without an account of the much more visible ruptures. At first sight, then, Mauss's reflections seem more likely to raise doubts about the idea of a distinctively Japanese civilization than to aid in theorizing it. It should nevertheless be noted that Mauss adumbrates a line of argument that may lead to other conclusions: he speaks of societies 'singularizing themselves' in relation to other parts of the same civilizational area. If we regard self-singularization within a civilizational context as an aspect (more or less pronounced) of the self-constitution of society, it seems legitimate to ask whether it can go far enough to generate a variant or alternative version of the shared pattern. Mauss does not raise this question, but it is not out of tune with his approach, and it has – as we shall see – a particular bearing on the case to be discussed below.

But civilizational perspectives on the Japanese phenomenon must be grounded in contemporary theory. Although the program outlined by Durkheim and Mauss has proved conducive to progress in different directions, connections with later authors are not always easy to trace, and another important source must be given its due. In brief, it seems to me that the most representative recent versions of civilizational theory are based on Durkheimian foundations inasmuch as they seek (in selective ways) to broaden the spatial and temporal horizons of sociological analysis, but that the specific contents of their claims to that effect are better understood as partial (albeit innovative) reinterpretations of the Weberian legacy. From this point of view, we can more easily distinguish two very different types of civilizational theory and assess the prospects of synthesizing their insights. We will then be in a better position to approach the Japanese case without one-sided preconceptions.

Among the classics of the sociological tradition, Max Weber's work stands out as the most ambitious and seminal contribution to the comparative study of civilizations, but his concrete analyses of civilizational complexes and their trajectories were not accompanied by any sustained reflection on the conceptual status and criteria of the civilizational units in question. In that respect, his ideas are less relevant to later debates than those of Durkheim and Mauss. His comparative studies focussed on rationalizing processes and the more or less significant socio-cultural breakthroughs resulting from them; although the widely varying contexts and directions of rationalization are underlined, the cultural background is never thematized in a systematic and balanced fashion, and this has often led critical readers to interpolate universal criteria of rationality. As a result, the multi-civilizational perspective is overshadowed by an explicitly or implicitly evolutionistic model. One of the two main contemporary types of civilizational theory may be seen as a response to this streamlining of the Weberian project. Its foremost representative is S.N. Eisenstadt, whose work is probably the single most decisive post-Weberian contribution to the comparative study of civilizations. Eisenstadt moves beyond Weber's analysis of diverse religious cultures to develop a more systematic account of the comprehensive cultural frameworks that set civilizational complexes apart from each other. In contrast to functionalist conceptions of culture as a programming and controlling instance, Eisenstadt stresses both its order-maintaining and order-transforming effects; but to underline its ultimate constitutive role, he uses terms like 'cultural cosmologies', 'basic ontological conceptions', 'cultural visions of the world', and other similarly accentuated ones. Some of his formulations might seem reminiscent of the cultural determinism which he criticizes on other levels. His theoretical project has, however, proved capable of generating extensive comparative research into the cultural traditions of major civilizations, the interplay of traditions and transformations in premodern history, and the impact of civilizational legacies on modernizing processes. Moreover, Eisenstadt has tried to locate Japan within his comparative framework and developed a very distinctive interpretation of Japanese uniqueness.

The other version of civilizational theory is also grounded in a critical appropriation of Weberian ideas; in this case, the neglected theme brought to the fore is the long-term transformative and rationalizing dynamic of power structures. Long-term rationalizing processes thus become much less dependent on pre-existing patterns of rationality than they were in Weber's view, and correspondingly more intertwined with the metamorphoses of power. Norbert Elias's analysis of the civilizing process – and of state formation as its central component – is the pioneering and paradigmatic example of this approach. Here the concept of civilization serves to highlight the historical depth of the processes in question as well as their all-round impact on the human condition. In contrast to Eisenstadt, comparative perspectives are much less evident, and Elias's attempts to anchor his historical sociology in an evolutionary framework did nothing to strengthen them. But as some of his less dogmatic followers have shown, the interpretive history of Western Europe from early medieval to early modern times – that is the concrete content of *The Civilizing Process* – can be taken as a starting-point for the study of contrasts and parallels with the trajectories of other civilizations.

Eisenstadt's conception of civilizational pluralism centres on cultural patterns, more precisely on cultural constructions of world order, and he is more interested in large-scale civilizational frameworks than in long-term civilizing processes.[3] But a culturalist orientation does not *ipso facto* lead to narrowly culturalist explanations: Eisenstadt is careful to emphasize that cultural models only become effective in conjunction with the strategies of social actors who serve to control resources and implement institutional rules. The interconnections of culture and power are thus in principle acknowledged as a key theme of civilizational theory. We can, however safely say that the distinctive features and directions which emerge at this level have so far figured less prominently in Eisenstadt's typology of civilizations than the cultural foundations as such, and we may surmise that the imbalance is due to choices built into Eisenstadt's very conception of culture; the strong emphasis on models (and the counter-models of protest) tends to devalue the more complex, ambiguous and mutable aspects of the cultural context. This suggested line of criticism will be reinforced by specific lessons from the Japanese experience. For the time being, let us note that Eisenstadt develops Weberian and Durkheimian themes well beyond the limits of classical thought, but in a fashion better suited to the reconstruction of overarching cultural traditions than to the analysis of historical transformations.

Conversely, Elias combined an innovative conceptualization of power with a concrete account of its long-term historical dynamics, and did so in a way which provokes further questions about the role of cultural factors, although his own work shows a marked inclination to minimize and marginalize them. The result was a distinctive paradigm of civilizational theory, less comprehensive and less diversified than Eisenstadt's, but complementary to it in certain respects, and more productively attuned to some aspects of the classical legacy. To sum up, we can therefore describe post-classical trends in the sociological discourse on civilization as separate but synthesizable moves towards a theory that could confront the tasks outlined by Durkheim and Mauss; if we want to envisage an effective fusion of the two paradigms in the field (or a critical combination of their insights), the question of adequate ways to theorize culture and power, as well as their interrelations, is obviously of prime importance.

These introductory remarks should help to avoid any misunderstanding of our claims on behalf of civilizational theory. But the sketch of sociological alternatives may also indicate the main source of such misconceptions. The contested character and marginal status of the sociological paradigm of civilization made it easier to develop an extra-disciplinary version of comparative analysis which has had a much greater impact on public perceptions of the field. Oswald Spengler and Arnold Toynbee are the best known representatives of that tradition; critics have tended to reject their work – as well as that of some less influential authors – as a fanciful and retrograde variant of the philosophy of history.[4] For present purposes, the insights or suggestions which might – contrary to blanket dismissals – still be found in works of this origin are less relevant than a pervasive bias which sets them apart from the sociological perspective to be explored here. It is not the idea of civilizational pluralism as such that is at issue, but rather the over-totalized conception grafted onto it: civilizational traditions and complexes tend to appear as closed worlds governed by their own unitary and comprehensive logic. Spengler's interpretation of cultures as monads is the most extreme case (it is immaterial to our concerns that he preferred to speak of cultures rather than civilizations, and reserved the latter term for phases of decline), but the more nuanced models constructed by Toynbee and others are still strongly slanted in the same direction.

The over-totalized image of civilization – more precisely: of civilizations in the plural – lends itself easily to ideological uses. In more or less close conjunction with a similarly accentuated concept of culture, it has often functioned as an ingredient of or substitute for nationalist discourse. The indigenization of Western notions of culture and civilization in Japan provides a particularly instructive example, and by the same token a clear indication of the pitfalls which a more critical civilizational theory must avoid.[5] But before confronting this all-too-familiar ideological tradition on its own ground, we must underline some further general points in contrast to its theoretical premises. One of the most obvious weaknesses of the over-totalized conception is its tendency to ignore or minimize 'intercivilizational encounters' (this term was coined by Benjamin Nelson with explicit reference to the sociological classics), i.e. the transformative impact of separate civilizational complexes on each other; interaction between such complexes is not *ipso facto* conducive to internal transformation, but developments of that kind have often been of major historical importance, and Japan is surely a prime case in point. A sociological theory of civilization, based on the abovementioned sources, can easily accommodate this question as a significant but variable part of its problematic. Similarly, it can allow for varying levels of internal coherence and homogeneity: civilizations can be more or less marked by a differentiation of central and peripheral traditions, and more or less open to the polarization of orthodoxy and heterodoxy.

The Chinese background

Those who reject the idea of a separate Japanese civilization, without contesting the general premises of civilizational analysis, tend to treat Japan as a part of the Sinic or Far Eastern civilizational area (this was, for example, Toynbee's original position). Conversely, any defence of Japanese originality against such claims must be based on evidence of deviation or primordial independence from the Chinese pattern. For the argument to be developed here, the question of the Chinese model and its impact is of particular importance: as I will try to show, a constitutive relationship to Chinese sources and criteria of civilizational identity was characteristic of the Japanese tradition from the outset of its recorded history, but the distinctive way of accepting and adapting a pre-given external paradigm sets the Japanese case apart from less autonomous variants of the Chinese pattern and lays the foundations for a line of development which can be seen as a civilizational constellation *sui generis* (in the double sense outlined above). This thesis represents, in a sense, a middle position between the idea of a unitary Sinic civilization and that of a self-contained Japanese core. We can describe Japanese civilization as derivative in the sense that it took shape within the orbit of an enduring centre and on the basis of a dominant regional model, but not in the sense of a mere imitation or diffusion of invariant patterns (and to call it a satellite civilization, as Toynbee did in the revised version of his typology, seems incompatible with the level of autonomy evident in its history). Further elaboration of this point must begin with a closer look at some key characteristics of the Chinese tradition; their implications and interconnections will help to understand the ascendancy as well as the adaptability of a cultural model in a regional context.

Other reasons of a more general kind speak for focussing on the Chinese background. It can be argued that this case provides a privileged starting-point for civilizational theory: it exemplifies a continuity of cultural orientations and corresponding political formations which fits the framework envisaged by Durkheim and

Mauss even better than other historical complexes of a comparable type (such as Islamic, Hindu or Western civilization). Civilizational foundations ensured the unity of the Chinese world throughout a phase of exceptionally intensive interstate competition (the 'warring states' from the eighth to the third century BC) as well as the unusual solidity of imperial structures after unification and in spite of successive major changes to the structures of Chinese society. The course of China's transformation into a modern nation-state shows how different the traditional form of unity was from the integrative mechanisms theorized (and transfigured) by mainstream sociology; the description of twentieth-century China as 'a civilization pretending to be a state' (Lucian Pye) may be misleading in that it minimizes the genuine (albeit inconclusive) changes that have taken place, but it does highlight a very important aspect of the problematic. As for the regional dimension, the civilizational resources of the Chinese centre enabled it to exercise more or less effective control far beyond the limits of conquest; cultural hegemony served to legitimize the 'tributary system' as a distinctive mode of interstate relations. In this way, subordination to Chinese cultural standards was combined with an elusive but not irrelevant recognition of political sovereignty; and even where the latter aspect of the model was rejected in principle (as in Japan), Chinese guidelines for state-building could still be used by indigenous elites. In short, the Chinese case convincingly meets the two conditions specified by Durkheim and Mauss: unity across political boundaries and continuity across historical passages.

If we consider the specific cultural premises of this historical record, they seem – as Benjamin Schwartz has argued – to centre on a particularly comprehensive, emphatic and resilient conception of order.[6] More precisely, the general notion of a primacy of order in both the cosmic and the human spheres culminates in 'the idea of a universal, all-embracing socio-political order centering on the concept of a cosmically based universal kingship'.[7] This central imaginary signification of order (to use the term introduced by Castoriadis) is open to divergent interpretations and adaptable to changing historical contexts. As Schwartz stresses, the mainstream of traditional Chinese thought is a shared problematic rather than a binding orthodoxy; different schools of thought develop distinctive variations on the theme of order, but the underlying common ground is strong enough to allow for combinations and cross-fertilizations on a much larger scale than in more polarized traditions. At the same time, the understanding of order and the cosmological grounding of social order are sufficiently flexible to accommodate protest within tradition. Finally, the traditional (and tradition-building) conception of order proved capable of re-elaboration at a higher level of reflexivity, in response to the impact of a more other-worldly religious culture (Buddhism) and by means of extensive borrowing from this rival source, but without problematizing its own fundamental continuity; this was the main achievement of the Neo-Confucian turn.

The Chinese conception of order, encapsulated in the notion of the Way, is – as Schwartz puts it – holistic and immanentistic. At the same time, it is characterized by ambiguities and elasticities that will be easier to understand if we consider the historical background. Although the present author cannot claim any independent expertise in this field, it seems clear that some theoretical lessons can be drawn from available work on Chinese intellectual and political history. We can, in particular, distinguish the case for shared and enduring cultural orientations from the more discredited notions of an invariant cultural essence or an unchanging social order. The underlying problematic of order is inherently ambiguous and conducive to tensions between different intellectual choices and traditions. Universalism and culturalism – the claim to represent an inclusive socio-cosmic paradigm and the emphasis on particular virtues derived from a privileged place within that framework – were complementary aspects of the Chinese tradition, rather than clear-cut opposites, and changing circumstances could strengthen one orientation at the expense of the other. Culturalist attitudes came to the fore when the Chinese empire had to retreat to a less dominant position within the region (from the tenth century onwards) and when it found itself on the defensive against the expanding West. This constellation differed from Islamic and Christian universalism as well as from the polarization of Hindu culturalism and Buddhist universalism within the Indian tradition. Similarly, the controversy about the religious core of the Chinese tradition in general and Confucianism in particular reflects an inbuilt ambiguity of the beliefs in question: for observers from other religions cultures, the sacred dimension of the Way was less obvious because of an early shift from theocentric to cosmocentric visions, and the most sociocentric version of the latter could be mistaken for a purely secular mode of thought. Those who took this view tended to neglect the Daoist tradition, more explicitly religious but less central to the dominant Chinese self-image than the Confucian one, and now more widely recognized as a formative cultural force than it was in earlier stages of Chinese studies. The question of Chinese religiosity (within the 'great tradition', not to be confused with the problematic of popular religion) must thus be linked to a historical analysis of implicit meanings shared by interconnected traditions and adaptable to changing priorities. Finally, the particularly emphatic and resilient notion of sacred kingship – inseparable from the imaginary of the Way – is both complemented and counterbalanced by another model of human harmony with cosmic order: the sage. A synthesis of these two ideals of human perfection was not inconceivable but it was projected into a mythical past; the distance maintained in historical times was one of the factors militating against the fusion of moral and cognitive authority in one centre (critical observers have suggested that the Chinese version of the 'cult of personality' under Mao Zedong had something to do with a reactivated mythical model of the emperor as sage).

The Chinese tradition is, in short, characterized by basic and recurrent ambiguities within a distinctive and durable framework. But we can also distinguish successive phases of elaboration and identify some major landmarks. Interpretations of the most archaic formative phase (the Late Bronze Age culture of the Shang dynasty in the second half of the second millennium BC) have highlighted two aspects which played a decisive role in the whole subsequent development of the tradition. On the one hand, a close connection between sacred kingship and imaginary kinship prefigures the later association of imperial authority with a family-centred image of society; on the other hand, the Shang monarchy had already secured the primacy of royal over priestly authority and confined the religious elite to the subordinate role of specialists in divination, but the growth and rationalization of this activity – with its emphasis on reading and interpreting natural signs – was conducive to a gradual transformation of the world-view towards a more supra-personal conception of an integrated socio-cosmic order. The Zhou state which replaced the Shang dynasty at the end of the second millennium inherited these cultural orientations and imposed further rationalizing shifts on the social as well as the cosmic side (the notion of a mandate of Heaven may date from this phase). The Zhou legacy was, in turn, assumed and reinterpreted by the various schools of thought which responded to the experience of political fragmentation and interstate competition from the seventh to the third century BC. Two striking features set this period of intellectual ferment and innovation apart from the otherwise comparable transformations which took place within other major civilizations during the same centuries: a particularly strong emphasis on a paradigm of order identified with a known historical period (not just with a mythical past) and a particularly close and positive relationship to the political order perceived as a normative framework of social life (it is not the case, as some interpretations have suggested, that classical Chinese thought is uniformly state-centred, but the dominant currents do affirm the primacy of political order, and the apparent deviations from that line are sometimes linked to the mainstream in less obvious ways).[8] The imperial unification of China and the construction of a correspondingly ambitious model of socio-cosmic order led to a reconfiguration of the intellectual field, but the model favoured by the new imperial centre was an eclectic combination of classical currents, with a strong emphasis on Confucian ideas (but more so on the level of official form than with regard to underlying content). There is no need to discuss later developments at length; two landmarks should, however, be noted because of their particular importance for Japanese responses to the Chinese model. When the Chinese empire was rebuilt by the Sui and Tang dynasties (in the late sixth and early seventh century) after a prolonged phase of fragmentation, the ideological framework imposed by the new imperial centre differed from traditional precedents in significant ways. Confucian teachings remained important, but at the same time, acceptance and protection of Buddhism served to legitimize the empire in more universalist terms, and Daoism became more closely associated with the reigning dynasty than at any earlier or later stage. The three traditions seem to have been combined in relation to three aspects of the imperial domain: if Buddhism symbolized the hegemonic reach of the reborn and now more ambitious empire, Confucianism represented its Chinese sources, whereas Daoist religious institutions functioned more effectively on a local or regional level. But the obverse of this pluralism was a more prominent ideological role of the imperial centre and court as such: it claimed support from and authority over all three traditions, but was not identifiable with any one of them. The most cosmopolitan and pluralistic period in Chinese imperial history was thus also characterized by a higher visibility of the imperial centre as the ultimate embodiment and guarantee of socio-cosmic order. A later retreat from hegemonic ambitions coupled with more intensive internal development under the Song dynasty (from the late tenth century onwards) led to ideological readjustment. A reconstructed version of Confucian thought made a stronger claim to encompass the whole of the Chinese tradition and represent Chinese civilization to the outside world.

The Japanese trajectory as a civilizational constellation

The above bird's eye view of Chinese history is a necessary background to further discussion: as I will argue, inventive transformations of Chinese patterns are crucial to Japan's civilizational identity. This is a very striking – perhaps the most clear-cut – case of civilizational differentiation through singularization within a shared field. As we have seen, Mauss hinted at this theoretical possibility but did not deal with any specific examples. It is, however, not being suggested that the question raised at the beginning can be answered in unqualified positive terms. Rather than describing Japan as a civilization *sui generis,* we might say that a distinctive – but neither self-explanatory nor all-embracing – civilizational pattern was involved in the making of the Japanese tradition and the dynamic of Japanese history, and that its relative weight varied in the course of time. If we trace the beginnings of this pattern back to a formative encounter with Chinese civilization at the moment of imperial reunification in the sixth and seventh centuries, we must by the same token attribute a crucial role to the very small minority of rulers, priests and scholars who engineered the transfer of cultural models. There is indeed no denying the formative and durable impact of strategic choices made in the course of the transformation of the Yamato state into imperial Japan. But the frameworks put in place by a state-building elite had a logic of their own and proved capable of developments which took them far beyond the original setting. It is this interplay of elite construction and institutional dynamics that will be central to the following discussion.

To clarify the civilizational dimensions of the patterns and processes in question, we should first focus on the long-term twist given to the relationship between Japan and China from the seventh century onwards [1]. The interpretive and practical appropriation of the Chinese model was accompanied by an inventive definition of Japanese identity [2]. The framework put in place during the seventh-century transformation – centred on cultural definitions of order, authority and power – proved both adaptable and resilient enough to shape the relationship between change and continuity in the later course of Japanese history [3]. Finally, the set of orientations that grew out of the encounter with China could be adapted to a new global constellation which called for a relocation of models to follow and a redefinition of the relationship to them [4]. In all these respects and at all stages of the Japanese historical experience, the imperial institution was of crucial importance. Its role is so central to the Japanese historical experience that it might be described as a meta-institution, or perhaps more precisely as a civilizational nucleus.

(1) The seventh-century transformation of Japanese society, state and culture was not only guided by Chinese institutional models, but also by the vision of socio-cosmic order which served to systematize and legitimize them.[9] Several aspects of this cultural transfer should be noted. First and foremost, it did not – as in many other cases of integration into the Chinese civilizational sphere – result in unconditional acceptance of Chinese cultural hegemony. The emerging Japanese state rejected not only Chinese claims to symbolic sovereignty, but also the concomitant image of the Chinese empire as the sole embodiment of superior order. Imperial Japan construed itself alongside China and through autonomous use of Chinese inputs to restructure indigenous tradition into an ostensibly pristine paradigm of order. As in China, sacred kingship was central to the vision of socio-cosmic integration; there were, however, two significant changes to the original model. On the one hand, the Japanese imperial institution claimed authority over a particular collectivity and territory which it at the same time demarcated from the multi-ethnic domain of Chinese imperial power. This was not simply a shift from universalism to particularism: on the Chinese side, changing combinations of universalistic attitudes with more identity-conscious ones were – as we have seen – characteristic of successive historical periods, and on the Japanese side, the notion of an exclusive link to sacred sources could in principle – although this possibility remained latent for a long time – serve to transfigure particularism into more world-embracing projects. In short, the Japanization of the Chinese model changed the balance between opposite aspects, but left some scope for variation. On the other

hand, the Japanese imperial institution claimed divine descent where the Chinese one invoked the mandate of heaven, and sociocosmic integration was thus redefined in terms of natural continuity rather than meta-moral principles. In contrast to the Chinese pattern, the cosmic source and the social recipient of legitimacy were too closely linked for any tension between them to be possible. But precisely this direct divinization of hereditary rulers could – in the course of further changes – be used to rationalize and justify a new division of power. The imperial institution came to represent incontestable sacred authority, as distinct and separate from effective control. Restorationist ideologies could then – when circumstances permitted – appeal to the former against the latter, and thus reintroduce a certain degree of tension between the principles and practices of domination. In view of these nuances, we can agree with Eisenstadt's analysis of the Japanizing process as a de-transcendentalizing and de-universalizing turn, but it must be stressed that this change was carried out in such a way that it did not exclude a certain reactivation of trends pointing beyond given contexts of social life, even if they had to be articulated within a more limited framework.

Early imperial Japan was thus more than another local variant of the Chinese (or Sinic) civilizational pattern. But it was not only the maintenance of distinctive identity and of claims to equal (if not eminent) rank that set it apart. The 'Japanese synthesis of China',[10] not to be confused with a mere borrowing of Chinese models, grew out of the same encounter as the imperial self-definition. The Chinese model was internalized and institutionalized as a paradigm of cultural perfection, although it was never allowed to absorb or undermine the distinctive identity that had been established at the same time. This constitutive presence of China within the Japanese cultural world is best understood as an interplay of imagination and reality. On the one hand, the image of China was identified with the really existing Chinese empire, and thus with the institutions and traditions of an exceptionally massive and durable power structure. On the other hand, the model – albeit reinforced by the power and prestige of the regional super-state – remained open to selective and autonomous reception. The seventh-century transformation coincided with the most markedly pluralistic phase of the Chinese tradition (as noted above, the Tang empire combined Confucian, Buddhist and Daoist inputs in a more systematic fashion and on more overtly equal terms than any earlier or later dynasty), but in the

Japanese context, the Buddhist component was from the outset more central than in China and became even more dominant during the Nara and Heian epochs. The renewed flowering of Japanese Buddhism during the Kamakura period drew on Chinese sources, but the trends that had now been marginalized on the mainland had a much more formative impact on Japanese religious culture. And as historians of Tokugawa thought have now shown, the early modern Confucian turn was no mere alignment with a pre-existing orthodoxy: both institutional limits and interpretive innovations set the Japanese versions of Neo-Confucianism apart from the Chinese ones.

(2) The seventh-century transformation was not simply an adaptive transfer of Chinese ideas and institutions to a Japanese setting. Rather, the constitution of Japan as a separate and self-defining geographical, ethnic and cultural entity took place at the same time as – and in close connection with – the appropriation of the Chinese model. On the geopolitical level, this involved far-reaching changes to the regional power structures. From the early third to the late sixth century AD, the fragmentation of China had been accompanied by the formation of a more peripheral state system which encompassed the Korean peninsula and parts of the Japanese archipelago. This constellation – more fluid and multi-central than at any other time in East Asian history – gave way to the triangular pattern (China, Korea and Japan) which has been characteristic of the region since then. But whereas China was reunited under imperial control and with more lasting results than before, the 'pen-insular system' (as some historians have called it) was divided between two main centres, one of which abstained from further involvement in mainland affairs. The emerging Japanese state brought a large part of the archipelago under effective control and went onto annex more outlying territories, but did not – after 660 – aspire to any conquests beyond the islands.

The unification of the archipelago was achieved through cultural strategies as well as military and political ones, and it is – in retrospect – difficult to disentangle their respective roles. Recent historical research has highlighted the multicultural character of early Japan; traces of different traditions have been found in the official accounts of mythology and dynastic history, and studies of early Japanese religions have stressed the specific features of local religious cultures. But this growing evidence of underlying diversity makes the success of cultural integration and centralization all the more striking. The new state imposed its synthesis of adapted Chinese patterns and reconstructed Japanese ones, and this combination became a durable basis for further assimilation. The imperial institution – i.e. the whole complex of sacred kingship, dynastic continuity, court culture and founding myths – was crucial to this process. Its role as an 'exemplary centre', a supreme source of authority, prestige and collective identity, is in some ways reminiscent of sacred kingship in other Asian traditions; but as Joan Piggott has shown, the model of rulership that emerged from the seventh-century transformation must be analyzed as a particularly elaborate fusion of the Chinese paradigm with the multiple forms of kingship that had come to the fore at various moments of Japanese prehistory (they included shamanistic as well as military role models, but also the attempts to impose a monarchic superstructure on alliances of kinship groups).[11]

Although the imperial institution was, first and foremost, an integrative and legitimizing focus for aristocratic society, it was from the outset embedded in forms of social integration and collective identity which proved capable of extension beyond the original limits. A close connection between familial and political structures, backed up by the cult of ancestors and the ideology of sacred kingship, had been characteristic of Chinese civilization from a very early stage; the Japanese variant of this pattern – an imaginary fusion of kinship, kingship and cosmogony – was based on a more direct application of the familial imaginary to social organization. In view of what we now know about the background to the seventh-century transformation, this should be seen as a systematic and inventive archaization of the Chinese model rather than a perpetuation of pre-existing conditions. The result was, as Beonio-Brocchieri argued, a far-reaching deviation from Chinese images of the people and the political community: 'The people is not, as in China, one of the elements which contribute to the formation of the country on the level of nation and state (together with other components, such as the emperor, the territory, a specific ideology etc); it is, rather, the whole collectivity of the Japanese as an essential and fundamental element of the nation'.[12] We might object to the somewhat anachronistic terms of this description: Beonio-Brocchieri's own analysis shows that the incorporation of the whole collectivity into the framework first devised to unify aristocratic society around a new centre was no simple matter (he argues that during the medieval period, the familial principle became a centrifugal factor and favoured the proliferation of sub-units which later had to be reintegrated into a more complex pattern of unity). But it seems clear that the turn taken in the seventh century was conducive to developments which gradually broadened the scope of integration and legitimation in kinship terms (the last stage on this road was the modern ideology of the family-state). In this altered version of the Chinese model, the relationship between community and ruler was – or could become – closer but also more subaltern than in the original context; the 'people' had no legitimizing role to play.

The civilizational framework that grew out of the seventh-century transformation was closely linked to geographical and geo-cultural images of Japan. As critical historians (especially Amino Yoshihiko) have recently emphasized, a strong and durable conception of Japanese identity – centred on imperial sovereignty and rice-growing peasant communities – took shape at this early stage and survived later changes to social conditions and power structures; its influence on Japanese historiography is most evident in a tendency to neglect groups and subcultures which do not fit into the scheme (especially those linked to seaborne trade and other maritime activities). But if we follow the interpretation proposed by Philippe Pelletier, this set of constitutive images may be seen as one aspect of a more complex picture.[13] The particularistic construction of Japan as a separate and self-contained collectivity is inseparable from the image of insular unity; but the idea of Japan as one island (*shima*) was superimposed on a multi-insular reality. This imaginary fusion ignored – or served to minimize – the plurality of the central islands and their traditions, the particular role of outlying islands in the history of Japanese relations with the continent, and the very close connection with the Korean peninsula. At the same time, however, the effort to appropriate the Chinese model without any cession of sovereignty led to the adoption of a more continental notion of territoriality. To put Japan on a par with its overwhelmingly powerful and prestigious neighbour, the island polity was imagined as a country (*kuni*) with its own version of imperial rule and sacred order. The imperial institution and its mythology drew on both images and aspired to bridge the gap between them. But in the long run, the duality of *shima* and *kuni* became a problem as well as a resource for elaborations of Japanese identity.

(3) As suggested above, civilizational patterns can be analyzed in connection with processes of state formation in general and empire building in particular. On the other hand, the civilizational aspects of such combinations develop – in varying ways and degrees – an autonomous dynamic beyond the reach of political centres. From this point of view, two lines of comparative analysis are particularly relevant to our concerns. Civilizational models, achievements and visions can spread beyond the boundaries of the political units with which they are most closely associated; they can also remain in place and maintain cultural identities over time which help to contain or counterbalance centrifugal political dynamics. In both respects, China stands out as characterized by a particularly close link between civilizational and political structures. No comparably influential and durable civilization identified as strongly with a model of imperial rule as a mediating link between social and cosmic order. But some qualifications are worth noting. Although Chinese cultural patterns were inseparable from a political context, adaptation to power structures of a different kind could – as the Japanese and Korean trajectories show, albeit not in the same ways – give rise to new formations. And within the imperial domain, it seems clear that the persistence of a strong civilizational framework helped to defuse the subversive potential of a society that became increasingly complex and resistant to traditional methods of control. The civilizational commitment to an imperial vision made it easier to rebuild the real empire after a breakdown and shield it from confrontation with new social forces.

The Japanese version of the relationship between state formation and civilization was strikingly different from the Chinese one. On the one hand, there was no civilizational expansion beyond the boundaries of the Japanese state: the cultural assimilation of the archipelago was, as we have seen, a long-term process, but it took place within the limits prefigured by the seventh-century withdrawal from continental affairs, and it accompanied the extension of political control by successive Japanese power centres. But on the other hand, basic cultural premises and core institutional components survived more radical structural changes and phases of more far-reaching fragmentation than in China. Since the imperial institution played a key role in maintaining this continuity, it may be described as a civilizational nucleus. Its relationship to the forces which exercised – or aspired to – effective power is not always easy to define, and the concept of legitimacy must be used with care because of its Western connotations, but it seems safe to say that the imperial dynasty and its symbolism remained central to the frame of reference for any claim to superior prestige and authority.

If we confront this continuity of basic cultural orientations and their key institutional embodiment with the dynamics of Japanese history, the most salient point has to do with the long-term trajectory of the Japanese state. In contrast to China, the Japanese pattern of state formation is characterized by a clear divide between primary and secondary phases.[14] From the late twelfth century onwards, a new power centre created by a military elite (but capable of pursuing projects and strategies which transcended its original social basis) developed alongside the imperial court and underwent changes which culminated in the intricate power-sharing system of the Tokugawa period. The imperial institution was first confined to a subordinate political role and later deprived of all power, but continued to function as a part of the cultural foundations for the new power structure. This is not to deny that the military counter-state had a civilizational agenda of its own; it imposed new rules on various areas of social life. But the fact that it adapted to the civilizational legacy of the primary phase had far-reaching implications. Basic cultural premises were perpetuated across a major historical divide.

Changes to the structure and social identity of state power were not the only challenge to the imperial tradition. One of the most striking features of late medieval Japan – from the fourteenth to the sixteenth century – was a general strengthening of centrifugal social forces; village communities, Buddhist sects and local warlords participated in a long-drawn-out power struggle which made this period very different from both earlier and later ones. But although this was also a time of noteworthy cultural innovations, none of the actors or organizations involved reached a point of explicit rupture with the imperial myth. The same pattern of flexible continuity is characteristic of the whole history of Japanese religions: major shifts could take place within the framework of the pluralistic religious culture that first took shape at the same time as the imperial state, but they did not affect the privileged role of the imperial institution. Both its particular relationship to a suitably reconstructed indigenous tradition and its ability to draw on other sources remained intact.

It is not being suggested that civilizational continuity is self-explanatory. The institutionalized meanings at the core of the Japanese tradition did not simply endure as underlying and determining premises of socio-cultural life; rather, a more detailed analysis – which cannot be undertaken here – would have to deal with the historical actors, forces and conditions involved in the ongoing reproduction of constitutive patterns. Civilizational constants should, in other words, be seen as more or less formative aspects of historical constellations: in the Japanese case, the transformation of the imperial nucleus was linked to other long-term developments, and at certain historical turning-points, more far-reaching changes seem to have been within the bounds of possibility (or at least perceived as such by some of the protagonists). Direct imperial rule was clearly envisaged by the architects of the most important seventh-century reforms, and although it soon proved incompatible with the realities of the power structure, the tension between ambitions and constraints could give rise to strategic as well as ideological visions of rectification. From this point of view, one of the most interesting episodes in the history of the imperial institution took place in the early fourteenth century: representatives of two rival branches of the imperial dynasty – one in theory and after abdication, the other in practice and as a reigning sovereign aspiring to rule – broke new ground and pursued projects which were ignored or misunderstood by later historiography.[15] The retired emperor Hanazono (1297–1348, reigned 1308–18) embarked on an extensive reexamination of Chinese thought and history; if his thought had reached the level of fully-fledged ideology, it would obviously have entailed a major reinterpretation of the imperial myths and a shift towards more Confucian ideas of rulership. At the same time, his successor Go-Daigo (1289–1339, reigned 1318–39) was trying to establish a new kind of monarchy, ostensibly based on an emphatic reaffirmation of the founding myths but in fact guided by some knowledge of Chinese developments under the Song dynasty and responsive to changes in Japanese society.

The failure of Go-Daigo's project (the Kenmu restoration) put an end to imperial initiatives. But the victory of his adversaries did not settle the question of ultimate authority once and for all. It seems clear that the idea of deposing the imperial dynasty was considered when the Ashikaga shogunate was at the height of its power, and that Nobunaga's treatment of the imperial court prefigured a more radical break with tradition than the policies eventually adopted by the Tokugawa regime. The symbiosis of the two centres – the products of primary and secondary state formation – was always problematic, the question of their relationship could be reopened as historical circumstances changed, and in the end, it became a symbolic focus for the transformative potential of the Japanese tradition.

(4) So far, our line of argument has linked the civilizational question to Japan's unusually self-contained history. The geopolitical fact that there was no foreign conquest in recorded history prior to 1945 (and, except for an unsuccessful invasion of Korea at the end of the sixteenth century, no Japanese expansion on the continent from the mid-seventh to the late nineteenth century) has no direct bearing on the question. Isolation is neither a necessary nor a sufficient condition for the emergence of a distinctive civilization, but it may – in certain contexts – be conducive to civilizational formations of a specific kind. In the Japanese case, it would seem that the civilizational patterns discussed above transfigured a self-contained history into a more comprehensively self-contained order. The model represented by a more advanced civilization was incorporated in such a way that it became an integral part of the Japanese tradition and could be upgraded or devalued in response to internal developments. The continuity of cosmic and social order was defined in such a way that the particular identity of the Japanese collectivity became a privileged part of the whole; and the fundamentals of a cultural framework for political power were maintained throughout successive phases of social change.

But the fourth and final issue raised above – the relevance of a civilizational approach to the understanding of Japanese patterns of modernity – takes us into a different field of inquiry. Now we are dealing with exceptionally rapid and radical transformations of Japanese society, accompanied by equally fundamental reorientations in the global arena; although the Japanese trajectory after 1868 may have been – for most of the time – more autonomous than other non-Western paths to advanced modernity, it was certainly not self-contained in the same sense as the earlier phases. This does not mean that no case can be made for civilizational perspectives, but they will have to be adapted to the new dimensions of historical change. Analysts of Japanese modernization have frequently noted both the importance and the adaptability of traditional factors within modern frameworks; for those who regard premodern Japan as a distinctive civilization, such connections are reason enough to claim at least a partial continuity. The problem is somewhat more complicated if Japan's civilizational identity is – as I have tried to show – inseparable from its relationship to China. On this view, we would have to establish a link between the traditional role of the Chinese model and the modern turn to the West; evidence of civilizational continuity would, in other words, have to be found in ways of appropriating and adapting external paradigms. The parallel between learning from China and learning from the West is, of course, too obvious to have been overlooked. What remains to be seen is how far we can go beyond the loose analogy that is familiar to all students of the field. A few concluding remarks may serve to clarify some aspects of the question.

Both sides to the Japanese modernizing process – the Westernizing and the nationalist – have been of such dimensions that we can plausibly speak of civilizational dynamics. On the one hand, the architects and activists of the great transformation that began in 1868 were from the outset remarkably interested in all aspects of Western civilization – not for the purposes of unconditional imitation (the 'Kemalist' current was always marginal), but from a position which could combine learning with the search for equivalents or counterweights to the unadaptable or unacceptable elements of the Western civilizational complex (a classic example of the effort to construct functional equivalents is Itō Hirobumi's defence of the imperial myth as the only conceivable Japanese counterpart to Western religion). On the other hand, the totalizing ambitions of Japanese nationalism and its exceptional capacity to absorb or defuse ideological alternatives are well known; its critics have accused it of making the nation the measure of all things. In a more value-neutral vein, the concept of the 'civilizational nation'[16] has been coined to describe the particularly self-contained identity and historical continuity seen as characteristic of some Asian nations, notably India, China and Japan. The term seems, however, in some ways more easily applicable to Japan than to the other cases – at least in the sense that Japan can more plausibly claim to have built a national identity of civilizational dimensions.

The two sides of Japanese modernity have interacted in complex and original ways: if it is possible to speak of Japanese reinventions of Western institutions (most notably those of capitalism), this is the result of strategic reasoning guided by a nationalist imagination. Moreover, the shifts of focus and direction on the Westernizing as well as the nationalist side are no less noteworthy than the overall strength of both currents. The Westernizing project that led directly and unquestioningly to expansion and empire-building was very different from the course followed after the 'embrace of defeat'[17] in 1945. As for the mutations of nationalism, the most convincing analyses of postwar economic development have also thrown light on this question: the 'strategic economy' that has been central to the Japanese economic system reflects a fundamental reorientation – but not a termination – of nationalist policies.

In short, the dual frame of reference that has been characteristic of Japanese modernity clearly lends itself to civilizational interpretations, even if this line of argument has yet to be developed in detail. And it is tempting to see the interplay of the two trends as a more dynamic, reflexive and adaptable version of the long-standing pattern first developed in relation to China. This view will be easier to defend if we can point to specific developments and show that they paved the way or set the course for a transition from the traditional to the modern version. It seems to me that several interconnected trends of this nature were already at work during the Tokugawa period. As regards the relationship with China and the role of the Chinese model, the notion of a neo-Confucian orthodoxy dominating early Tokugawa thought has been subjected to effective criticism.[18] There was undoubtedly a new upsurge of interest in Chinese (and more particularly Confucian) thought after the consolidation of the Tokugawa regime, but no wholesale alignment with a hegemonic Neo-Confucian mode of discourse. Rather, aspects of the mainland tradition were appropriated without their specific institutional basis and often combined with indigenous themes; most importantly, this new round of selective borrowing from Chinese culture took place at a time when practical contact with the mainland had been reduced to a minimum and no political relations were maintained. If it can be said that the Japanese engaged with the Chinese model as an internalized other and on their own terms, this was markedly more true of the Tokugawa period than of any other phase in Japanese history. In that sense, it can be argued that a relativization of the Chinese connection was in progress beneath the surface of an intensified Sinocentrism. And at the same time, a reappropriation of Japanese traditions and a redefinition of Japanese collective identity were preparing the ground for claims to equality or even superiority in relation to China. This current, central to the prehistory of Japanese nationalism and to the (at first symbolic) reaffirmation of the imperial institution, found its most articulate expression in the School of Native Learning (*kokugaku*), but it influenced – directly or indirectly – the whole spectrum of Tokugawa thought and culture.

In short, a multiple reinterpretation of the relationship with China was changing the Japanese self-image and creating preconditions for a more practical reorientation in the regional (and ultimately global) arena. A much less visible minority group, interested in the Western world for both intellectual and practical purposes, added to the transformative potential which remained latent until the mid-nineteenth century. Although Western learning (*rangaku*) was too marginal and suspect to become a fully legitimate part of Tokugawa culture, the need for more knowledge of the West was obvious enough to prompt a shift to more permissive official policy in the early eighteenth century, and the results were significant enough to contribute a major cultural resource when conditions were ripe for a radical change. Cognitive foundations for the turn to the West were laid well before the political breakthrough.

Finally, the position of the Tokugawa regime – the last and by far the most elaborate version of the military state – within the ideological field was in some ways indicative of new developments. The political centre did not identify with an orthodoxy. A policy of qualified pluralism was proclaimed on various occasions; the Tokugawa rulers cultivated links with the established religious traditions, and at a later stage, they allowed a limited intellectual opening to the West. Their ideological strategy was more structured and balanced than those of earlier military regimes. On the other hand, the Tokugawa state could not claim (and did not have to assume) the specific cultural identity and centrality that remained a prerogative of the imperial institution. This constellation – a political centre capable of working with changing combinations of cultural orientations, without an exclusive commitment to any particular one – was already a significant step towards the civilizational shift discussed above.

As I have tried to show, there are valid reasons to speak about Japan as a distinctive civilization. But the pattern that sets it apart is neither self-contained nor unchanging. Japan's civilizational identity is inseparable from ways of relating to the outside world, first developed in the course of a formative encounter with China but much later transferred to a more global context, and it is best understood in connection with successive historical settings, rather than as an invariant paradigm. This line of argument should, of course, be confronted with other approaches; but further discussion in that vein is beyond the scope of this paper.

5 State Formation in Japan and the West

The concept of state formation is now widely used in social theory and historical sociology, but often without reference to its most significant source: the work of Norbert Elias, especially his analysis of the civilizing process in medieval and early modern Europe. As a result, some important aspects and connotations of the problematic in question tend to be overlooked.[1] It must be admitted that this unacknowledged diffusion of an impoverished idea is partly due to shortcomings of the original formulation. Although Elias made it clear that his reconstruction of the 'long Middle Ages' of Western Europe was to be seen as the first step towards a more extensive comparative study of civilizing processes, he did not systematically link his argument to this project, and the absence of a broader framework often leads to explicit or implicit over-generalizations of the European experience. As a result, *The Civilizing Process* does not easily lend itself to extrapolation for comparative purposes; its impact in this field has been delayed and fragmented. The following reflections will suggest some ways of establishing a more direct link with comparative analysis, with particular reference to the Japanese experience.

Japan has – for obvious reasons – often been singled out as an exceptionally interesting case for comparison with the West. The two themes that have traditionally been highlighted in this context are the common feudal background and the dynamics of capitalist development; medieval Japan is – or was until recently – widely regarded as the only fully-fledged example of feudalism outside Europe, modern Japan is indisputably the most outstanding case of capitalism in a non-Western setting, and it seems plausible to assume that the first fact has something to do with the second. Although this approach was by no means exclusive to the Marxist tradition, it was most emphatically defended by Marxist historians, and it has been affected by the decline of Marxist influence on Japanese studies.

Historians of premodern Japan have become more suspicious of 'European analogue theories', even if they do not explicitly reject the very notion of feudalism, and analysts of Japanese capitalism have tended to opt for either of two viewpoints that are equally at odds with comparative models of developmental patterns: they emphasize the embeddedness of the Japanese economy in a unique set of institutions or its exceptional conformity with universal rules of economic reason. If we look for a more promising strategy of comparative analysis, one of the possible starting-points is the key role of state formation in Japanese history. It has been highlighted by recent research and aroused some theoretical interest, but little has been done to clarify structural contrasts and parallels with the West.[2]

The following discussion will focus on this issue; it begins with a critical reading of Elias's genealogy of the Western state and goes on to suggest some additions, which can then be applied to the Japanese case. But the limited scope of the article should be noted: it is meant to outline a research programme to which the present author can only make a limited contribution and which would have to be tackled from several different angles.

Theoretical and historical perspectives

In the German original the first chapter in the second volume of *The Civilizing Process* is subtitled 'On the sociogenesis of occidental civilization', and the title of its second section refers to a 'sociogenesis of absolutism'.[3] The close connection which Elias establishes between these two themes is crucial to his project; as he sees it, earlier accounts of the unity and specificity of Western civilization have neglected the specific contribution of the absolutist state and its cultural framework (his analysis of court society deals with one of the most important aspects of this problematic).[4] He emphasizes the uniformity of absolutism, rather than its varying and context-bound trajectories, and the continuity of post-absolutist history (especially with regard to the permanent patterns of interstate competition), in contrast to more conventional accounts of the modern transformation. This levelling of later developments serves to highlight the creativity and dynamism of medieval Europe, and thus to justify the restructuring of Western history around the concept of the 'long Middle Ages'. Elias is, in other words, particularly interested in the long-term process that culminated in the formative but relatively transient episode of absolutism. His account of this subject is one of the crucial contributions to the twentieth-century discovery of the Middle Ages.[5] It invites two kinds of comparison: with the work of other authors in the same area and with parallel or at least partly analogous results of research on other civilizations. The first task is beyond the scope of this article, and our discussion of the second will be limited to preliminary remarks on a particular case. As I will argue, the theory of state formation – the cornerstone of Elias's interpretive history – calls for further conceptual distinctions; it can be shown that the issues in question were neglected because of their relative marginality in the medieval Western context, and their significance becomes clearer from a comparative point of view.

More precisely, there are five main conceptual dichotomies that can serve to develop and expand the theory of state formation. I am not implying that the themes to which they relate are wholly absent from Elias's work (we could probably find more or less explicit allusions to most of them), but they are not systematically integrated into his theory, and they are never tackled at the level of basic concepts.

First, it seems convenient to begin with the distinction between primary and secondary state formation. There is, in other words, an obvious difference between the emergence of states out of primitive (i.e. by definition stateless) societies and the rebuilding of states after the collapse of earlier ones and a temporary regression to lower levels of political organization. The radical changes brought about by primary state formation have been highlighted in recent work, especially by Pierre Clastres and other French authors who have elaborated on his insights.[6] From the viewpoint of historical sociology, however, this transformation must be understood as a process, rather than an abrupt break; the work of S.N. Eisenstadt and his associates offers some promising clues.[7] Elias's general conception of state formation as a long-term process is indirectly relevant to this issue, but his direct concern was with a process of secondary state formation which he did not define as such. Although he was certainly not unaware of the prehistory of Western European feudalism (i.e. the fall of the Roman empire in the West and the subsequent civilizational collapse), his analysis of medieval developments fails to address this question in a systematic way. He explains the rise of feudalism as a result of the Carolingian collapse, but there is no discussion of the background to the short-lived Carolingian restoration of empire.[8] From this point of view, his genealogy of feudalism is open to the same criticism as other versions of the traditional view. Historians now tend to see the late tenth and early eleventh century as the turning-point of the feudal transformation; on that view, it was much less directly related to the fragmentation of the Carolingian state than earlier accounts had suggested, and the doubt cast on this privileged connection makes the need for a broader historical perspective all the more obvious.[9] If we can speak of a 'feudal revolution', we must give due consideration to its long-term prehistory.

In general terms, processes of secondary state formation differ with regard to the characteristics of the breakdowns which precede them and of the more or less significant legacies left behind by earlier state structures. In the Western context, the latter aspect was of particular importance. The image of imperial power survived and remained strong enough to inspire recurrent projects of restoration; they all ended in failure, but their direct and indirect effects were an integral part of the process which gave rise to the European state system. Ethnic units and regional kingdoms, based on the fusion of imperial fragments and barbarian conquerors during the final crisis of Roman rule in the West, continued to play a key role in the process of state formation which began anew after another phase of fragmentation. Impoverished but enduring centres of urban life linked medieval Europe to its Roman past and served as foundations for a second flowering of urban communities and city-states in the West; the degree of continuity is a matter of debate, but some recent work on the subject suggests that it may have been more fundamental than historians often assumed. A more crucial component of the Roman legacy was the institutional framework of Christendom. The Catholic Church, evolving in interaction with other forces of the feudal world, made a significant impact on several levels: as a transmitter of preserved or rediscovered cultural traditions, as the embodiment of a civilizational unity which transcended political divisions, and – especially from the eleventh to the thirteenth century – as a pioneer in the creation of governmental models and techniques that could he appropriated by secular powers.[10] Last but not least, the reactivation and adaptation of Roman law gave the emerging state structures a normative frame of reference which became progressively more important.

All these features of medieval European history are well known, and they were obviously included in Elias's overall picture of the Middle Ages. But they are not given their due in the context of his analysis of state formation (and to the best of my knowledge, there has been no later attempt to integrate them into a suitably expanded version of his theory). In particular, they remain under-theorized as aspects of a specific relationship between primary and secondary state formation. It may be suggested that an exclusive focus on Western Europe is likely to obscure this question: the breakdown of the original political framework was too complete and the lasting elements of its legacy too disparate for the connection to stand out in relief. A comparative perspective will help to highlight it.

Second, a further distinction can be made between autonomous and dependent processes of state formation. I use the first term to refer to the development of separate power centres which interact and compete on relatively equal terms (state formation is never wholly self-contained); by contrast, the dependent variant takes place on the periphery and under the dominance or pressure of stronger centres. In this sense, dependent state formation occurs primarily within imperial zones of influence or in state systems where hegemonic powers have control over client regimes. Elias does not use these terms, but the Western European pattern of state formation – as analyzed in *The Civilizing Process* – is clearly marked by a plurality of autonomous processes within the region as well as by the autonomy of the region as a whole with regard to a broader geopolitical context. On closer examination, however, it seems that this was not simply a given condition; ways of blocking or neutralizing a more dependent development played a major part in the consolidation of Western Christendom as a civilizational complex. To begin with, the elementary institutions of feudalism (which became the starting point of state formation) were created during an era of acute external threat from several sides. When the danger of foreign conquest receded, the internal dynamics of Western society led to a counter-wave of expansion and colonization, but this did not result in empire-building; rather, the most notable outcome was the emergence of new states established by conquerors who turned the existing techniques of rule to particularly effective use (the Norman conquest of England, the Norman kingdom in Sicily and the principality of Brandenburg are obvious cases in point; the abortive but not irrelevant experience of the crusader states is also worth noting).[11] In other words, the effect of conquest – within the Western region, on its outer margins or at the expense of its Islamic adversaries – was to establish new centres of autonomous development, rather than imperial formations. Elias did, of course, deal with the last wave of barbarian invasions before 1000 AD as well as Western expansion during the High Middle Ages, but not from the angle suggested here. And he does not relate this part of his narrative to another conspicuous feature of the Western trajectory: the repeated failure of imperial projects from within. Together with the other developments mentioned above, the blocking of empire (with the partial and temporary exception of the papal monarchy) epitomizes the obverse of Western state formation. Developments that might have given rise to dependent patterns were contained or diverted by the forces which favoured a multi-central configuration and – in the longer run – a self-maintaining state system.

There were, of course, some significant exceptions to this rule. In particular, conquered territories could serve to strengthen imperial projects. The kingdom of Sicily was the main basis for Frederick II's unsuccessful but historically significant attempt to transform the fiction of the Holy Roman Empire into reality.[12] More importantly, the Christian reconquest of the Iberian peninsula culminated in the rise of Spain as an imperial power. But the long-term result of this successful move from local resurgence to global expansion was to separate Spain from the mainstream of Western European history. Neither of these two episodes is analyzed in Elias's work.

The second of the above distinctions should not be confused with a third one: that between endogenous and derivative processes of state formation. In this case, the focus is on the cultural contexts and directions of political development. Endogenous processes generate their own interpretive and practical models. The level of reflexivity and articulation varies widely, but there is always some interaction between the dynamics of power structures and the semantics of the cultural patterns involved in their constitution (China in the second half of the last millennium BC is an outstanding example of an early process of state formation with a high level of reflexivity; one of the landmark developments of the twelfth century in Europe was a more reflexive turn in state formation). By contrast, derivative processes are based on the systematic application of models borrowed from elsewhere. It is true that the adopted guidelines are always adapted to circumstances. In that sense, the contrast between endogenous and derivative processes is a matter of degree, and this distinction should perhaps be qualified more strongly than the others. But it can serve to underline important differences. They are probably more pronounced in the East Asian region: the process that led to the unification of China after a long-drawn-out struggle between several contenders for hegemony was – as a whole – indisputably endogenous, whereas the Korean kingdoms of the sixth and seventh centuries and – even more strikingly – Japan during the seventh and eighth centuries are prime examples of derivative state-building. East Asian history also exemplifies the point that dependent and derivative patterns do not necessarily coincide. In the sense defined above, state formation in Japan took a derivative turn at a decisive moment, but since China never exercised any political control over Japan, we cannot speak of a dependent process. By contrast, Korean states – before and after the unification of the peninsula – were not only organized along Chinese lines, but also from time to time exposed to direct Chinese intervention. Some phases of a derivative process can therefore he described as dependent. And the Inner Asian political formations that emerged in response to the rise of the Chinese empire were more dependent than derivative: they mostly functioned on the basis of a partly predatory and partly client relationship with the Chinese state, but they could only to a very limited extent imitate its institutions, and it was – paradoxically – only when these frontier polities conquered large parts of Chinese territory that their structures became more derivative.[13]

If we consider the Western European trajectory from this point of view, its endogenous aspects are evident, whereas the derivative elements are – for specific historical reasons – less visible and more likely to merge into the background when the regional pattern is studied in isolation. It is possible to reconstruct the intellectual history of state formation in the West in terms of more or less creative responses to problems posed by the increasingly complex power structures and their impact on social life. The external sources involved in this process were mainly of two kinds. On the one hand, the Roman legacy was reactivated in different and divergent ways. Although the mirage of imperial renewal was, as we have seen, a major force in medieval history, it functioned as a mythical vision of supreme power, rather than a model for practical purposes. Roman law was, of course, much more important in the long run, but less so in connection with imperial strategies than in the context of state-building on a more limited territorial basis; it played a key role in conjunction with other factors, but did not constitute a fully fledged model in its own right. On the other hand, the question of inputs from other more advanced civilizations has proved difficult to answer. The main obstacle is the 'ideology of silence', as one historian has called it, i.e. the tendency of Western Christendom to misrepresent or deny its borrowings from the cultures which it regarded as heretic or infidel.[14] The term was coined to describe the response to Islamic influence or dominance in frontier regions of the West, but it seems applicable to the relationship between Western and Byzantine civilization. There is no doubt that the sixth-century Codex Justinianus was the single most important Byzantine source of Western statecraft (Helmut Koenigsberger describes it as 'the intellectual basis of the absolutism of the Western monarchies of the sixteenth, seventeenth and eighteenth centuries'[15]); it is, however, best understood as a link to the Roman legacy, and the later impact of more distinctively Byzantine influences is more elusive.[16] As for the Islamic connection, the role of the Norman kingdom in Sicily as a pioneering transmitter is crucial, and one of the questions that have been raised about it concerns the indirect influence of Chinese bureaucracy through Islamic channels.[17]

Fourth, it seems useful to distinguish between two contrasting patterns of the relationship between the process of state formation and the broader social context in which it is embedded; they might he described as immanent and transformative. In the first case, the state appears as part of a more comprehensive power structure and the dynamics of state formation operate in close connection with other relatively autonomous developments. In the second, the ascendancy of state over society is more pronounced; it gives rise to more or less rationalized and more or less effective projects of adapting the social order to the imperatives of state construction and interstate competition. Needless to say, this contrast is no less relative than the others. The state is never a mere by-product or instrument of social forces, and society is never a passive object of political intervention. But in the European context, the transition to absolutism exemplifies the difference. In comparison with the less interventionist medieval monarchies, it represents a transformative turn. Although it is true that the scale and scope of state intervention during the absolutist era was – by more advanced modern standards – very limited, a new concern with the organization and mobilization of society was characteristic of this phase. One of its expressions was the idea of the 'well-ordered police state', more activist in spirit than the term might suggest, and particularly important because of its influence on the Petrine revolution in Russia.[18] The latter event is one of the most striking cases of a transformative turn in a long-term process of state formation. But in assessing the absolutist state as a historical phenomenon, we must also take note of its role in paving the way for more radical visions and strategies of state intervention, including both the Jacobin and the Bonapartist offshoots of the revolution which destroyed it.

Elias has little to say about the transformative ambitions of absolutism. The logic of his project leads him to treat the absolutist state primarily as the final result of a long-term process, rather than a turning-point which opens up new possibilities. It appears as a complex and intricate network of balancing mechanisms, based on a particular constellation of social forces, and some of the cultural devices developed to maintain it as a going concern (especially those linked to court society) became lasting achievements of the civilizing process. The consolidation of the absolutist regime turned out to be the prelude to radical change, but for Elias, this has to do with the vulnerability of its structures rather than with the innovative potential of its strategies. Absolutism had pushed the state-building monopolization of key resources to a point where the royal monopoly was ripe for conversion into a public one. Because of the growing interdependence of state and society, functional democratization was the logical outcome of the process which at first had led to an unprecedented concentration of power. To repeat: the emphasis is on a structural predisposition to rapid change, not on transformative visions that could be reactivated and reinterpreted in a new context.

The fifth and last dichotomy has to do with patterns of political integration and their significance for the dynamics of state formation. It can be found in the work of historians of early modern Europe, but a more general formulation may be appropriate in the present context. Helmut Koenigsberger was, to the best of my knowledge, the first to draw attention to the importance of composite states in sixteenth- and seventeenth-century Europe, and he did so in connection with a critical reconstruction of Elias's theory; J. H. Elliott has discussed the phenomenon at greater length and in relation to its historical background.[19] As both authors emphasize, dynastic expansion often brought countries with different traditions, institutions and customary laws under the control of one ruler. The early modern monarchs tried in various ways to cope with this diversity, but the superficial unity that some of them achieved fell far short of later standards set by unitary nation-states. The difference between the two phases is thus crucial to the formation of the modern state. While some composite structures developed into more unitary ones, this outcome cannot be construed as an evolutionary norm: the absorption of Scotland into the United Kingdom, the much more short-lived union of Spain and Portugal, and the history of Habsburg rule in Bohemia exemplify the different trajectories of composite states.

A more detailed typology of composite states would have to include more anomalous cases – such as Switzerland and the Netherlands – besides the monarchies. But there is no doubt that dynastic expansion was the key factor involved in this distinctive phase of state formation. On the other hand, the dynastic rulers were building on older foundations, and a closer look at the latter may help to define the contrast between composite and unitary patterns in more general terms, as well as to explain why Elias did not deal with this issue.

Elias was, as is well known, most directly concerned with the development of the French state. Early modern France was clearly a composite monarchy, but it developed particularly sustained and effective strategies of assimilation. Elias was more interested in the overall direction than in the obstacles that had to be overcome, and this is in line with his view on the essential continuity of the whole process of state formation. The emphasis is on the similarities between medieval, early modern and advanced modern trends, rather than on any changes to basic patterns. A comparative approach might have thrown more light on significant differences; in particular, English and French variants of medieval monarchy could be seen as incipient cases of the uniform and the composite type. In England, the Norman conquest gave rise to a relatively strong centre which imposed a correspondingly uniform regime, whereas the French kings had to pursue a much more improvised and fluctuating strategy of piecemeal absorption. This did not predetermine the whole subsequent history of the two states: the seventeenth-century British monarchy was more thoroughly composite than the French one. But the early modern shift towards the composite end of the spectrum is most clearly evident in the rise of a major power which is conspicuously absent from Elias's account. The Habsburg empire was the composite state par excellence.

In brief, Elias's paradigm case was a state that must – prior to its revolutionary transformation – be described as composite, although his stress on the dynamics of unification and their long-term effects led him to minimize this feature and its implications for comparative analysis. The contrasts stand out more clearly if we consider the experience of other European states. Unitary and composite states can then be seen as fully developed embodiments of more elementary trends: state formation can proceed through assimilation by one strong centre or a more or less asymmetric juxtaposition of several ones. The distinction between the two types is thus linked to general conditions and alternatives, even if it is more directly predicated on specifically modern developments than are the other concepts discussed above.

To conclude this part of the discussion, let us note some common implications of the above comments. If it can be argued that Elias's theory of state formation is in general weighted towards power at the expense of culture, the distinctions proposed here should be linked to that claim.[20] The connection is most obvious in the last case. Cultural traditions are built into the customs and institutions which coexist within a composite state, and the construction of unitary states requires cultural assimilation. The derivative and transformative patterns of state formation are – in different ways – characterized by a strong and direct involvement of cultural models, and this is one of the factors that set them apart from their respective opposites. Derivative state formation is, by definition, guided by an external authority that operates through cultural rather than political channels, and transformative turns call for cultural articulation of their goals. As for the first dichotomy, there is always a cultural side to the relationship between primary and secondary state formation, although the relative weight of culture varies: it is to some extent through a cultural legacy that primary processes continue to affect the course of secondary ones. This was a particularly significant aspect of Western European developments. Finally, cultural factors also have some bearing on the contrast between autonomous and dependent processes. If this dichotomy is most obviously applicable to imperial formations (they combine a highly autonomous centre with dependent processes on the periphery), specific examples are by the same token related to the diverse cultural patterns of imperial power.

State formation in Japan

As we have seen, a typology of processes of state formation throws some light on underdeveloped themes and unexplored perspectives in Elias's work on European history. It remains to be seen how useful it is for a comparison of Europe and Japan. The following discussion will deal with five successive phases of Japanese history and use the categories defined above to clarify contrasts and parallels with European developments. The chronological divisions in question are well established and generally accepted, but the historical interpretation of each epoch as well as of the whole sequence has undergone some changes in recent years. The first phase includes the seventh-century transformation as well as the Nara and Heian periods (710–94 and 794–1192 respectively; the fifth and sixth centuries can, for our purposes, he treated as a prelude to this chapter in the history of the Japanese state); the second and third are roughly coextensive with the Kamakura and Muromachi shogunates (1192–1333 and 1336–1573 respectively), whereas the fourth one begins with the unification of Japan in the second half of the sixteenth century and ends with the demise of the Tokugawa regime in 1868. The fifth and last comes to an end with defeat and occupation in 1945. This paper will not deal with the question whether the five post-war decades should he seen as an intermezzo or as the beginning of a new phase, and it will not go beyond a brief comment on the present constellation.

Before the seventh-century transformation, a primary process of state formation had been under way in the Japanese archipelago and the neighbouring continental regions. The Yamato state (it would be an anachronism to speak of a Japanese state before the seventh century) was part of an emerging state system which also included the Korean kingdoms; moreover, since China was going through a long phase of fragmentation, there was no imperial centre, and the whole East Asian region came closer to constituting a multi-central state system than at most other times.[21] We can therefore speak of a whole complex of relatively autonomous processes (the view that the Yamato state was created by conquerors from the mainland is a minority opinion which I do not find plausible). As for developments within the archipelago, it seems clear that they correspond to Elias's account of the early phases of state formation, even if the process he was dealing with was a secondary one. The Yamato rulers strove to control key resources, i.e. primarily land and population (with particular emphasis on the latter); the gradual strengthening of the centre was accompanied by more intensive rivalry among the remaining contestants (the ascendancy of the Soga family as a partner and potential adversary of the ruling dynasty is a case in point), and it seems that both territorial and kinship-based power structures were involved in the struggles.

But it is the seventh-century turning-point in the Japanese process of state formation that raises the most interesting theoretical issues. Elias's basic concepts are obviously applicable to this case. The attempt to establish effective fiscal and military monopolies and adapt political institutions to this purpose was a key component of the reform process.[22] A more elaborate and elevated form of sacred kingship served as the symbolic foundation for this strategy. However, the most striking features of the seventh-century transformation are best described in terms of the additional conceptual distinctions proposed above. A primary process of state formation was accelerated and completed in an exceptionally rapid and sweeping fashion. Although some radically new arrangements were introduced, the strategy as a whole was a continuation of earlier efforts by other means. Its success was due to the systematic borrowing of institutional patterns from the more advanced Chinese civilization. They were adapted to the Japanese context (in particular, the combination of aristocratic and bureaucratic elements was more strongly weighted in favour of the former in Japan than in China), but there is no doubt that the impact of the Chinese model was real and massive; there is hardly a comparable case of a premodern state undergoing a wholesale reconstruction of the basis of an imported blueprint. The autonomy which the Japanese ruling elite nevertheless showed in learning from China was even more evident in foreign policy. As the Japanese state assimilated lessons from political development on the continent, it withdrew from continental affairs; it rejected any form of political subordination to China as well as any idea of overseas expansion. At the very moment when the process of state formation took a derivative turn, it thus became even more autonomous than it had been. As for the fourth dichotomy, the implications of the seventh-century reform seem beyond dispute: although historians are now inclined to treat key institutions of pre-reform Yamato as by-products of state formation, it was only after the middle of the seventh century that the process entered a transformative phase. The result was a compromise between the new imperial centre and the social forces which it tried to absorb, and the long-term consequences differed from the visions of the reformers, but the whole subsequent history of Japanese society was profoundly affected by the changes set in motion from above. One of the more peculiar features of this process was the effort to counterbalance its cultural impact by reconstructing a native tradition which served as a safeguard of continuity. The religious traditions imported from the continent reinforced the push for political change, but in the cultural domain, their effects were muted by the symbolic power of the very institutions which they helped to strengthen. From a comparative point of view, this constellation is an interesting example of the often complex relationship between cultural breakthroughs and innovative state formation.

The last stage of the first phase was a long-drawn-out decomposing process. Despite the real successes and lasting effects of the reform, the new regime as a whole was too alien to the Japanese environment and its ambitions too far in excess of its resources for the system to survive intact. But its decline was much less rapid and straightforward than earlier Western interpretations and comparisons with Europe would suggest. The parallel with the Carolingian empire in Europe and the subsequent shift to a decentralized feudal order (suggested, for example, by Marc Bloch) now seems misleading: historians disagree on many questions concerning the long history of the Heian state and its changing power structures, but it is generally accepted that the developments which in the end led to its downfall were – in contrast to the almost instant collapse of Carolingian power – both complex and protracted, and that they had more to do with internal dynamics than with challenges from outside. Briefly, the decisive factor was a progressive privatization from within and above (it might perhaps he described as state formation in reverse); aristocratic houses and factions carved up the state, appropriated resources and privileges, and emptied the imperial institution of power, but continued to operate within the framework of the imperial court and its broader institutional context. This analysis raises some intriguing questions with regard to the last of our typological distinctions. There is no doubt that the seventh-century reformers had envisaged – and to a significant degree achieved – a momentous step towards unitary statehood (surely one of the most impressive premodern developments of this kind), but the concessions made to the aristocracy as well as to the Buddhist establishment made the system more multi-central in practice than in theory. It is true that the rivalry between sub-centres of power and privilege was channelled into court politics, rather than regional conflicts, but the building of provincial power bases by court factions and religious institutions was an essential part of it. We might, in other words, say that the post-reform polity had – from the outset – some of the hallmarks of a composite state, and was thus exposed to further fragmentation.

This new – and now prevalent – perspective on the origins of medieval Japan is incompatible with the notion of a warrior class – the samurai – emerging out of the ruins of the imperial regime to expropriate and displace the court aristocracy.[23] Provincial warriors were part of the system from the outset, never fully assimilated to the new institutions put in place during the reform era, but long constrained by a power structure which set limits to their upward mobility. The decisive shift in the balance was the result of a crisis of the whole regime, rather than a frontal collision of courtiers and warriors, and the establishment of the Kamakura shogunate – the first warrior government – in 1192 was therefore not so much the end of a class conflict as the beginning of a new phase of state formation: 'the coming together of men of the provinces to create a locus of authority that was both physically and institutionally distinct from the capital city and imperial control'.[24] This was, in other words, a secondary process of state formation; it differed from the primary one with regard to its geographical basis, its formative mechanisms and its developmental patterns. And it has some significant affinities with the process analyzed by Elias, especially in that it also unfolds in the context of a feudal order (admittedly, the question of Japanese feudalism is controversial in many respects, but the present paper cannot deal with it). As Elias showed, feudal institutions functioned both as obstacles to and instruments of state-building. The same duality is characteristic of the Japanese case, but the connection between the dynamics of feudalism and those of state formation is even closer: the military counter-state was more thoroughly immersed in the feudal world than the European kingdoms which had survived in residual form from pre-feudal times and became the focus of renewed state-building.

The other side of this situation, however, was that the results of the primary process continued to coexist with the foundations of the secondary one, and thus to perpetuate 'a system of government approximating a dyarchy'[25] which had no parallel in the West. As we have seen, oversimplified constructions of similarities between Japan and the West must he abandoned, but we can still treat these two historical examples as two exceptionally clear-cut cases of transition from a primary to a secondary process of state formation (there was, by contrast, no such transition in premodern China). In the Japanese case, the survival of the imperial institution and the court organized around it meant that the primary process had left a more unified, symbolically charged and directly reactivable legacy than in Europe. Its relationship with the military counter-state – the embodiment of the secondary process – varied from phase to phase; during the Kamakura era, it took the form of two interdependent but competing power structures.

The Kamakura regime began with an attempt to build political structures on the traditions and practices of the warrior class, and its initial phase can therefore be said to represent a more endogenous process of state formation than its imperial predecessor. But as it developed a more complex apparatus of government, it came to rely on court experts and traditions. The derivative aspect was, however, most evident on the level of legitimacy: the claim to rule was based on a fictitious delegation of power by the imperial court, and the reference to the primary process thus remained essential to the self-image of the new state. But although the principle of imperial sovereignty was never contested, the Kamakura regime was indisputably the stronger partner (especially after a brief civil war in the early thirteenth century). Within the limits set by the dyarchic structure, it was essentially autonomous. Despite its impressive success in imposing its authority on an increasingly complex society (legal innovations played an important role in this respect), the overall pattern must he described as immanent rather than transformative. The military counter-state emerged in conjunction with a changing balance of social power, accompanied by agricultural growth and commercialization; it was beneficiary and a co-ordinator rather than a sovereign initiator of social change. Finally, the dyarchy as such was a composite state, and although the main division of power was between court and samurai, other players – such as the main Buddhist monasteries – could conserve or expand their power bases.

Paradoxically, it was the weaker partner in the dyarchy that first tried to adopt a more transformative strategy with the aim of building a more unitary state. This is at least a plausible interpretation of the policies of Emperor Go-Daigo during the short-lived Kenmu

Restoration (1333–36). He seems to have envisaged direct imperial rule, based on a disparate alliance of social forces (some of his allies pursued the more anachronistic goal of restoring power to the court aristocracy); the result would have been a reactivation of the primary process and a neutralization of the secondary one. But he also seems to have drawn on information about the more bureaucratic form of imperial rule that had prevailed in China under the Song dynasty (960–1279). His innovations were, in other words, inseparable from another derivative turn.

The restoration failed, and the conflict ended with a victory of the samurai and a return to military rule. There are, however, some reasons for regarding the Muromachi shoguns as inheritors of the more innovative elements of the Kenmu Restoration. In any case, historians now emphasize that this second samurai regime – a 'military government which for the first time gained possession of all aspects of secular authority'[26] – began with a major effort to build a more centralized state.[27] The military rulers moved to the imperial capital, and the available evidence suggests that they planned to dethrone the imperial dynasty, but failed to do so for lack of support in their own ranks. In short, their strategy seems to have aimed at a complete absorption of the primary process of state formation by the secondary one, and this would have been the foundation for a more vigorous reassertion of state control over society. The long-term result was the exact opposite: causes and effects are a matter of debate among historians, but in general terms, there is no doubt that the Muromachi project backfired and culminated in an unprecedented fragmentation of the Japanese state. The process of state formation had to begin again on a more limited basis and in a more dispersed manner. Local warlords – the *daimyō* – now became its main protagonists; although their methods of mobilizing resources and securing control over their domains varied considerably, and some cases reveal a more rationalizing and experimental spirit than others, they fit into Elias's conceptual framework inasmuch as the construction of monopolies and competition with other state-builders were their main concerns.[28] It seems appropriate to describe the *Sengoku* era – from the late fifteenth century to the early second half of the following one – as a decentralized phase of the secondary process of state formation. The key developments were endogenous (they were shaped by the needs and ambitions of local military elites), and the configuration of autonomous processes – in contrast to the more unified patterns of earlier phases – was in some ways reminiscent of the prehistory of the European state system. Within the domains, the new apparatuses of power had a stronger impact on local social life than the more remote centres of imperial or shogunal power, and we can therefore speak of a more transformative turn in a restricted context. Finally, the domain rulers were, even if on a very limited scale, experimenting with techniques and institutions that would later serve to recreate the foundations of a unitary state.

The astonishingly rapid unification of Japan during the second half of the sixteenth century marked a new turn in the process of state formation. This had something to do with Western influence: firearms were brought to Japan by Westerners and became an important asset for those who were quickest to make use of them. In this sense, the first encounter with the West can be said to have accelerated state formation in Japan (it seems likely that the rejection of the West was also prompted by developments at this level: the involvement of Christianity in power struggles within Japan, especially the possibility of a Christian state emerging in Kyushu, posed a more acute threat than Spanish expansion). But apart from this contingent factor, the changes of the preceding century had clearly paved the way for a leap from fragmentation to unity. A comparison of the strategies of the three successive unifiers – Nobunaga, Hideyoshi and Ieyasu – suggests that the unifying process could have taken different directions. The policies adopted by Nobunaga and Hideyoshi are in some ways indicative of a more ambitious and innovative project than the one which eventually prevailed. In the present context, however, this question will have to be left out of consideration; I will only deal with some aspects of the regime put in place by Tokugawa Ieyasu and perfected by his successors.[29]

As historical research has shown, the social and political order of Tokugawa Japan was based on a complex combination of different socio-cultural patterns and principles of organization. If crucial phases of state formation in Japan and the West were characterized by the dynamic interaction of feudalism and centralizing forces, the Tokugawa regime represents an unusually sustained attempt to devise a stable synthesis of both these factors. The result was, however, a gradual transformation of the feudal elements under the impact of state-centred and state-building developments; the urbanization, bureaucratization and intellectualization of the samurai, often noted by historians of Tokugawa Japan, is the most conspicuous aspect of this process, and the most decisive for the later course of Japanese modernization. Another noteworthy feature of Tokugawa Japan is the combination of two levels of state formation, institutionalized in the *bakuhan* system. The central authority of the Tokugawa dynasty was superimposed on *daimyō* rule in the domains, but the latter were still in many ways more like separate political units than parts of a unitary state. Comparison with European history has often led to misleading views of this constellation. Elias's comments on the divergent trends of state formation in France and Germany can perhaps be used as a starting-point for more adequate description. The French line of development led to the gradual absorption of feudal domains by a centralizing monarchy, whereas the failure to establish an imperial centre in Germany was followed by fragmentation into smaller states. The Tokugawa regime can – up to a point – be regarded as a combination of both these patterns, but in a very distinctive context. More importantly, the two-tiered structure of state formation was reflected on the level of the two basic monopolies. Within the domains, taxation and military resources were under the direct and exclusive control of the *daimyō* and his functionaries; the central government did not try to replace the regional monopolies with a central one, but a very large part of the country was brought under the direct control of the Tokugawa house and guidelines enforced by the centre imposed severe constraints on the use of fiscal and military monopolies by the regional rulers. This is most obvious with regard to military matters, but the overall structure of the Tokugawa order also prefigured and limited the methods which the *daimyō* could use to extract resources from their domains.

Finally, it can be argued that the Tokugawa regime combined the different types of state formation, as distinguished above. By recognizing the symbolic supremacy of the imperial institution while barring it from the exercise of power, it achieved a durable synthesis of the primary and secondary process; but, as events were to show, the imperial institution could still – in a crisis – serve to legitimate a challenge to this power structure and a rebuilding of the state on new foundations. The two-tiered *bakuhan* system combined the autonomy of the centre (enhanced by an exceptionally thorough strategic withdrawal from international politics) with dependent development in the domains. During the last phase of the regime, some of the domain rulers greatly extended their elbow-room, and this factor was to play an important role in the final crisis. As for the distinction between endogenous and derivative patterns, there is no doubt that the construction of the Tokugawa state was essentially an endogenous process, but derivative aspects are more evident in the model which it tried to impose on Japanese society. The rigid hierarchy of four estates, known as *shi-nō-kō-shō* (samurai, peasants, artisans and merchants), was derived from the Chinese tradition, although its origins may – in contrast to the conventional view – have been less Confucian than Legalist. From another point of view, the Tokugawa regime used transformative methods – a far-reaching and systematic re-fashioning of the social fabric – in order to embed the state in a stable socio-cultural context. Its fundamental goals were thus more in line with what was described earlier as the immanent type of state formation; but the long-term and largely unintended effects of this double-edged strategy – the bureaucratization of the samurai, the commercialization of the economy and the consolidation of national unity – were to prove conducive to rapid change when external conditions called for it. Finally, the Tokugawa regime was based on a very unusual mixture of the features characteristic of unitary and composite states. Inasmuch as the domains retained their own foundations and symbols of statehood, they were in some ways more self-contained than the separate parts of composite states in the West. But the uniform and comprehensive order imposed by the centre, combined with its exclusive control over such key areas as foreign affairs and relations with the ultimate course of legitimacy (the imperial dynasty), made the whole system more like a unitary state. The streamlined and circumscribed autonomy of the domains enabled them to construct their own bureaucratic apparatuses and exercise more effective local control than the Tokugawa government did, but not to maintain separate political traditions or invent original strategies of state-building.

The exceptionally rapid and successful transition to a centralized nation-state after 1868 was – in terms of our theoretical framework – the final triumph of the unitary over the composite model. The leadership that presided over this landmark transformation was keenly aware of the cultural prerequisites: a mythical vision of the national community (*kokutai*), with particular emphasis on homogeneity and uniqueness, served both to impose a higher level of integration and to conceal the limits to it. But the strategy of the

Meiji bureaucrats was also innovative in regard to other aspects of state formation. Most importantly, it was based on a definitive fusion of the primary and secondary processes: the imperial institution became an essential part of the modern state. Direct imperial rule remained a fiction, but even in that capacity, it changed the whole pattern of legitimation. The reactivation of the imperial tradition was, moreover, an effective way of symbolizing the autonomy which the samurai activists wanted to defend against Western encroachments. The continuity of the dynasty highlighted the fact that state formation in Japan had never been dependent on an external centre (it was only after 1945 that it went through a phase of dependence). But if the architects of the Meiji state managed to avoid political dependence, there was no way around cultural borrowing for political purposes. Even if there was an endogenous background to the revolution of 1868, in the sense that the internal crisis of the regime called for a radical restructuring of the state, the post-revolutionary system of government and administration drew extensively on Western models. Historians have often underlined the similarity with the seventh-century reform: a derivative turn in state formation was motivated by the desire to maintain autonomy. At the same time, the main residue of the primary process – the imperial institution – provided an endogenous counterweight. The Meiji oligarchs enshrined imperial sovereignty and divinity in a constitution otherwise modelled on the more authoritarian Western versions of the rule of law. But the importance and adaptability of the imperial legacy is perhaps most obvious in relation to immanent and transformative aspects of the Meiji state. As a symbol of sacred authority, a guarantee of continuity and a focus of collective identity, the imperial institution served to embed the new state in an older tradition and thus to strengthen its immanent character. On the other hand, radical change could be disguised as return to imperial rule, and the incorporation of the dynastic myth into the ideology of the nation-state was to prove a very effective device of mobilization. In this regard, the imperial connection enhanced the transformative potential of the state. The category of the 'developmental state'[30], as defined by Chalmers Johnson, may be applicable to other countries besides Japan, but one of the factors that fitted the Japanese state for a pioneering role in this area was the unusual combination of traditional and modern resources: the '*tennō* system' protected a strong and purposeful bureaucracy from contestation and enabled it to dispense with ideological inventions. A strategy of development was perceived and justified as a defence of identity.

To conclude, we must briefly discuss the impact of the modern Japanese state on the East Asian sphere. The internal transformation after 1868 was bound to affect other states as well as interstate relations in the region. This spillover effect, inherent in the modernizing efforts of the Meiji regime, stands in marked contrast to all earlier phases. The most decisive turning-point in the history of the Japanese state – the seventh-century reform – coincided with a virtual withdrawal from the East Asian state system; cultural and economic contacts were maintained, albeit not without fluctuations, but Japanese involvement in political and military affairs on the mainland came to an end with the retreat from Korea in the 660s. A change of course seemed imminent on two later occasions. At the beginning of the fifteenth century, the shogun Ashikaga Yoshimitsu accepted the title of 'King of Japan' from the Chinese Emperor; this move, which might have led to major changes in Japan's relationship with China, was obviously linked to the growth of trade with the mainland and probably to Yoshimitsu's plans for more concentration of power, but no further steps followed. More significantly, the invasion of Korea at the end of the sixteenth century was meant to pave the way for a conquest of China and thus for Japanese rule over the whole region; this attempt failed, and the Tokugawa regime then reverted to isolationist policies. The early modern pattern of foreign relations (1600–1868) is best described as a more restrictive version of the traditional one. The notion of the 'closed country' *(sakoku)* is misleading, and it is particularly inadequate with regard to the East Asian context. Within the region, the Tokugawa rulers pursued a policy of limited and regulated contact, rather than total isolation; they used this minimalist strategy (controlled trade with China and Korea as well as exclusive diplomatic relations with the latter) to maintain – for domestic purposes – an imaginary regional order centred on Japan.[31]

There is no comparable Western case of a long-term process of state formation without involvement in a state system. But the regional impact of the rising Meiji state is also without parallel in Western history. It is true that the whole European state system was repeatedly affected by changes in the strength and orientation of its major components; both revolutionary France and unified Germany were, however, confronted with rivals of essentially the same kind, whereas Meiji Japan faced no serious competition from its neighbours. Both China and Korea were – for different reasons – taking a much more tortuous and difficult road to modernity. Contrary to popular notions of an inbuilt and permanent imperialism, the evidence suggests that this obvious strategic advantage did not translate into certainty or consensus about the course to follow. It was self-evident that the modernized Japanese state would exercise more power and influence on the mainland, but there were different ways of doing so, and disagreement on this issue was – in an intricate and sometimes unexpected fashion – linked to other conflicts within the Japanese power elite. As a classic account of Japanese policy in Korea has shown, uncertainty and high-level discord were characteristic of Japan's new regional strategy during its formative period.[32] And the presence of Western powers aggravated the problem: Japan's turn to a more active foreign policy and a more ambitious conception of its regional role coincided with a new phase of Western expansion and intra-Western rivalry in East Asia. The Japanese ruling bloc had to adapt to an unprecedented interlocking of global and regional affairs. The victory over Russia in 1905 was a significant success, but not a definitive breakthrough.

The situation was further complicated by the impact of Soviet power and the Soviet model on East Asian politics after the First World War. But it was precisely in this context that Japan's regional project took a more distinctive and explosive turn. The policies of the ultra-nationalist and militarist phase – from the end of the 1920s to the end of the Pacific War – must be seen as a counter-challenge to both Western patterns of modernity and their Soviet adversary (the affinity with Fascist regimes in the West was significant, but it should not obscure the differences). This double thrust was important for the ideological impetus of the project, for the mobilization of domestic support and – to some extent – for the appeal to nationalist elements in various Asian countries. But the ultra-nationalist alternative was double-edged in another sense, and this was reflected – in different ways – in its internal as well as its external results. With regard to the Japanese polity and its principles of organization, ultranationalism accepted Western techniques of maximizing power and proposed to use them more effectively against the West, but rejected even the most muted versions of the liberal-democratic model and tried to replace them with ideological and political constructions of radical particularism. In terms of the conceptual framework sketched above, the primary autonomous and endogenous aspects of the Japanese state were invested with new meaning, and this served to block further Westernization of its institutions. There is no doubt that the ultra-nationalist adaptation of the imperial myth was a very effective antidote to both liberal and socialist dissent at a crucial historical moment. The combination of Western methods turned against Western power and anti-Western visions in response to Western models did not work as well in the international arena: Japan's military successes could be seen elsewhere in Asia as further proof of the efficacy of instrumental Westernization, but the extreme particularism of Japanese ideology was an obstacle to political mobilization on the same scale, and it was conducive to disastrous misperceptions of the balance of forces.

In brief, ultra-nationalism abroad was inevitably a less coherent proposition than at home. This does not mean that its impact on Asian history was negligible. The Japanese onslaught on the mainland weakened Western colonialism in South and Southeast Asia beyond repair. It also paved the way for revolution in China: the Communist victory in 1949 would not have been possible without the damage inflicted on the Guomindang regime by the Japanese invasion. The defeat of ultra-nationalism thus seemed – at first sight – to entail a major victory for the Soviet model as a global alternative. But in retrospect, it can he argued that the emergence of a second Communist centre marked the beginning of the end for Communism as an international movement: it was only a question of time when the reality of two imperial powers would prevail over the phantasm of ideological unity. Finally, the failure of ultra-nationalism condemned Japan to a prolonged phase of incomplete statehood and subaltern foreign policy.[33] The erstwhile pioneer of modern state-building and modern imperial strategy in the region became an economic superpower with a self-limiting political agenda.

The long-term repercussions of these developments are at the centre of present changes in the East Asian regional power structure. American hegemony, always an uncertain substitute for earlier Western domination, is undergoing a redefinition of ends and means in response to the post-Cold War constellation; the failure of the Soviet model is as incontestable in East Asia as elsewhere, but the distinctively Chinese version of post-Communism is only beginning to take shape; Japan's changing relationship with America and its new economic power on the mainland, especially in Southeast Asia, have yet to find an adequate political expression. An implication of particular relevance in the present context should he noted: the fluid and uncertain state of affairs in East Asia has made it clearer that the modern phase of state formation in the region is uncompleted, and different patterns and directions of future development – with correspondingly different attitudes to Western models – can be envisaged. This applies to China, where further adaptation of the post-Communist imperial state to the emerging capitalist economy seems inevitable in principle but impossible to predict in detail, and to Korea, where reunification is overwhelmingly likely but its modalities uncertain; it is also true of Japan, where an overdue transformation of the relationship between economic and political power, at home and abroad, could yet be carried out in different ways. The complex synthesis that has been characteristic of Japanese state formation, especially its early modern and advanced modern phases, is – in other words – likely to produce new variations. But more specific scenarios are beyond the scope of this article.

6 Elias in Japan: State Power, Military Elites and Organized Violence

There is – as far as I can judge – no evidence that Norbert Elias saw Japan as particularly relevant to the foundations or to further development of his theory of civilization and state formation. *The Civilizing Process* contains only one significant reference to Japan: a footnote to the chapter on the 'dynamics of feudalization.'[1] It begins with a brief mention of an American author who noted parallels between European and Japanese feudalism; this point is then linked to Otto Hintze's more general discussion of the preconditions and characteristics of feudal societies; and Elias goes on to quote Ralf Bonwit (probably on the basis of a private conversation, since nothing is said about a text) on the 'astonishing similarities' between the institutional dynamics of feudalism in Western Europe and Japan. To sum up, it seems clear that Elias's ideas about comparing Japan and the West centred on a common experience of feudal society, but his comments on this rely on the work of other authors, and they do not suggest strong views on Japanese exceptionalism. Japan is for him a particularly striking case of feudal structures developing in a non-Western historical context, but clearly not – as it was for some comparative historians – the only significant one. His references to 'Homeric warrior society' and to 'living societies' resembling the medieval West show that he wanted to apply the concept of feudalism to a wide range of historical phenomena; although this view should not be confused with the Marxist conception of feudalism as a universal stage of social development, it does allow for far-reaching generalizations across historical and geographical boundaries. The brief discussion of Homeric Greece and its 'knightly society' (*Rittergesellschaft,* used with reference to ancient and medieval times) is particularly interesting in that it highlights a presumed case of feudal institutions and attitudes which underwent a transformation very different from the later Western one analyzed in *The Civilizing Process*.

In short, the Japanese case is subsumed under a much broader category which would – if Elias had pursued this line of argument – presumably have served to guide a comparative study of both structural similarities and developmental contrasts with the West. But as I will try to show, there are good reasons to conclude that specific aspects of the Japanese experience are of particular relevance to the theoretical model developed in *The Civilizing Process*, and that they raise questions of particular importance for further development of the paradigm outlined but not completed by Elias. More precisely, I will argue that if we confront the argument of *The Civilizing Process* – more precisely: the explicit theory of state formation – with the pattern of Japanese history, the latter appears to be characterized by several striking anomalies. I shall then briefly consider traditional historical accounts of the trends and forces involved in these – by Western standards – atypical developments, and go on to outline a new picture that seems to be emerging from recent research; finally, I will discuss some implications of this revised account of the Japanese experience for the interpretive framework of Elias's theory of state formation.

Japan as a counter-example

Let us start with the above-mentioned anomalous phenomena. There are at least five well-known aspects of the Japanese historical experience – from the seventh-century transformation of the Japanese state to the nineteenth-century opening to the West – that should be mentioned in this context.

(1) The historical relationship between military society and court society differs markedly from the West. As is well known, Elias analyzed the rise of court society and its role as a model for more comprehensive civilizing processes in connection with long-term trends of state formation: the court was an essential instrument of the absolutist state, in that it served to complete the pacification and disciplining of the military elites which had dominated European society during its earlier phases. More recent scholarship in the field seems to stress the cultural and representational aspects of court society rather than the strictly strategic ones; this is in line with a more general growth of interest in the cultural frameworks

of state formation.² But in Japan, a complex court society with a correspondingly elaborate culture is characteristic of an early phase of state formation; it was created in the course of the seventh-century transformation. Later developments led to a transfer of power from the court aristocracy to a military elite; although this process was – as we shall see – more complex than earlier historians tended to believe, there is no doubt about the long-term militarization of power and authority. It would not, however, suffice to say that in Japan (in contrast to Europe), court society gives way to military society. An important point to be added is that the power centres of military society envisaged and experimented with different strategies in relation to court society. The first phase (from the late twelfth to the early fourteenth centuries) was characterized by an uneasy coexistence of the court and the military counter-state. Subsequently (during the fourteenth and early fifteenth century), new military rulers attempted to take over the court and merge the two historical layers of the power structure at the top. The failure of this project led to a fragmentation of military society, and to efforts to create substitutes for court culture and society on a much smaller scale, while at the same time trying to implement new principles of social organization. The solution which prevailed after the late sixteenth-century unification of Japan was less innovative than some of the approaches tried before: The traditional centre of court society was integrated into the legitimizing framework of military society, in a symbolically prominent but materially marginal capacity; and at the same time, the unified military state became the focus of a new civilizing process, different from but not directly contrary to the court-centred one.

(2) The final outcome of an exceptionally self-contained process of state formation – the early modern Japanese state, from the beginning of the sixteenth to the middle of the nineteenth century – differed from analogous regimes in Europe (i.e. the absolutist states) in some fundamental ways. As Elias showed, the distinctive characteristics of the early modern state in the West had to do with success in imposing the twin monopolies of taxation and violence, and the achievements of the absolutist monarchies in this regard paved the way for their transformation into nation-states, more or less capable of further functional democratization. But in Japan, the infrastructures of Tokugawa rule fell far short of effective monopolies of taxation and violence, and this was not merely a matter of less effective pursuit of the same goals as in the

West; rather, a strategy of combining concessions to political sub-centres at the most elementary level of social power with compensatory mechanisms of control in other areas added up to a specific pattern of state formation. We might speak of partial functional equivalents of the basic monopolies, but then it needs to be added that as a result, the overall configuration became different. As Mary Elizabeth Berry puts it, aspects of the state in the Weberian sense (she does not refer to Elias) 'remain problematic in early modern Japan – whether we are concerned with a public treasury, a separate judiciary, or a national bureaucracy.'[3] She goes on to underline the importance of 'private attachment' – personal bonds within and between ruling houses at different levels of the power structure – as part of the system of control. It is worth noting that this enhanced personalization of authority ran counter to the logic which is – according to Elias – central to the modern phase of European state formation, i.e. the conversion – gradual and at first latent – of private monopolies into public ones. There were, of course, other trends at work within the Tokugawa order, and as events were to show, it was in some ways even more amenable to transformation into a nation-state than its Western contemporaries; but the role of 'private attachment' was certainly one of the factors which made the Japanese transition from early to advanced modernity different from the Western one.

(3) This brings us to the third point: in the Japanese case, the relationship between feudalism and state formation did not develop along the same lines as in Elias's account of the West. It is surely one of Elias's most important – but still not fully appreciated – contributions to the sociological understanding of European history that he relativized the concept of feudal society; if we follow his line of argument, it is no longer possible to speak of a 'transition from feudalism to capitalism', as if we were dealing with two equally self-contained and dominant social systems. For Elias, the feudal institutional context is important as a matrix of state formation, and it has a lasting impact on the form and direction of the state-building process; but on the other hand, the dynamic of state formation is from the outset uncontainable within the feudal framework and conducive to changes which paved the way for a different social order. In brief, the cumulative impact of state formation de-feudalized the social context in three fundamental ways. The progressive monopolization of violence and taxation laid the foundations for a re-concentration of sovereignty at the top, i.e. in

the hands of the monarchic state (by contrast, the parcellization of sovereignty had been a key characteristic of feudal institutions); the pacification and disciplining of feudal elites changed their behavioural patterns and value-orientations; and new cultural models, linked to the institutional complex of court society, replaced or absorbed feudal traditions. From a long-term perspective, the Japanese case resembles this Western pattern in that the centripetal dynamic of state formation prevailed over the centrifugal one of feudalism; but the constellation that was stabilized for two and a half centuries in early modern Japan was very different from the one that was evolving at the same time in the West. At the political level, feudal forms of power were systematically conserved and used to strengthen the control of the ruling Tokugawa house over the subaltern centres of power. At the socio-economic level, they were no less systematically eliminated and replaced by a more bureaucratic, centralized and impersonal control of the military state over the peasantry (and as more recent research has shown, this change left considerable scope for development and differentiation within the rural society from which the military elite had now been separated). This paradoxical combination has made it difficult for Western historians to define early modern Japan in typological terms. Those who focused on the most visible part of the Tokugawa power structure tended to see the whole system as a feudal order, artificially consolidated and conserved in the face of historical pressures for change; those who noted the obviously non-feudal aspects of Tokugawa Japan were tempted to conclude that the country must have entered a post-feudal (by implication bourgeois and/or capitalist) stage of development. But neither Western Europe nor Japan ever saw a comprehensively and exhaustively feudal society; there were only successive mixtures of feudal and non-feudal elements, and among the latter, the state structures in formation played a crucial role; but the particular combination of feudal and state-centred elements which prevailed in early modern Japan has no parallel in the West. [4]

(4) The relationship between the early modern Japanese state and the urban-commercial elite is similarly difficult to fit into a Western frame of reference. To clarify this point, it may be useful to recapitulate Elias's analysis of the Western European – more particularly French – pattern of interaction between absolutism and the bourgeoisie. As he saw it, the institution of the monarchy was at its strongest during a historical epoch when a weakening

nobility had to compete with ascendant bourgeois strata; and he went on to argue that the 'most representative and socially influential example of the bourgeois in the seventeenth and eighteenth centuries...is the middle-class servant of princes or kings, that is, a man whose nearer or more distant forefathers were indeed craftsmen or merchants, but who himself now occupies a quasi-official position within the governmental apparatus.'[5] It goes without saying that absolutism is still a very controversial phenomenon, and that new perspectives have been opened up in recent years.[6] But I do not think that the essentials of Elias's conception of the absolutist state have been invalidated: it was a power structure which transcended both feudal and bourgeois contexts, but could mobilize material and cultural resources from both sides. And the reference to rivalry between social forces (and the opportunities thus created for a self-strengthening state) should not be misunderstood: Elias's analysis is fundamentally different from the Marxist view (contested, of course, within the Marxist camp) of the absolutist state as based on nothing more than a prolonged balancing act between aristocracy and bourgeoisie. For Elias, a relative equilibrium between rival forces is important, but it is only one side of the story; the other is the ability of the absolutist state to transform both forces (in different ways and to a different extent, but with significant effects on both sides), and to translate the inputs from them into its own language. If we now confront this model with the Japanese experience, it seems clear that there was no comparably far-reaching interaction within the framework of the Tokugawa regime. It is true that relations with merchant elites in Edo and Osaka were an important part of Tokugawa strategy; there were some temporary shifts towards greater merchant influence (especially during the rule of the minister Tanuma Okitsugu in the second half of the eighteenth century); and intellectuals with a merchant background made an important contribution to Tokugawa thought. But even allowing for all this, it still seems beyond doubt that socio-cultural barriers between the Tokugawa elite and the urban strata were more durable and effective than in the West. This fact is particularly noteworthy if we set it alongside two others. First, the early Tokugawa regime presided over what was probably the most massive urbanizing process in premodern history, including the transformation of a minor castle town into the world's largest city (Edo). Second, the lasting divide between military and commercial elites did not – in the long run – lead to unmitigated involution or paralysis of the state dominated by the former. When the whole political and social order had to be restructured in response to a changed global environment, the decisive impulse came from within the many-layered Tokugawa power structure.

(5) The fifth and last anomaly which I want to consider has to do with the relationship between state formation and state system. Elias's account of the Western European pattern suggests – in brief – a fundamental continuity and homogeneity of the two levels. The original context of state formation can be seen as a state system in miniature: the process begins with competition between unstable and small-scale power centres, and the emergence of stronger ones reproduces rivalry on a larger scale. Territorial states develop together with a European state system, and in the last instance, the competition between nation-states follows the same basic pattern as that of power units within the early medieval world. In the Japanese case, we can of course observe some interconnections between the two levels. During phases of fragmentation, Japan became in some ways more like a state system than a unified state, and some important innovations took place within that context. This applies, in particular, to the *sengoku* period (from the late fifteenth to the second half of the sixteenth century); but it is also worth noting that the condition of Japan during a few crucial years before 1868 was somewhat similar. The anomaly appears when we consider the relationship of the Japanese state to the East Asian region: decisive turning-points in the process of state formation coincided with withdrawal from political involvement beyond the archipelago. This was the case in the seventh century, when the creation of the imperial state took place at the same time as a definitive retreat from the continental political arena. But for present purposes, it is more important to note that the same pattern was repeated in a more radical fashion at the beginning of the early modern era. In completing the unification of Japan, the Tokugawa regime also abandoned all plans for expansion on the continent; and this policy culminated – after some hesitation – in a very thoroughgoing minimization of contact with the outside world. It is true that the traditional notion of a 'closed country' is more than a little misleading, but we can still speak of a remarkably radical isolationism. And at the same time, the combination of central Tokugawa authority and autonomous domain rule retained some aspects of a state system within Japan, but in a way designed to

eliminate active competition between the quasi-states. We can, in other words, speak of a double detachment – internal and external – of state building from interstate competition.

The mutations of the samurai

These characteristics stand out when Japanese history is analyzed in the light of a theory which emphasizes the autonomous dynamics of state formation. But the formerly dominant views of Japanese history did not follow that line, and the phenomena in question therefore seemed less significant. They were, to cut a long story short, incorporated into the narrative of samurai ascent and domination. This stratum or class – the terminology varied – was seen as the central collective actor of Japanese history for almost a millennium. From this point of view, the transition from court society to military society reflected the victory of a new elite of professional warriors over the old civil aristocracy; the infrastructural weakness of the Tokugawa state could be interpreted as a symptom of the collective strength of the samurai, who strove to assert their power over the rest of the population without unduly empowering the state which represented them; the persistence of feudal forms and of obstacles to fusion with bourgeois society also seemed indicative of an exceptional strength and resilience of the military elite; and the isolationist policy after 1600 made sense as a part of a more comprehensive strategy of protecting samurai domination against disruptive influences.

This vision of Japanese history can be traced back to traditional beginnings: the earliest observers of the changing power balance in medieval Japan saw it as a matter of samurai challenge to the court establishment, and this was of course a real and important part of the story. In modern historiography, this perspective has been applied and developed from different angles; there is, in particular, a Marxist as well as a non-Marxist version of it. The Marxist interpretation emphasizes the class character of the samurai and draws some specific conclusions from that premise, but it shares the underlying conception of long-term historical trends with other schools of thought. And the image of the samurai as a sovereign historical actor is not easily discarded, even when new perspectives are opened up on a more theoretical level. For example, the introductory chapter of Eiko Ikegami's recent and seminal work on the samurai and the state contains the following statement: 'The history of Japan since the emergence of the samurai class can be summarized as a process during which the samurai collectively legitimated their hegemonic position as those who were able to enforce peaceful behavior on others'.[7] But this claim seems more compatible with the traditional view than with the emerging new interpretation, to which Ikegami's book makes a particularly important contribution.

This new interpretation (it has been taking shape in the recent work of various authors) is, as we shall see, more favourable to comparative analysis along Eliasian lines. It does not deny that the samurai – and their collective action in pursuit of power – played a key role in Japanese history; the point is, rather, that the samurai-centred accounts of this history have tended to neglect the other side of the coin: the contexts in which samurai action took place, the dynamics of the historical forces unleashed through the initiatives of samurai actors, and the structural logic of long-term processes which have transformed the cultural orientations and behavioral patterns of the samurai and given unintended twists to their apparent triumphs.

The following discussion will briefly consider three aspects of this problematic. First, the question of the origins of the samurai and the conclusions that can be drawn from some recent work in the area; second, the particular characteristics of samurai identity and self-image as they took shape against the background of historical origins; and third, the dynamics of samurai-based state formation, conditioned by the broader context in which it unfolded.

The emergence of the samurai must be analyzed in connection with the preceding phase of state formation, i.e. the process which began with the construction of the *ritsuryō* state in the seventh century and eventually led to the fragmentation of aristocratic power and the decline of central authority in the eleventh and twelfth centuries. According to the traditional Marxist thesis, more or less dominant during the first phase of postwar Japanese historiography, the samurai appeared and began their long rise to power within a social vacuum opened up by the decline of the *ritsuryō* state: they were independent landowners who took advantage of the state's inability to implement central control, and then proceeded to arm themselves and increase their share of social power at the expense of the court aristocracy. It could be argued that the later (and explicitly anti-Marxist) theory of *ie* society, proposed by Murakami Yasusuke and his associates, is essentially a variation on the same theme: here the samurai appear as 'developer-lords', active in a part of the country no longer subject to any central control (the east and the northeast), and inventors of new organizational forms corresponding to new economic foundations (the distinctive institutional arrangements of the *ie*, a quasi-familial corporate group organized along hierarchical but at the same time functional lines).

Contrary to these two approaches, it now seems clear that the emergence of the samurai should be seen as a more direct outcome of the transformation of state structures between the seventh and the twelfth centuries. This is not to suggest that the samurai were simply a fragment of the state apparatus – its military arm – which became autonomous when the *ritsuryō* regime disintegrated. More generally speaking, it is misleading to describe the trajectory of the *ritsuryō* state simply as a disintegrative process, due to an initial imbalance or discrepancy between a state-building project inspired by the Chinese model and a social environment which did not lend itself to restructuring on that scale. In fact, the *ritsuryō* project already involved a far-reaching and inventive adaptation of the Chinese model, and the changes which it underwent during the following centuries were double-edged: decomposition and reconstruction went hand in hand. Moreover, the *ritsuryō* model had combined integration and exclusion in a way that had to be modified in response to a changing context. The constitution of the samurai as a separate social group with a specific power basis and a distinctive identity must be understood in the light of these trends.

On the one hand, the military specialists within the aristocratic elite were increasingly marginalized by the court families which appropriated imperial power, and by the pronouncedly anti-military ritual culture which this ascendant oligarchy created around itself. On the other hand, the *ritsuryō* model of state and society was – as many historians have emphasized – based on an ideological scheme which highlighted the relationship between imperial authority at the top and rice-growing peasantry at the bottom, and by the same token obscured the role of non-peasant strata (such as hunters and seamen) in social and economic life. It seems a plausible hypothesis that the constitution of the samurai had something to do with the mobilization and unification of marginal elements on various levels.[8] This does not mean that the samurai had no roots in rural society; we must, in all probability, allow for multiple origins, but if the background was diverse, the unity achieved through the fusion, redefinition and reevaluation of previously marginal elements was all the more essential.

In brief, the emergence of the samurai was one of several results of the development described above as a combination of decomposing and reconstructing processes. Among other important trends, let us note the consolidation of the Buddhist establishment as a more autonomous power bloc than it had been during the early phase of the *ritsuryō* state; the ascendancy of the Fujiwara family at court; and the attempt of the imperial house to distance itself from the imperial institution and transfer power to retired emperors. But most importantly, the imperial institution survived as the focus of legitimate authority and as the centre of the whole cultural framework of the political order. It is in relation to this background – the survival of an institutional core that is best described as a civilizational nucleus – that we must consider the question of samurai identity.

Eiko Ikegami has rightly emphasized the exceptional importance of samurai honor culture. As she sees it, four main aspects of the honor complex can be distinguished. The notion of honor was central to the ideology of vassalage; it was, in other words, a moral resource that helped to sustain feudal mechanisms of control, but also to defend the element of reciprocity which they contained. Second, it served to emphasize the dignity and sovereignty of the *ie*, or house, that functioned as the elementary structure of samurai power: 'each *ie* held some degree of statehood', and the honor culture gave an ideological expression to that state of things. Third, the notion of honor was central to samurai military culture and its 'distinctive social consciousness of military skills, power and discipline.'[9] Fourth, the definition of the collective identity of the samurai and of their relationship to other social forces came to centre on their unique culture of honor. The latter was, of course, not without its internal tensions; most importantly, the core values of autonomy and loyalty were open to conflicting interpretations.

This analysis of the honor culture complex seems to me unobjectionable. But some comparative perspectives might throw further light on it. It is surely unusual for such a broad spectrum of ideological functions to be associated with an honor culture, and a plausible explanation for that can be found in the broader cultural and political context. The comprehensive character, integrative potential and institutionalized continuity of the ideological framework constructed around the *ritsuryō* regime – and capable of surviving its transformations – made it extremely difficult to develop or even envisage an alternative ideological project. The hegemony of the pre-existing paradigm was further reinforced by its affiliation with a superior and enduring civilizational model: the Chinese empire and its culture. It is true that this permanent reference to an external source provided a certain opening for variation: the appropriation of the Chinese model was never complete, and it was possible to experiment with new directions as well as changes in emphasis. The special relationship between the warrior elite and the Zen Buddhist monasteries after the establishment of the Kamakura regime in 1192 shows that the particular orientations and preferences of the samurai could to some extent be articulated in this context. But the effect was limited, and only one of several parallel developments. The doctrinal and organizational innovations of Kamakura Buddhism can, in general, be seen as results – among other things – of more sustained and autonomous appropriation of Chinese sources, and the tends that can be linked to a specific samurai background played no hegemonic or synthesizing role.

Under these circumstances, the ideological self-assertion of the samurai could only take the form of a particularistic valorization of their honor culture. To clarify the implications of this, a brief comparison with the military elite of the medieval West may be useful. There are some undeniable and significant similarities. In both cases, a privileged warrior stratum grew out of the fusion of groups of diverse social origin; a distinctive ethos served to define its collective identity and emphasize its unity; and a combination of military power and control over land gave it a privileged social position. But three fundamental contrasts should also be noted. First, the development of knighthood in the West involved a much more comprehensive reorganization and reorientation of a pre-existing nobility: the military elite of the High Middle Ages absorbed older layers of aristocracy, whereas the samurai emerged alongside the court aristocracy and remained different from it. Second, the ideology of Western knighthood was to a large extent articulated and systematized by an institution which had no parallel in Japan: the Catholic Church. This made it possible to integrate the rules and values of knighthood into an innovative and comprehensive feudal ideology (or 'feudal imaginary', to quote G.

Duby), also without parallel in Japan. Third, this ideology of knighthood could develop into ambitious and universalistic projects of conquest (crusade) and/or imperial state building, and thus – in the latter capacity – lead to alliances or conflicts with the Church on which it was at the same time dependent (let us note in passing that it is misleading to talk about conflict between sacred and secular power: the papal monarchy and the imperial monarchy were different combinations of sacred and secular authority).[10]

To sum up the implications of those similarities and differences for the long-term dynamics of state formation, it may be suggested that the cultural profile of the samurai was on the one hand – in comparison with the Western nobility – more conducive to small-scale experiments in state-building, potentially very effective within their limits; but on the other hand less capable of putting its mark on large-scale and long-term projects of that kind.

The twelfth-century samurai breakthrough can also be compared to another case of a military elite aspiring to political power, much closer to Japan in geographical and cultural terms. In a recent work on military rule in twelfth- and thirteenth century Korea, Edward J. Shultz suggests – in very general terms – parallels with the Kamakura regime, but his analysis of the events that began with a military conspiracy against the ruling Korean monarch in 1170 shows that in fact the contrasts are more significant. The Korean case may be said to resemble the Japanese one in that a crisis in state structures prompted a bid for power by the military elite, previously even more emphatically subordinated to the civilian one than in Japan; but the context and the sequel were very different. In Korea, the seizure of power by military leaders was closely linked to widespread social unrest, and the first decades of military rule seem to have aggravated the problem. But the second phase – the rule of the Ch'oe family from 1190 to 1258 – was marked by efforts to re-stabilize the social order and re-unify the power centre. Although the Ch'oe rulers created new instutions to secure their house's hold on power, there was no parallel state; rather, the military rulers now sought integration on more equal terms. They even established an examination system for military officials. As Shultz puts it, 'the fatal flaws in the Ch'oe structure were its cultivation of civilian officials and its failure to devise a new ideological basis for its system.'[11] In contrast to Japan, a rift between civil and military elites did not – because of the very different social setting – spiral into a new dynamic of state formation.

But if we want to consider the relationship between samurai identity and state formation from a comparative angle, we should first spell out some conceptual preliminaries. It is one of the key theses of *The Civilizing Process* that state formation follows a logic of its own, irreducible to any specific class strategies (and the defence of this insight in concrete historical terms is surely one of Elias's most important contributions to sociological theory). One of the fundamental reasons why this logic prevails over class-based counter-trends – despite the prima facie broader basis of the latter – is that it is much more easily translated into unitary and coherent strategies (collective action by united classes is much more exceptional than the mythology of the class struggle would have us believe). In principle, state formation transcends the configurations of class action, and in practice, it takes advantage of conflicts and divisions within dominant classes. One of the tasks of comparative analysis is to examine the impact of contextual factors – including the cultural frameworks – on this asymmetric relationship: they may enhance or minimize the primacy of state formation, or channel it in specific directions.

In the Japanese case, the constraints and options of the military counter-state (founded in Kamakura at the end of the twelfth century) were, to begin with, decisively affected by the continuing existence of the primary imperial state. This coexistence set limits and imposed demands which co-determined the development of the new regime from the outset. But the older imperial partner and rival also prefigured goals and initiated projects which affected the trajectory of the military counter-state, most significantly through a failed attempt to restore direct and exclusive imperial rule (in a self-reforming version) in the 1330s.

Furthermore, the intact ideological framework determined the cultural parameters of state formation. Not that there was no scope for experiment and manoeuvre; in particular, the restored military regime of the Ashikaga (1336–1573, but in decline after the mid-fifteenth century) seems to have aimed at replacing the imperial dynasty and transferring its legitimizing framework to itself), whereas the phase of fragmentation (mid-fifteenth to mid-sixteenth century) allowed the smaller centres to experiment with ideological innovations.[12] But as unification progressed, a more definitive ideological strategy had to be adopted; and the alternative that prevailed was a systematic reconstruction of the traditional framework, conservative enough to sustain a myth of continuity, but flexible enough to allow early modern Japanese thought to explore some new themes.

In view of all these contextual factors, it seems clear that the military counter-state was from the outset both more and less than an expression of the collective samurai quest for hegemony. More, because it operated within and had to adjust to a framework external to the particular interests and cultural orientations of the warriors; less, because this involvement tended to bring it into more or less acute conflict with its samurai constituency. The 'paradoxical nature of Tokugawa state formation' (Ikegami) should thus be seen in the light of a much longer paradoxical trajectory that goes back to the twelfth century. On the one hand, it is true that the samurai maintained a more lasting privileged role in state formation than any comparable elite in the West. On the other hand, the state structures created on this basis constrained samurai action, curtailed samurai autonomy and transformed samurai identity in particularly complex ways. The processes of state formation unfolded in the shadow of earlier achievements and their Chinese model; when the links between centre and periphery loosened to the utmost (during the *sengoku* period), the new possibilities open to local samurai groups were counterbalanced by tighter forms of organization and a more intensive dynamic of competition. The Tokugawa regime inherited the accumulated legacies of all previous phases and combined them in a hybrid pattern, half state and half state system.

At the most general level, then, the Japanese experience appears as a particularly promising test case for Eliasian approaches. As I have argued, the model which Elias extracted from Western European history is not directly applicable, but the most basic insights into the autonomous dynamic of state formation seem exceptionally relevant to Japanese history, and the comparative perspective would highlight factors which the exclusive focus on European cases has tended to obscure.

7 Multiple Modernities and Civilizational Contexts: Reflections on the Japanese Experience

The following discussion will first deal with different comparative approaches to the modern phase of Japanese history, and then move on to consider the underlying conceptions and criteria of modernity; it will finish with some tentative directions for further comparative analysis. It should be noted that the three successive strategies of comparison, summarized below, are neither mutually exclusive nor limited to the historical conjunctures which made them seem particularly relevant. Rather, they relate to different levels of analysis and layers of historical significance, highlighted by changing circumstances; all of them have to some degree been applied throughout the long-standing debate on modern Japan, and the task of theoretical reflection is to synthesize their respective insights and rationales, not to choose between them. Similarly, the images of modernity that have served to anchor comparative perspectives can to some extent be seen as alternative models, but not as incompatible paradigms. As I will try to show, it makes more sense to speak of steps towards contextualization. An initially dominant but fundamentally inadequate conception of modernity must be overcome without losing sight of its relative truth-content. And the construction of a more complex theoretical framework is closely linked to better understanding of the specific case in question: as the idea of multiple modernities acquires clearer contours and firmer theoretical foundations, the originality of the Japanese experience becomes more visible and significant.

Strategies of modernization

The first of the three comparative perspectives which I want to discuss has to do with Japan as an example of non-Western responses to Western expansion and domination. In that context, the Meiji transformation – together with its sequel – stands out as a particularly effective counter-project, and its exemplary results were the main focus of references to Japan during the early phase of postwar modernization theory. The most instructive comparative analyses undertaken on this basis stressed the affinities as well as the contrasts between Japan and states with a much longer record of direct contact with Western powers. Both Russian and Turkish trajectories of modernization were extensively compared to the Japanese one and used to illustrate general patterns as well as possible variations.[1] The same line of argument could even be extended to Germany, inasmuch as that country's relationship to more advanced western and northwestern neighbours prefigured later patterns of unequal development on a global scale. But modernizing latecomers within or on the margins of the Western world are not the only relevant cases. The Japanese achievement, although undeniably outstanding in the Asian and African world, could be compared to the much less impressive efforts of a few other countries which also escaped colonization. Earlier accounts of Thailand and its exceptional record in the Southeast Asian context tended to overdraw parallels with Japan; as more recent critical reappraisals have shown, Thailand was in fact too dependent on Western powers to be regarded as a case of autonomous development.[2] In a more idiosyncratic vein, Anthony Giddens has compared Japanese and Ethiopian responses to the Western challenges.[3] Finally, the analysis of the Japanese modernizing process can throw some light on developments in major Asian countries whose road to modernity was more affected by foreign domination. Their modernizing strategies were – to a more or less significant and lasting extent – influenced by the Japanese precedent and thus conducive to indirect Westernization through emulation of the state that had gained unique prestige by pioneering an innovative method of matching Western power.

As for the specific themes and issues that may be tackled from this comparative angle, the contrasts and parallels drawn between Japan, Russia and Turkey are probably most revealing. In all three cases, the need to import and/or imitate Western ways of rationalizing the pursuit of power appears as a catalyst of more far-reaching changes; the first steps of strategic modernization lead to unintended consequences and unexpected pressures for more radical moves, but the ability to cope with this expanding horizon of change varies significantly from case to case. In general terms, however, the state can be seen as the central factor of both the initial modernizing turn and the subsequent transformative phase. The fundamental similarity of state-centred modernizing processes does not exclude major divergences. In that regard, some distinctive aspects of the Japanese experience can serve to exemplify broader issues. The sustained dynamism and autonomy of the Japanese modernizing process since 1868 are all the more remarkable in view of the fact that it had been preceded by a long phase of strategic withdrawal and minimized contact with the Western world, which in turn had followed a brief but by no means insignificant first encounter. By contrast, the Russian and Turkish trajectories were characterized by more continuity of contact with the West but less continuity of the collective identity and the imaginary frame of reference that lent cultural meaning to the strategies of response. Furthermore, the Japanese pattern of ideological orientation – a particularly radical but adaptable version of nationalism, going far beyond the Western model which antedated it – can be contrasted with the Turkish retreat from imperial and religious universalism towards a more unconditionally Westernizing nationalism, as well as with the Russian invention of a universal counter-paradigm of modernity to challenge the West in global terms. Finally, the specific characteristics of Japanese modernity cannot be analyzed without posing the question of their traditional preconditions, more visibly important – and more explicitly invoked – in Japan than in the West. The Japanese case thus becomes a starting-point for relativizing the contrast between tradition and modernity, and for rethinking a distinction grounded in Western experiences (and reinforced by one-sided readings of the latter). This line of argument would seem to represent the most radical use that can be made of our first comparative perspective.

The second one has so far been less in evidence among modernization theorists. It is mainly advocated by comparative historians, and their principal reasons relate to developments during the Meiji epoch, seen as comparable to changes unfolding in advanced Western societies at the same time.[4] On this view, the historical conjuncture of the 1850s and 1860s may have put Japan in a position akin to other countries threatened by Western expansion, but the exceptionally rapid reorientation of Japanese global strategy made the sequel more similar to innovations within the Western core. The trends and policies in question have to do with the socio-cultural ramifications of state-building, and the Japanese pattern can be compared to other ascendant powers; in this context, Germany is seen as a core state aspiring to hegemony, rather than an internal periphery of the West, but parallels can also be drawn with Britain, France and the United States. What these key players of the global state system have in common is a multi-faceted agenda of national integration, mobilization and accumulation. If there were some distinctively Japanese ways of pursuing these goals, they can be explained in terms of specific constraints as well as inventive approaches to the problems of advanced modernity. From the former point of view, it seems particularly significant that Japan had to carry out an industrial revolution in conjunction with the restructuring of state and society (this constellation is reminiscent of rapidly advancing latecomers within the Western region, but the linkage of capitalist accumulation and bureaucratic state-building was probably more methodical and effective than anywhere else). And the simultaneous turn to imperial expansion, inseparable from the broader economic and political transformation, took place in a more exceptional context: contrary to the global reach of Western colonial empires, Japanese colonialism had to operate within a region of which it had previously been a marginal part. As for the other differentiating factor (innovations based on specific historical resources and experiences), the most obvious case in point is the emergence of a particularly inclusive and pervasive version of nationalism, backed up by reconstructed traditions and translatable into strategies of state control.[5]

Another very important offshoot of this second comparative perspective should be noted. If the Meiji transformation entailed changes of essentially the same kind as those undergone by hegemonic Western states, the question of endogenous sources and preconditions must be posed. Growing interest in the Tokugawa antecedents of Meiji Japan has led to better understanding of the early modern epoch as a distinctive historical phase. The mid-nineteenth-century return of Western powers to the region thus seems to have precipitated a transition whose outcome reflected more internal trends: from a country developing independently of the West and inventing original solutions to some of the same problems, Japan was transformed into an exceptionally receptive but also uniquely autonomous borrower of Western techniques and institutions. Historical analyses of the early modern background have opened up a particularly interesting field of comparative studies. Some of the most interesting work in this area has been done on early modern Japan and France, but A. Macfarlane has recently – in a somewhat overdone fashion – tried to construct long-term parallels between English and Japanese history.[6] In any case, the question of similarities and differences between early modern Japanese and Western lines of development is open to further research. And it is obviously one of the main starting-points for a more general debate on trends in the whole Eurasian region.[7] The theoretical issue, more or less fully articulated, is of prime importance: it is being suggested that we can speak of modern or proto-modern patterns, as well as of processes with modernizing implications and outcomes, in regions beyond the reach of significant Western impact and epochs prior to the decisive breakthrough of Western expansion. This claim has far-reaching consequences for the whole problematic of Westernization and modernization, but the contributions of comparative history have yet to be fully integrated into the mainstream of theoretical debates.

The third approach I want to discuss is less developed than the other two; but as I will try to show, it can be linked to very fruitful theoretical ideas. With the rise of new developmental centres in East Asia (first Korea and Taiwan, then parts of mainland China), the modern Japanese achievement – although unequalled – came to be seen as less unique and more comparable with other projects drawing on a shared regional background. This trend was reinforced by growing awareness of the specific patterns of East Asian history and the regional responses to Western hegemony. To interpret the Japanese experience in this context is to pose two interrelated questions: how significant is the common East Asian heritage for the overall regional configuration of modernity, and how to account for the features which set the Japanese trajectory apart from the rest of the region? These developments are too recent for alternative positions to have taken clear shape, but we can at least distinguish two very different lines of argument. On the one hand, the manifest resurgence of the whole region has led many observers to stress the most familiar and official part of its heritage. The notion of a 'Confucian region' has thus gained some currency; a representative work written before the demise of Communism made the claim that Confucian ideology was to East Asia what liberalism was to the West and socialism to the Soviet bloc.⁸ Although things seem decidedly less clear-cut in the post-Communist world, the idea of a specific Confucian connection between tradition and modernity in East Asia has not disappeared, and there is no reason to doubt that Confucian patterns of thought and models of behaviour were in many ways relevant to the recent and contemporary history of the region; here I only want to indicate the main difficulties with a strong version of the thesis. First, the case for a Confucian economic ethic involved in late twentieth-century capitalist development cannot be made without a complementary account of traditional inaction. If there is a developmentalist side to the Confucian ethic, it must be one that could be effectively neutralized for a long time by contextual factors (or countervailing tendencies internal to the same tradition). Second, the East Asian tradition was not simply or unequivocally Confucian; rather, the Confucian strand (always marked by internal diversity) was a crucial but never exclusive component of a more complex tradition, adapting to other currents and redefining itself in the process, but striving with notable success to impose an orthodox self-image which obscured the underlying plurality. Third, historical research has cast doubt on earlier assumptions about the homogeneity of the region, especially on the construct of a uniformly Neo-Confucian early modern phase, and drawn attention to the varying destinies of Confucian doctrines in China, Korea and Japan. In particular, it seems that the misconception of Tokugawa Japan as dominated by Neo-Confucian orthodoxy and integrated into a Neo-Confucian regional culture has been effectively demolished. Finally, claims on behalf of the Confucian legacy must also come to grips with the difficult task of establishing and explaining its survival throughout modern upheavals in both continental and insular parts of the region. The defeat of the Taiping rebellion in China is arguably as important for the subsequent history of East Asia as the success of the Meiji Restoration in Japan.⁹ And the revolutionary phase – or intermezzo – of twentieth-century Chinese history can hardly be treated as a temporary deviation from Confucian patterns. The comparative study of revolutionary crises and ruptures in the region is still in an early stage.

In view of the difficulties faced by advocates of historical or civilizational continuity, some authors seem inclined to take the opposite tack and stress the transformative dynamism that has been so much more characteristic of the East Asian world than of other regions reacting to Western hegemony. From this point of view, modern Japan – from 1868 onwards – can be seen as a pioneering innovator which brought irreversible change to other parts of the region.[10] Japanese rule in Korea destroyed the traditional order and paved the way (unintentionally and unevenly) for more independent development. Similarly, Japanese colonization of an outlying Chinese province (Taiwan) and the creation of a client state in a peripheral region (Manchuria) had far-reaching consequences for the course of Chinese history. Most importantly, there are good reasons to doubt that a Communist revolution would have taken place in China, had it not been for the shattering impact of Japanese imperialism on the half-consolidated nationalist regime. If we add to these considerations the point that a Japanese institutional invention – the capitalist developmental state – has (in different ways at different historical junctures) played the role of precedent and model on a regional scale, there seems to be a strong case for interpreting modern East Asian history in terms of a Japanese 'big bang' and multiple but comparable repercussions throughout neighbouring countries.

But this does not dispose of the questions raised (however one-sidedly) by defenders of the Confucian thesis. Japan's road to modernity, including the radical turn taken in the second half of the nineteenth century, has a prehistory which cannot be understood without reference to the regional context and Japanese ways of relating to it. Analogously, the role of long-term trends and durable legacies in the responses to the Japanese bid for empire calls for closer examination. In brief, the problem of the relationship between civilizational background and contemporary change remains on the agenda.

Patterns of modernity

Let us now turn to the second problematic mentioned at the beginning: the underlying interpretations of modernity that inform and orient comparative study. It seems easy to identify the interpretive premises of the first approach. If the modernizing processes and strategies exemplified by the Japanese case are, first and foremost, marked by more or less effective learning from Western precedents (mainly in the domains of wealth and power), and more or less far-reaching effects of the applied lessons, the general idea of modernization can be defined in cognitivist and technological terms: it refers to the sum total of the socio-cultural effects of the growth and defusion of applicable knowledge. This view is explicitly stated in some seminal works on modernization theory and implicitly presupposed in others. The most obviously relevant applications of knowledge have to do with the most visibly effective instruments of power; derivative strategies of modernization – i.e. those constructed in response to and in defence against pioneering projects – are therefore likely to begin with military, administrative and industrial innovations. But the ramifications of strategic learning extend to all areas of social life.

It is hardly necessary to underline the particular relevance of this conception to the Japanese case. Japanese modernization – including its self-critical accompaniments – is to an unusually high degree centred on strategic learning processes. This orientation was already characteristic of the emerging Meiji state, committed to 'seeking knowledge throughout the world' for self-strengthening purposes. A more thoroughgoing version of the same strategy was advocated by those who wanted to push the appropriation of Western knowledge beyond the limits of power-centred pragmatism; the notion of *bunmei kaika* (civilization and enlightenment) served to define the goal of uncompromising modernization. Learning from Western experience in order to contest Western ascendancy was no less central to later phases of Japan's transformation; it seems clear that the capitalist developmental state matured on the basis of lessons drawn from the interwar breakdown of Western capitalism as well as from the totalitarian responses to it. At the same time, the critical idea of uncompleted enlightenment crystallized into a more explicitly negative diagnosis of the dominant trend. This is a key theme in Maruyama Masao's seminal essay on 'thought in Japan': modern Japan may have excelled in borrowing ideas and techniques from the West, but it has yet to assimilate a more structured and cumulative model of the growth of knowledge.[11] Last but not least, the role of Marxism in modern Japanese thought and culture should be seen in this light. If Japanese Marxism was both the most original offshoot of the Marxist tradition outside Europe and the most representative oppositional ideology inside Japan (the latter fact has perhaps been more widely understood than the former), both aspects are obviously related to its claim to represent a systematic and definitive self-knowledge of modernity.

In short, this first interpretive model – let us call it the cognitivist conception of modernization – is eminently applicable to the

Japanese experience. If we want to determine its limits in that regard, a brief glance at basic conceptual problems may be useful. The first point to note is that the idea of modernity which we have been discussing is by no means incapable of further development and differentiation. In particular, it can be argued that it contains *in nuce* a notion of reflexive modernization, and that the latter concept is therefore neither as new nor as challenging as some contemporary authors have argued. If the overall modernizing process is analyzed as a dynamic configuration of intended and unintended effects of cognitive progress, it seems logical to assume that there will be historical conjunctures characterized by attempts to update the cognitive program of modernity in response to cumulative dynamics of unintended consequences (both aspects, the confrontation with endogenous but unexpected problems and the articulation of significantly altered but still modern projects, have been stressed by theorists of reflexive modernization). In that sense, the concept is clearly applicable to nineteenth-century Western states and societies: new ideologies of modernity took shape against the background of conflict-laden and disintegrative modernizing processes. And the same thing is doubly true for Japan. The strategies of modernization after 1868 were based on observation of the troubles encountered by Western models and anticipation of the specific problems likely to be caused by the transfer of the latter to the Japanese context. It can thus be argued that Japanese modernization entered its reflexive phase in 1868. Needless to say, no value-judgment is implied. The concept, as used here, does not have the connotations of a higher, more complete or more liberating type of modernization.

There is, furthermore, no unbridgeable gap between the claims of the cognitivist conception and the language of systems theory. A suitably diversified notion of cognitive growth can be translated into systemic models. The well-known Parsonian model can be read in this way; here we cannot go into detail, but it may be suggested that the idea of adaptive upgrading (the main criterion of evolutionary progress) applies not only to the economic dimension, but also to other subsystems, inasmuch as their structures and functions are adapted to the rules and tasks inherent in the overall systemic pattern. The organizational codes of mutually complementary subsystems are, in a sense, objectified and programming patterns of knowledge whose application leads to improved performance. Systemic logic shapes the course of social change and evolution in a way fundamentally analogous to the effects of cognitive progress. It is in keeping with this background affinity that Parsons's account of Japanese modernization arrives at much the same conclusions as those who work with more straightforward cognitivist models: the Japanese record of learning from West (the latter being taken to represent the 'main pattern' of modernity) is unequalled, but the results so far are notably one-sided, and a comparable effort will be needed to create a balanced modern society.[12] Whether later developments in systems theory (especially the work of Niklas Luhmann) have led to a more radical break with the ideas discussed above is – for present purposes – an open question, and in any case, the absence of any significant references to Japan makes them less relevant to our theme.

I have referred to the core premise of the first comparative approach as an image or interpretation of modernity; but it is a self-relativizing image in the sense that modernization – *qua* cognitive progress of a more or less linear kind – becomes primary, and modernity can only be defined as a condition which gives free rein or minimizes obstacles to the modernizing process. By the same token, this frame of reference excludes the notion of multiple modernities. There is nothing in the cognitivist conception that would allow us to talk about significantly different durable configurations of modernity. That idea only makes sense if we can distinguish several components of the modern constellation, as well as different ways of relating them to each other, with more or less significant effects on their internal logics and constitutions. And such assumptions can, in turn, only be sustained if differences due to historical contexts are integrated into the paradigm: the historicity of modernity is irreducible to general models and theories. Multiple modernities are, by definition, historically conditioned, shaped and circumscribed modernities.

As I will try to show, this pluralistic conception of modernity can be linked to the second of our comparative perspectives. The connection is less straightforward than the first one, but the distinctive features noted by historians may point to theoretical issues familiar from other contexts. More specifically, the developments associated with state-building after 1868 add up to a comprehensive pattern of institutional and ideological formation which sets Japan apart from other societies in a similarly advanced phase of modernization. As S.N. Eisenstadt stresses in his recent work on Japanese civilization, the analysis of Japanese modernity should begin with the construction of the Meiji state, its relationship to the various social factors and arenas of the modernizing process, and the tensions subsequently generated by the very success of the interventionist 'schoolmaster state'.[13] For our purpose, it seems convenient to begin with the relationship between *state and economy*. If it is analyzed in terms of a gradual but not linear growth of the developmental state (including phases of experimentation, retreat and malfunctioning), it raises important questions about boundaries and interconnections between social spheres. The institutions of capitalism and the bureaucratic state are mutually integrated in a peculiar way, and this arrangement is not simply superimposed on a standard pattern of differentiation; rather, the interconnections affect the internal constitution of each side in fundamental ways. The obvious originality of Japanese practices in this area has led some observers to question the very validity of Western-style concepts of state and capitalism; but as indicated above, the most promising line of interpretation – exemplified by the work of Chalmers Johnson – presents Japanese economic development as a reinvention of capitalism, actively assisted and oriented by the bureaucratic state.

A broader overview of the relationship between *state and society* throws further light on the pattern of integration or differentiation. Here we can draw on arguments developed by Murakami Yasusuke, without necessarily accepting their entire theoretical framework.[14] A closer look at the Japanese case helps to establish the nation-state as the main modern agency of integration (and as the historical reality behind the idealizing constructs of mainstream Western sociology); the main reason why Japanese experience can thus serve as a basic corrective to Western theory is that it constitutes an exceptionally clear-cut case of a nation-state extending its scope of activity without taking the trans-national ideological turn which has been typical of other ambitious state-centred projects. As Eisenstadt has emphasized, the Meiji state pursued the twin goals of control and mobilization in a way comparable to Western regimes of revolutionary origin, and this remains true of its successors. At the same time, this twofold strategy of enhanced integration was combined with an imported model of modern society which reflected Western standards and visions of differentiation. In the course of the modernizing process, these two aspects interacted in complex and changing ways, including strategic adjustment on both sides (e.g.

the retreat from early Meiji ideas of the unity of state and religion as well as from a comprehensive state control over the economy) and attempts to upgrade the integrative framework, so as to make it more resistant to the side-effects of its own success. And it seems a plausible claim that growing tensions between them played a key role in the incomplete (and soon to be reversed) changes which set Taishō Japan apart from the much longer and more formative Meiji period.

The discussion of integrative and differentiating factors, central to any analysis of modernity, would be inconclusive without some comments on the cultural dimension, i.e. the self-interpretation and self-affirmation of differentiated spheres as well as the interpretive and legitimizing aspects of the integrative forces. In this context, the distinctively Japanese relationship between *state and nation* is of particular importance. It is generally agreed that the modern Japanese construction of national identity and the ideological projects built on that basis differed from European counterparts in significant ways. Maruyama Masao's seminal analysis of Japanese nationalism contains insights which have yet to be fully assimilated by Western theorists, but his specific accents and his choice of the term 'ultra-nationalism' reflect a somewhat one-sided – albeit understandable – concern with the militarist phase that had come to an end in 1945. A more balanced approach would have to do justice to the exceptional totalizing capacity as well as the adaptability of Japanese nationalism; it should also account for both affinities and differences between modern nationalism and traditional Japanese patterns of collective identity. As for the latter, S.N. Eisenstadt and B. Giesen have proposed the term 'principled primordiality'.[15] More specifically, a model or order borrowed from a more advanced civilization (China) was used to consolidate and transfigure an ethnic particularism which thus became more resistant to universalist alternatives. The transition to modern nationalism, triggered by the threat from Western nation-states, was a complex process which opened up various and in part contrasting possibilities.[16] During the Meiji period, a high-powered conception of national identity and integration took shape and was imposed against other currents; its continuing dominance was to some extent obscured by the more visible liberalizing trends of the Taishō interlude, but the subsequent militarist turn brought nationalism back to prominence and led critical observers to conflate the underlying pattern with its most extreme manifestations. A comprehensive interpretive history of modern Japanese nationalism – which no Western scholar has so far attempted to write – would need to account for reorientations before and after militarist rule without losing sight of long-term constants.

In the present context, it is the integrative logic of nationalism and its interaction with the modernizing dynamic of differentiation that should be underlined; let us note a few points which fit the emerging picture of a distinctive pattern of modernity. First, the strong and sweeping claims on behalf of the national collectivity made it more difficult for universalist ideologies (liberal or socialist, secular as well as religious) to articulate and impose their principles; Western forms of ideological differentiation could thus only develop to a limited extent. Second, the systematic reference to the national collective as a legitimizing and mobilizing authority set limits to the self-articulation of social spheres and forces, with the result that Japanese patterns of institutional formation and social stratification differ substantially from the Western ones; neither functional nor normative rationalizations of claims to autonomy could play the same role (S.N. Eisenstadt has developed this analysis in much greater detail). Finally, the imaginary paradigm of the national community served not only to reinforce core political institutions, but at the same time to devalue or de-legitimize the more mundane and divisive aspects of political life. A major counterweight to the unfolding differentiation of the political sphere was thus built into Japanese political culture. And it could function in two complementary ways: On the one hand, ethnic nationalism became an expression of protest against the authoritarian practices of the modernizing bureaucratic state, and of the wish for a more harmonious relationship between state and society.[17] On the other hand, the vision of national unity beyond political division and conflict lent effective support to strategies of totalitarian integration. It is probably true that Western scholars have tended to underestimate the first aspect; but it is also true that the anti-statist version of nationalism was to a very significant degree absorbed or neutralized by official ultra-nationalism.

These considerations should suffice to show that the Japanese case cannot be subsumed under a uniform pattern of advanced modernity. It remains to clarify the implications of the third perspective for the problematic of plural modernity. As noted above, the results of recent work on the regional background are less conclusive than those of better-established approaches; but it can at least be said that the question of the East Asian civilizational legacy and its formative impact on modern history has been put on the agenda, even if we have at the same time become more conscious of the pitfalls and short-circuits to be avoided when tackling this theme. On a more general theoretical level, it is the problem of civilizational frameworks of modernity – or, in cautious terms, the role of civilizational factors in the diversification of modernity – that we have to confront. This is not the place for detailed conceptual analysis; suffice it to say that we are using the concept of civilization in a sense outlined most convincingly by Durkheim and Mauss. In their language, the term refers to large-scale and long-term units of social analysis; civilizations transcend societies both in space and time. Although the comparative study of civilizational complexes must begin with different clusters of cultural features (capable of defusion and more or less open to modification within a civilizational area), the arguments adumbrated by Durkheim and Mauss also suggest that cultural definitions of power (reflected in political structures) are of particular importance. In brief, interrelated patterns of culture and power can be seen as the core constituents of civilizational identity, and the following remarks should be read in that sense.

Before going on to consider the relevance of civilizational theory to the analysis of Japanese modernity, it seems advisable to note some basic caveats and qualifications that follow from the above discussion – especially with regard to the problematic of the East Asian region, but also in the light of more general points made about conceptions of modernity. To begin with a very elementary observation: as the difficulties of the Confucian model show, civilizational frameworks should not be identified with orthodox, representative or programmatic ideologies. Clusters of collective representations (or imaginary significations, to use the more specific concept proposed by Castoriadis) are by definition central to civilizational analysis, but their capacity to crystallize into ideologies and claim the status of orthodoxy should be treated as a variable, dependent on intrinsic as well as contextual factors. Comparative studies have shown that some civilizational patterns are more conducive to the formation of orthodoxy than others, and some orthodoxies are more exclusive than others (or more capable of containing dissent and heterodoxy). Within one civilizational complex, some societies may differ from others in both degree and kind, as regards the construction of orthodoxy; here the contrasts between China, Korea and Japan seem particularly interesting. Another lesson to be learnt from the East Asian case concerns the question of inbuilt transformative capacity (or predisposition to social change). This should also be treated as a key variable, and civilizational patterns can differ not only in respect of their ability to develop it, but also in the sense that the potential for change may be more or less dependent on activation by external factors. Historical research has disposed of the idea that East Asian societies stagnated before the nineteenth-century encounter with the expanding West, but it still seems possible to speak of particularly effective structures and strategies of containment. As for the changes that did take place in the aftermath of Western intrusion, the East Asian record of radical change is surely unsurpassed by any other region. This is most obviously true about Japan; as for China, the story of its protracted revolutionary crisis is a familiar one, but some doubts remain about its meaning. A prominent authority on the subject has argued that the Chinese experience reflects an underlying resistance to radical change: it took a whole series of upheavals and convulsions to make Chinese society ripe for revolution.[18] But if we consider the whole trajectory since the mid-nineteenth century and the variety of successive or competing projects (from the Taiping rebellion to the rival twentieth-century strategies of imperial reconstruction), a rather different diagnosis seems to suggest itself: the long-drawn-out collapse of the old order released a broad spectrum of forces aspiring to radical change. And in a very different setting, the rapid transformations – in incompatible directions – that have taken place in independent but divided Korea point to similar conclusions.

The problem of social change and its civilizational preconditions is closely related to another issue: the varying openness to and ability to cope with intercivilizational encounters. The latter term, coined by Benjamin Nelson, refers to episodes of particularly formative – very often one-sided – interaction between civilizations. This is one of the more important but less developed themes of civilizational theory; a persistent tendency to over-emphasize civilizational closure has led some of the most prominent authors in the field to neglect the other side of the picture. Here we must limit ourselves to a few observations regarding East Asia and the particular position of Japan within the regional context. The first thing to be noted is a long early phase of relative isolation: the formation of the East Asian civilizational complex, centred on China, was a more self-contained process than other comparable developments in the Eurasian world. In the later history of the region, phases of heightened receptivity alternate with inward turns and active isolationism. East Asia became the most important outlet for the expansion of the only non-monotheistic universal religion (Buddhism). But during the epoch of global Western expansion, East Asian states had reverted to cultural closure and political detachment; this is all the more striking in view of the material and cultural resources that could in principle have sustained a more activist strategy. As for later changes in the wake of direct encounters with a more powerful West, the vigour and originality of East Asian responses stand out in contrast to other regions. No East Asian state was colonized by the West (the idea of China having been reduced to quasi-colonial status is very misleading), but Western models were appropriated in a selective fashion and applied in a distinctive context (most strikingly in Japan and China, but the same can – *mutatis mutandis* – be said about the development of the two Koreas within the bipolar system dominated by Western rivals for hegemony). Twentieth-century East Asian history is noteworthy for the wide range of Western political projects – liberal democracy, socialism, communism, nationalism and fascism – that have been imported and/or reinvented, and sometimes radicalized beyond the original versions. Some observers might question the inclusion of liberal democracy in this list. But the postwar Japanese experience is surely a significant case, and the recurrent questions about the reality or authenticity of Japanese democracy are misleading; the point is, rather, that the institutions of liberal democracy have been adopted with important modifications, and the restrictive aspects of the latter do not add up to a systematic perversion.

In a sense, the Japanese trajectory exemplifies the regional pattern on a smaller scale but in a more intensive fashion. The history of Japan's relationship with continental East Asia (and thus also with the imported traditions that had become an integral part of the East Asian world) is reminiscent of the interplay of closure and opening which marked the interaction of the whole civilizational complex with the outside world. But in the Japanese case, the appropriation of the Chinese model led to an irreversible reconstitution and self-redefinition which Buddhism never achieved in China. Similarly, Japan can be seen as the most extreme case of the regional response to the West: the Westernizing process (self-controlled with the exception of the postwar American occupation) was more far-reaching and many-sided than elsewhere, and it could be interpreted as a definitive divorce from the Asian world; this self-image never prevailed over others, but it remained a part of ongoing debates.

Civilizational perspectives

With the above qualifications in mind, we should now turn to a more systematic discussion of civilization and modernity in the Japanese context. If the general idea of civilizational premises of Japanese modernity is accepted, there are three different ways of developing it further. The main focus can be on a shared East Asian background; on constitutive characteristics of Japan as a civilization in its own right; or on the civilizational duality inherent in the Japanese way of being involved in the East Asian civilizational complex without wholly belonging to it. These approaches are more or less clearly represented in recent literature on the subject.

In view of what has already been said about exaggerated and oversimplified notions of a 'Confucian heritage', we should look for a more critical version of the first position, i.e. one which acknowledges the historical importance of Confucianism without mistaking it for a self-contained civilizational framework. The task of civilizational analysis would, rather, be to reconstruct a substratum elaborated but neither created nor fully monopolized by Confucian thought and open to some alternative (up to a point subversive) interpretations. It seems to me that the most interesting argument of this kind is to be found in the work of Léon Vandermeersch; J.F. Billeter's condensed version of Vandermeersch's ideas, which includes some suggestions for future research, is also useful.[19] The texts in question deal with separate themes in very different ways; a detailed analysis of the origins of Chinese civilization (probably the most sustained work of its kind) is coupled with a more essayistic treatment of the 'Sinified world' as a whole, with particular emphasis on its modern transformation. Vandermeersch makes strong (and to my mind partly convincing) claims about the connections between the two fields of inquiry, but many questions about the long-term historical links remain open. We can therefore speak of elements for a theory, rather than a fully-fledged theoretical model; there are some obvious unfilled gaps, and as we shall see, the account of Japan's particular place and record is very incomplete. It may nevertheless be useful to outline the main points and potential reach of this paradigm, so as to contrast it with others which are in some respects more specific.

Vandermeersch's survey of the 'sinified world' begins with a uniquely integrative cultural trait: this is the region of Chinese characters. What makes this unifying feature so significant is the fact that the characters are not simply a distinctive way of writing (focused on the semantic rather than the phonetic articulation of language) which has survived in this region longer than elsewhere. Rather, they constitute a language *sui generis*, a written language uniquely different from and independent of the oral one. Because of its par excellence meaning-laden character, this separate and exportable language carries a strong cultural message – it is, in other words, charged with latent ideology and therefore eminently qualified to function as the bearer of standardized civilizational patterns. The specific character of this cultural content can, as Vandermeersch argues, only be understood in the light of very remote but lastingly formative origins: the essentials go back to the Chinese Bronze Age. Core components of the Chinese tradition took shape during the Yin period (i.e. the last centuries of the second millennium BC, also known as the later phase of the Zhang dynasty); they were re-consolidated within a more complex framework under the early Zhou dynasty at the end of the second millennium, and reformulated on a more sophisticated and reflexive level by the Confucian tradition.

The enduring core of Chinese civilization, as identified by Vandermeersch, can be defined in terms of a distinctive institutional configuration as well as a corresponding set of interpretive patterns. A particularly thoroughgoing fusion of kinship, politics and religion, centred on the institution of sacred kingship, was achieved at an early stage and successfully adapted to an increasingly complex social environment. The family served as a symbolic framework for the legitimation of royal authority and for the ancestor worship which was at the core of religious life; at the same time, the imaginary identification with the political centre and its religious framework made concrete family structures amenable to manipulation and modification from above. Given the early and effective monopolization of sacred authority by the monarchy, there was no place for an autonomous priesthood. The only religious specialists with a domain and a direction of their own were the diviners associated with ancestor worship (Vandermeersch has given a convincing account of the 'divinatory imaginary' as an omnipresent substratum of Chinese thought). Their gradual rationalization of religious beliefs culminated in a particularly powerful notion of cosmic order, open to further refinements and capable of absorbing countercurrents. To cut a long story short, this was the starting-point for a characteristic trend of the East Asian tradition: the sustained effort to elaborate and implement a mode of thought which Vandermeersch defines as 'morphological rationality', in contradistinction to the more familiar teleological model. His most succinct description of the morphological paradigm highlights the primacy of formality over finality. The most obvious expression of that approach is the pervasive ritualism of Chinese thought and culture, and the corresponding conception of human action stresses alignment with the patterns and tendencies of given situations, rather than the positing and pursuit of strategic goals. It is not being suggested that the whole tradition can be subsumed under this mode of thought; the cultural articulation of morphological rules did reach a level that stands in marked contrast to the Western emphasis on teleology, but this could not be achieved without institutionalized compromises with a less overtly developed strategic reason (the imperial combination of Confucian and Legalist models of statecraft is the most obvious example).

The traditional ritual framework collapsed together with other parts of the old order. As Vandermeersch argues, it can nevertheless be shown that the mindset behind it – structured and transmitted by Confucianism – continued to affect the modernizing projects and mechanisms which have shaped the recent history of the region.[20] It goes without saying that the developmentalist turn marks a massive and irreversible shift towards strategic rationality. But even in this changed setting the search for new models could reveal underlying affinities with the discredited ritualism of the past. At its most constructive, the morphological legacy is reflected in diverse ways of ensuring the social embedding of a dynamic economy (this point links up with widely accepted views on the network-based character of East Asian capitalism), as well as in a specific image of the state and its role in the modernizing process. Within the traditional framework, the state-centred social order was part and parcel of a cosmic one; the cosmological frame of reference has disappeared, but the functionalist (and as Vandermeersch notes, anti-political) notion of the state survives and serves to legitimize the emphasis on bureaucratic administration rather than representative government.

This brief summary should suffice to indicate the general thrust of Vandermeersch's argument. As he sees it, the most archaic layer of the East Asian tradition is also the most authentic common denominator of the region. Spatial and temporal continuity are inseparable; the unity of East Asian civilization is predicated on its ability to retain an unbroken link to very early origins. But when it comes to clarifying the role of this legacy for East Asian modernity, Vandermeersch focuses on a recent and relatively brief phase: the post-war crystallization of the developmental state in Japan, together with the distinctive variants that took shape in former Japanese colonies and tentative moves in the same direction on the Chinese mainland. Although the interpretive model in question is – as noted above – incomplete, it seems clear that a regional convergence of the advanced stage of modernity after markedly diverse paths from the mid-nineteenth to the mid-twentieth century is – at least in part – to be understood as a reactivation of shared archaic sources. This perspective obscures the key role of Japanese inventions and initiatives in the modern transformation of the region. In more general terms: if we want a theoretical approach that would do justice to the undeniable originality of the Japanese historical experience, before and after the decisive opening to modernity, Vandermeersch's model has some conspicuous shortcomings. It appears to rule out any significant civilizational input from indigenous Japanese sources, as well as any autonomous historical dynamic that would set Japan apart from the rest of the region and enable it to act as a transformative force in a broader context.

For these reasons, it seems appropriate to turn to the second of the three abovementioned approaches.[21] The most obvious merit of Eisenstadt's work is that it makes a strong case for a civilizational analysis of the Japanese phenomenon; but agreement on this general point does not rule out objections concerning the ways to theorize the civilizational aspects as well as their relationship to history. Within the limits of this paper, however, I can only outline the main reasons for questioning Eisenstadt's interpretation of Japan and urging consideration of the third alternative mentioned above.

Eisenstadt's model resembles Vandermeersch's in that it highlights a combination of archaism and modernity rather than the more commonplace interpenetration of tradition and modernity. They differ as to the definition and demarcation of the archaic component; for Eisenstadt, it is Japanese, rather than Sinic or East Asian, but it can be subsumed under the general category of non-Axial civilizations. That term can only be understood in connection with its positive counterpart. Eisenstadt's theory of Axial transformations and civilizations marked by them is too complex to be summarized here; its core idea is that some particularly formative cultures (most importantly Ancient Greece, Ancient Israel, China and India) experienced an unprecedented rupture and problematization of order, and that their common response to this experience (although not uniform in detail) was the construction of new models which involved a previously unknown distinction between transcendental and mundane levels of order. A non-Axial civilization is, by definition, internally impervious to these radical changes but not necessarily altogether outside their orbit: if it has to coexist and interact with Axial civilizations, its situation is ipso facto different from the pre-Axial condition. This is doubly true for Japan, which borrowed first from China and then from the West without losing its non-Axial identity (for Eisenstadt, China is – in contrast to Vandermeersch's view – one of the paradigm cases of the break with archaic patterns, even if the Chinese version of it may have been less radical than some others). Paradoxically, it was this particularly resilient non-Axial civilization which proved more capable of autonomous modernization than any other non-Western society. For Eisenstadt, that combination is the most conclusive evidence of Japanese uniqueness.

If we try to spell out the implications of the non-Axial identity which Eisenstadt attributes to Japan, the main point is obviously an emphasis on continuity in more than one sense of the word. *Ontological continuity* is characteristic of traditional Japanese cosmology: it emphasises the 'mutual embeddedness of nature and culture', as well as 'a perception of reality as structured in multiple, continually shifting contexts between which it flows', and it leads to 'a certain sanctification of the phenomenal world.'[22] In all these respects, the prevalent way of interpreting the world and situating the social domain within it stands in marked contrast to the Axial pattern of separation and tension. We can also speak of *structural continuity* inasmuch as the dynamics of institutional formation and change operate within a unifying framework: the powers and principles central to various areas of social life were continuously 'embedded and incorporated within the broad framework of the Japanese collectivity and its central symbols', and 'there were no criteria or values beyond this framework in terms of which new centers or collectivities could be constructed and their boundaries defined'.[23] As for the *historical continuity* between a tradition built around an archaic core and a modernity marked by that legacy, it is crucial to Eisenstadt's whole argument, but he is well aware of the particular qualifications that must be added at this point. It would be absurd to claim that the whole ontological framework of the tradition was left untouched by the modern transformation. Only a partial and fragmentary survival was compatible with the new principles imposed by the modernizing process, and if there is a civilizational side to Japanese modernity, it can only be understood as a component limited, counterbalanced and sometimes contested by others, rather than an intact and comprehensive paradigm. But as Eisenstadt argues, the cultural premises challenged by modernity could be re-articulated and translated into modern projects of integration and legitimation. The key connection between civilizational legacy and modern development is the socio-cultural complex briefly discussed in the second section of the paper: a form of collective identity which gave a very specific twist to the dynamics of differentiation and integration. Eisenstadt and B. Giesen use the term 'principled primordiality'[24] to describe this pattern. It was, in other words, a particularism all the more radical because it emerged in explicit contradistinction to more universal claims (represented from the outset by the Chinese model). Modern Japanese nationalism drew on this legacy and developed it further. But the exceptionally prominent role of the nationalist imagination in modern Japan – reflected in notions of identity as well as in ideological constructs based on them – highlights another aspect of historical continuity. The persistence of a radical particularism (not necessarily in a militant form), capable of containing or relativizing the universalistic logic of modernity, makes the Japanese transformation of Western models fundamentally similar to early borrowings from Axial civilizations, exemplified by Confucianism and Buddhism. Eisenstadt describes the Japanese response to the latter as 'de-Axialization', i.e. a sustained de-activation of universal and transcendental aspects; and since he interprets the cultural program of modernity as an ongoing transformation of

Axial traditions, the same term can be applied to the Japanese version of modernity.

A systematic examination of Eisenstadt's thesis would have to start with his theory of Axial transformations, which cannot be tackled in this paper; the following remarks will merely raise a few questions about the Japanese experience and its possible implications for an alternative approach to the field which Eisenstadt subsumes under the Axial paradigm. As we shall see, that line of argument will lend some support to the third civilizational perspective mentioned above.

The first point to note is the autonomous and constructive character of the Japanese response to the Chinese model: it was much more than reception up to a point and rejection beyond that. The framework established in the seventh century – open to significant redefinitions at later stages, but fundamentally intact until the transition to advanced modernity enforced radical change – combined inventive imitation of Chinese patterns with indirect use of them to consolidate Japanese identity in contradistinction to China. The Chinese model, as institutionalized in Japan, was strictly separated from the symbolic acknowledgement of Chinese sovereignty which otherwise tended to accompany it; it was based on a selective recombination of different components of the Chinese tradition; and it could be readjusted in ways that responded more directly to changes inside Japan than to those on the Chinese side (that applies, in particular, to the strengthening of the Confucian current, even if it fell far short of the orthodoxy which scholars formerly attributed to early modern Japan). On the other hand, the self-demarcating distinctively Japanese tradition was from the outset so imbued with Chinese elements that no clear line can be drawn between indigenous sources and unacknowledged borrowings; but neither the role of native premises in the construction of China nor the use of alien inputs in the self-definition of Japan prevented the Japanese tradition from maintaining a distinction between the two poles; the line was, however, drawn in a way which allowed new combinations as well as overall shifts of emphasis, particularly towards a stronger affirmation of Japanese identity.

Similar considerations apply to Japan's interaction with Western modernity. Contrary to dismissive accounts of Meiji Japan – the most formative phase of a much larger modernizing process – as a wholesale adoption of a Western model (more specifically a German one), the picture that emerges from historical research suggests a selective and synthesizing approach and a systematic use of preexisting patterns to contextualize and redesign key components of modernity. The Japanese version of capitalism is a particularly striking case of institutional reinvention, and the same can be said about the Japanese-style developmental state: it is based on a strategic rearrangement of elements essential to modern statehood, so as to maximize the autonomy and rationality of a bureaucratic core. As noted above, it is the combination of these two institutional complexes, together with the nation-centred cultural and ideological framework, that reveal most clearly the distinctive character of Japanese modernity, and it is best understood as a specific pattern of differentiation and integration. It seems clear that the interpretation of Japan as a non-Axial civilization is more attuned to the integrative aspect of this constellation than to the differentiating dynamic. It is, in other words, easier to impute an archaic logic to Japanese conceptions of national identity (and their ideological applications) than to the strategies of readjusted differentiation. If the latter part of the picture is given priority, the evidence of persistent archaism need not be discounted, but it will have to be seen in relation to other elements of a complex configuration, rather than as a foundational cultural feature in its own right; from this point of view the civilizational background to Japanese modernity might seem too diverse and ambiguous to be located on one side of the divide between Axial and non-Axial traditions. But further exploration of that issue is beyond the scope of this paper.

The two phases discussed above – the appropriation and ongoing reconstruction of the Chinese model as well as the inventive alignment with Western modernity – are interconnected. Japan's peculiarly ambiguous relationship to China and its civilizational sphere (in which it participated on its own terms and in such a way that a separate identity could be strengthened at the same time) prefigured an equally original response to the global modernizing push pioneered by the West. This does not mean that strategies and attitudes developed with reference to China were simply transferred to a new external model when the impact of Western expansion destroyed the old order in East Asia. To describe the modern reorientation in such terms – as some analysts have done – is to ignore a particularly interesting transitional phase which coincided with Japan's lowest level of involvement in both regional and global affairs. During the Tokugawa epoch, Japanese ways of relating self-identity to other cultures underwent a threefold change. Renewed efforts to appropriate the Chinese legacy, with an unprecedently strong focus on its Confucian core, went together with a policy of thoroughgoing disengagement from the Chinese world order; the enhanced sense of Japanese autonomy and centrality, inherent in the Tokugawa strategy, paved the way for a new affirmation and ideologization of collective identity (most importantly those of the *kokugaku* school) which went far beyond official policies and created a cultural reserve for future political use; at the same time, interest in the West and its achievements survived the setback to practical contact and led to growing knowledge of this potentially significant other. The overall result was a shift towards a more assertive particularism, accompanied by more flexible strategies of borrowing.

To conclude this discussion, and to underline the case for a civilizational approach, we should briefly consider the specific interplay of culture and power involved in Japan's relationship to the Chinese model and crucial to the more enduring patterns that grew out of the original encounter. The first point to note is that although the prestige of the Chinese model was in no small degree due to its association with an exceptionally durable centre of imperial power, the Japanese strategy of appropriation was from the very beginning – and more thoroughly than in any comparable case – based on a complete separation of cultural paradigm from political authority: apart from an isolated and inconclusive move on the part of the early Muromachi shogunate, Japan never accepted inclusion in the Chinese sphere of symbolic sovereignty. The systematic transfer of cultural patterns without any corresponding integration of power structures opened up a whole set of new possibilities for self-contained political development. At the outset (i.e. in the course of the seventh-century transformation), the cultural models and symbols borrowed from China served to strengthen an emerging centre and enhance its integrative capacity far beyond what indigenous power resources would have allowed. In the long run, however, the impact was more ambiguous. On the one hand, the strong cultural connotations of the new centre – the imperial institution – made it easier to disconnect its authority from effective power, and thus to consolidate an institutional pattern which has often been singled out as one of the most enduring characteristics of Japanese history. On the other hand, uncontested cultural primacy could – in more exceptional circumstances – be seen as a rationale for more direct rule. Such efforts were briefly successful during a crucial phase of the seventh-century transformation; an even more ambitious but also more extravagant fourteenth-century attempt (the Kenmu restoration, 1333–1336) was the last of its kind and led to a definitive marginalization of the imperial institution. But as recent historical research has shown, this does not mean that it was nothing more than a last act of resistance to the logic of history. Rather, this exceptionally radical bid to reunite authority and power was based on new lessons from the Chinese experience as well as on new solutions to the problems of Japanese society, and its failure should not obscure the fact that it had lasting effects on the whole context of state-building. The transfer of power from the imperial court to a military elite was irreversible, but it took the latter a long time to develop the institutions and techniques needed to maintain a power structure commensurate with the failed project of the imperial state. A stable version of the military counter-state did not take shape until the Tokugawa house completed the unification of Japan; after 1600, this resulted in the most systematic separation of imperial symbolism authority from the core structures of state power. That was, however, not the end of the story. By excluding the imperial institution from access to power, retaining it as part of a legitimizing framework, and avoiding a binding official definition of its role (the Tokugawa pattern of legitimation was based on a combinatory strategy rather than an orthodoxy), the new regime kept open a cultural space for re-interpretations of imperial symbolism. Visions of return to direct imperial rule within the traditional framework were no longer sustainable (the idea of 'restorationism' as a distinctive ideology developing during the Tokugawa period seems to have been demolished), but new interpretive constructs could – in due course – prove adaptable to innovative strategies when the whole Tokugawa order was thrown into crisis by forces beyond its control. The historically remote but genuine projects of direct rule could serve to sustain a new myth of direct rule which played a key role in Japan's externally induced but autonomously managed transition to advanced modernity.

These considerations should suffice to show that our third civilizational perspective can be linked to a pluralistic analysis of Japanese modernity. But I am not suggesting that it can – in the present phase of the discussion – provide a self-contained account of the issues arising in this context. An ongoing debate with the other approaches would seem the most promising line to take.

8 Miracles and Mirages: Comparative Perspectives on Japanese Capitalism

Old problems and new approaches

Historical circumstances have not favoured a comparative approach to the Japanese version of capitalism. During the imperial phase of Japanese modernization, cultural and political peculiarities of the emerging Far Eastern power were much more visible to Western observers than any noteworthy aspects of economic development. On the Japanese side, the dominant particularistic ideology was – in its specific and often elusive ways – also focused on cultural and political visions of self-strengthening. Developmentalist themes were important, but exceptionally closely linked to nationalist projects. As for the main counter-ideology which gained ground after World War I, Japanese Marxists were particularly interested in the theory of capitalist development and engaged in controversies about the specific problems of Japanese capitalism, but the very conceptual core of the Marxist tradition set limits to the theorizing of varieties or divergent paths. The Marxian frame of reference defined capitalism as a highly dynamic and self-contained economic structure, capable of imposing its logic across national, regional and civilizational borders; the Leninist way of bringing diversity back in led only to superficial adjustments, subordinated to tactical concerns and overshadowed by simplifying misconstructions of basic premises. On the other hand, some of the most original and least party-controlled contributions of Japanese Marxism – such as the work of the Uno school – were primarily aimed at distilling a systematic and uncompromisingly universal theory from Marx's unfinished analysis of capital.

After World War II, a capitalist developmental project became a much more central and visible part of the Japanese power structure than before. The undeniable and – to most observers – surprising success of the high-growth strategy provoked debate and inspired some seminal research on the historical and institutional background; results of this work remain central to ongoing discussions and will be important for the argument to be developed below. But the most widespread reactions to the emergence of Japan as an economic giant – with obvious implications of possible return to a more active stance in the political and military arenas – did nothing to encourage comparative inquiry. Explanations in terms of specific Japanese habits, mindsets or traditions – popular at home and abroad – short-circuited the complex relationships between cultural institutions and organizational aspects; the Japanese miracle was more easily perceived as a unique and total phenomenon than as a variant of more general patterns. Those who wanted to translate the miracle into a model (or feared that such a model might serve to impose Japanese hegemony) were more interested in global alternatives than in contextual variety. The two responses were not mutually exclusive: pioneering standards of modernity could be traced back to particular virtues or resources of the Japanese tradition.[1]

More recently, the time of troubles that began with the bubble economy of the late 1980s has changed both foreign and domestic perceptions of the Japanese economy. Earlier predictions of an unstoppable rise to global power now seem to belong to a bygone world.[2] The backlash – sometimes spearheaded by former eulogists of the miracle – has helped to resurrect another past: the tradition of liberal uniformitarianism, defended in more or less sophisticated terms by early modernization theory but incompatible with the later turn to a pluralistic view of path-dependent modern transformations. During the high-growth phase and its early aftermath, the Japanese economic achievement was one of the more obvious themes for reflection on non-European patterns of modernity; the setbacks of the 1990s are commonly seen as evidence of a return to the global normalcy of a liberal economic order. Critics of the Washington consensus have pointed out that popular notions of the Japanese crisis are – in the context of comparative perspectives on the last decade – vastly exaggerated, and that it is far too early for firm conclusions as to the capacity of the Japanese economy to cope with new global conjunctures in its own way. But the spectre of a total crisis, or even of the 'end of an economy',[3] is part and parcel of a broader trend towards de-legitimizing Japanese patterns of modernity and embracing a liberal overhaul as the only way forward. Attempts to portray the postwar economic regime as the last remnant of an oppressive militarist system draw their inspiration from this current, and they can link up with older arguments on behalf of liberal alternatives in waiting. Interesting but controversial episodes of liberalization, especially those of the Taishō era (1913–26), lend themselves to integration into a narrative of thwarted projects to be reactivated in a more benign environment.

On the other hand, recent developments in theoretical debates on capitalism have opened up perspectives with far-reaching implications for our understanding of the Japanese experience. Although the resurgence of Anglo-American models (and streamlined images of them) during the 1990s gave a new lease of life to notions of a universal capitalist paradigm of economic rationality, more reflective responses to the changing constellation focused on the varieties of capitalism and the need to analyze the global context in the light of interactions between them. The first typological analyses in this vein tended to stress basic contrasts between supposedly rival models of capitalism (often on the assumption that the question of their relative merits would be central to world politics after the demise of Communism), but the discussion has now become more sensitive to a broader spectrum of variations.[4] In the course of this historical and comparative turn, different views of the problematic and ways of dealing with it have emerged; there is, to the best of my knowledge, no systematic survey of the interpretive strategies applied to the question of varying capitalisms. The approaches to the field range from distinctions between historical forms of capitalism, premodern as well as modern (most easily developed on the basis of Max Weber's tentative definitions) to comparative analyses of local, national or regional responses to the dynamic of global transformations, and they include analyses of cultural backgrounds to capitalist development as well as of institutional frameworks and strategic choices made by key actors. National or state-contained varieties are not the only relevant cases: 'reinventions' of capitalism may take place in other settings, such as diasporic communities or cross-national networks of different kinds. But the enduring importance of nation-states lends particular weight to variations on that scale, and in that context, there can be no doubt about the exceptional significance of the Japanese case. Its record is striking enough to ensure that it remains one of the obligatory points of reference for the discussion, but it can nevertheless be argued that the fin-de-siècle setback made it seem less crucial than a long-term perspective will reveal it to be. The following analysis will suggest some ways of restoring it to a more central place.

There is another and even more recent line of theorizing about capitalism, so far developed without any sustained connections to comparative studies; it has not been linked to the Japanese experience, but as I will try to show, the potential points of contact are of major importance. The ideas in question are set out in Luc Boltanski and Eve Chiapello's work on the 'new spirit of capitalism', which also contains extensive concrete analyses of French developments during the last three decades.[5] Here I will only summarize the main theoretical points. The distinctive thrust of the argument has to do with three factors whose interplay is seen as the formative core of capitalist development: the structures, the spirit and the critique of capitalism. Boltanski and Chiapello base their account of this complex dynamic on what they call a 'minimalist' definition of capitalism – in the sense that it highlights the common denominator of otherwise variable forms and successive stages. Capitalism is, on this view, an economic regime centred on accumulation, i.e. on profit and its reinvestment on an expanding scale. This systemic principle can take various institutional and organizational forms, and modify them in response to changing conditions (the strong emphasis on the primacy of accumulation is reminiscent of Wallerstein's claims to the same effect, but the broader connotations differ; Boltanski and Chiapello are not arguing that all modern economies are uniformly locked into a capitalist world system). The other side of structural flexibility is a heightened need for cultural and psychological support: since the economic goal is not geared to concrete human needs, it calls for other ways to motivate and mobilize economic actors. The 'spirit of capitalism' is, in other words, a permanently necessary complement to the system, rather than (as Max Weber argued) a transitional factor that becomes redundant when structural maturity is achieved. This line of argument also differs from the Weberian one in that it makes a clearer distinction between cultural and psychological aspects. On the one hand, the imperative of accumulation can appeal to desires which seek infinite fulfilment – be it a matter of power, wealth or an endless quest for innovation (here the affinity with Durkheim's analysis of modern civilizational problems is obvious). But for Boltanski and Chiapello, as well as for our present purposes, the cultural side and its public expressions are more important. From that point of view, the spirit of capitalism must provide rationalizing visions and grounds for justification; its mobilizing role has to do with different social strata, but most directly with the executive cadres who implement the logic of the system.

The cultural – and more or less discursive – articulation of the spirit of capitalism can be condensed into historical paradigms. Boltanski and Chiapello distinguish two such models and claim that a third one has been in the making during the last three decades of the twentieth century. The 'first spirit of capitalism', supposedly central to nineteenth-century dynamics of industrialization and still active in early twentieth-century economies, is described in terms more reminiscent of Sombart than Weber. Its main embodiment is the heroic entrepreneur, understood as a fusion of calculating rationality with adventurous innovation. The German image of the *Gründer* is clearly visible; but references to the patriarchal and more conventionally bourgeois features of the 'first spirit' are more suggestive of French models. At this point, the question of national variations to the spirit of capitalism is implicitly raised, although Boltanski and Chiapello make no attempt to deal with it. Links to and inputs from nationalism would be the next theme to discuss; as will be seen, the Japanese experience is eminently relevant to both issues. As for the 'second spirit of capitalism', the language used to define it is more explicitly universal. The key figure is the manager of a large corporate organization, and the corresponding paradigm of economic culture is based on a bureaucratic and hierarchical model of rationality. This pattern evolved out of structural changes that began in the late nineteenth century, but it took final shape in the course of restructuring processes after the crisis of the early 1930s and reached its apogee after World War II. Here the implicit questions – also pertinent to the Japanese case – concern the interconnections between this bureaucratic redefinition of capitalism and the simultaneous changes to structures and functions of the state. Finally, the emerging 'third spirit' is – according to Boltanski and Chiapello – characterized by an adversarial relationship to the second. The emphasis is now on autonomy, flexibility and rapid adaptability as the main virtues of economic actors, and polycentric networks, rather than rigid bureaucratic structures, constitute the appropriate mode of organization. The new spirit has led to far-reaching structural changes, but it also finds expression in visions of mobilization and participation which go far beyond practical contexts. In other words, it has an imaginary dimension which draws on intellectual currents of the preceding decades. Boltanski and Chiapello speak of a 'connectivist' imaginary, underpinned by the widespread turn to relational approaches in contemporary thought. The fact that an inbuilt relational mode of thought has often been ascribed to the Japanese tradition (or to East Asian cultures in general) suggests connections worth exploring.

For Boltanski and Chiapello, the transformations of the spirit of capitalism cannot be understood without reference to its interaction with the third factor: the critique of capitalism. Critical responses have accompanied capitalist development from the outset; they draw on a whole range of reasons for discontent and take different directions. Two types of critique stand out as most influential – at least in the European context – and most capable of synthesizing the themes of protest. An 'artistic' critique – perhaps better described as aesthetic – condemns capitalism as a source of inauthenticity and disenchantment (caused by the subsumption of all values and experiences under the rule of the market), but also because of the restrictions which an increasingly powerful economic machine places on human liberty, spontaneity and creativity. A social critique, more congenial to the movements that have challenged capitalism on the political level, focuses on the inequality and poverty produced by the capitalist way of pursuing wealth (the critique of capitalism as a wasteful and anarchic economic order should perhaps be added to the list). As Boltanski and Chiapello argue, the two main transformations summarized above responded to critical challenges by appropriating substantial parts of the anti-capitalist imaginary. The 'second spirit' – the ethos of managerial capitalism – made far-reaching concessions to the social critique, both on the level of industrial relations and within the institutional framework of the welfare state. This historical experience, known in neo-Marxist parlance as the 'Fordist compromise', is not unfamiliar to analysts of twentieth-century capitalism. But Boltanski and Chiapello go on to propose a more controversial interpretation of the 'third spirit'. They see the radical movements of the 1960s – and especially the explosion in 1968 – as an epoch-making resurgence of the artistic critique; this was less obvious to contemporary observers because of the extensive use of ideological models and languages from the tradition of social critique, but the later development of a 'new individualism' has made this view more plausible. The changing balance between the two types of critique opened up new possibilities for defence on the part of the capitalist order; the new spirit represents a far-reaching and effective appropriation of the aesthetic critique, with results that have set new limits to the operative force of the social one. Here the two authors are clearly thinking of a more thoroughgoing internalization of the critique than in the case of the 'second spirit'. As they show, with particular reference to French developments after 1970, the changing structures and self-images of the capitalist enterprise reflect a sustained effort to learn from the adversaries in order to defeat them on their own ground.

The pluralistic conception of critique opens up promising lines of inquiry. To borrow a term from another universe of discourse, capitalism is an essentially contested economic regime; the countercurrents spring from multiple sources, enter into varying combinations and give rise to separate traditions; visions of a world beyond capitalism grow out of critical interpretations of the capitalist experience, but are neither inherent in the very idea of critique nor necessarily compatible with each other. The argument outlined by Boltanski and Chiapello could be developed along these lines. But for present purposes, it is the general idea of an interplay between capitalist development, anti-capitalist critique and adaptive changes to capitalist institutions, that should be noted and tested on the Japanese case. On the other hand, a closer analysis of Japanese variations to the common pattern will help to refocus attention on path-dependent diversity. Boltanski and Chiapello construct their historical narrative without any significant link to the unfolding debate on varieties of capitalism, and there is no readily available theoretical model that would allow us to combine their insights with comparative perspectives. But as I will try to show, Fernand Braudel's genealogy of capitalism may provide at least some tentative guidelines for that purpose. As a historian, Braudel was disinclined to pursue theoretical reflection beyond a strictly auxiliary level, and he dealt mainly with premodern and early modern forms of capitalism; but despite these limitations, his approach seems particularly conducive to a broad overview of our problematic.

As Braudel observes in passing, no misconception of capitalism is more serious than the notion of a self-contained economic system.[6] The emphasis is, in other words, on the permanent embeddedness of capitalist institutions in social, political and cultural contexts. But he was well aware of the other side of the capitalist dynamic (even if he did not discuss it in detail): the inbuilt and continually reproduced illusion of an economy governed by immanent laws. From that point of view, the theoretical construct of a self-regulated economic system is the culminating outcome of a historical shift which enhances the autonomy of economic institutions as well as the economic imaginary. Here it seems useful to link Braudel's line of argument to ideas put forward by Cornelius Castoriadis.[7] Capitalism is, as Castoriadis sees it, the first social regime to produce an ideological model of its own rationality; the basic principles of rational conduct and organization are equated with the supposedly constitutive rules of the economic sphere, and this conflation then becomes a rationale for the transfer of cognitive ideals from the natural sciences to the domain of social inquiry. The formation and development of this economic ideology represent another side to the spirit of capitalism.[8]

Further discussion of Braudel's more specific claims must begin with his distinction between three levels of economic life: material life, market economy and capitalism. The first level is the domain of production and consumption without insertion into networks of exchange. In all premodern and early modern economies, it constitutes an essential and enduring infrastructure of social life. The second is more or less synonymous with the sphere of exchange or circulation, seen as a complex of mechanisms and institutions which extend from elementary forms of trade to the specialized instruments of monetary economies. But Braudel insists on the specific features of a third level, which he identifies with capitalism and distinguishes from the more general category of the market economy. This 'superstructure', as he also describes it, crystallizes around the networks of long distance trade, centres on the quest for super-profits, and is mostly dominated by monopolies in close symbiosis with state power. In this sense, capitalism is – according to Braudel – a potential aspect of civilization in general, but different civilizations vary in regard to their capacity to realize it, as well as in the degree of capitalist diversification into other areas of economic activity.

Braudel's reasons for separating the capitalist superstructure from the more broadly based market economy should be summarized before moving on to specifics. First and foremost, the capitalist sector is the prime outlet for strategies and dynamics of accumulation: the pursuit of profit is at its most intense when it crosses socio-cultural boundaries and leads to the formation of 'economic worlds'[9] held together by trading networks. The enhanced commitment to accumulation presupposes a 'spirit of capitalism' in a more elementary sense than the cultural codes or mentalities associated with industrial capitalism. Although Braudel is markedly reluctant to enter into this debate at any length, we can reconstruct a line of argument which distinguishes the immanent cultural orientations of a capitalist economic sphere from the secondary constructs added to or imposed on it in particular historical contexts. For example, Braudel analyzes the preconditions for the capitalist breakthrough in Europe and stresses the importance of social power structures as well as mobilizable cultural traditions: in the medieval and early modern phases of European history, the social forces which embodied a capitalist ethos were still overshadowed by traditional elites, but they could act more autonomously in a more pluralistic social field than elsewhere, and their opposition to entrenched privilege enabled them to invoke 'moderation, wisdom and work'[10] as legitimizing values.

The primary and immanent spirit of capitalism, oriented towards accumulation but not *ipso facto* geared to industrial transformation, is best understood as an imaginary signification in the sense defined by Castoriadis.[11] But it is not identical with the vision of an 'infinite extension of rational mastery' which Castoriadis attributes to industrial capitalism. Rather, the economic imaginary focuses on visions of wealth to be gained by overcoming cultural and geographical barriers. This underlying orientation can – but need not – translate into rationalizing processes; Max Weber's contrasting categories of speculative and rational capitalism are applicable to different versions of the economic pattern that Braudel has in mind. The more rational type can draw strength from genealogical or institutional continuity. For Braudel, the quasi-dynastic character of families in control of major commercial centres or connections is an important part of the story. But when it comes to the European case, he sees the early modern overseas trading companies as key factors in the transformation which culminated in a unique breakthrough to industrial capitalism. More recent research on economic history seems to bear him out on this point.[12] The European trajectory also exemplifies a further connection which Braudel notes in no uncertain terms but does not explore as thoroughly as it merits: the trading monopolies were not only closely associated with the build-up of states in the forefront of European expansion, but also to some extent involved in state-building activities in their own overseas domains. This aspect of pre-industrial capitalist development is, in other words, linked to long-term and complex processes of state formation and variously affected by their dynamics. A more systematic discussion of such interconnections – going beyond Braudel's analyses – would have to consider the interaction of state structures and state-building strategies with the other levels of economic life. Impulses to the development of commercial networks, ways of containing their dynamic and efforts to benefit from their growth are integral to processes of state formation and relevant to the question of their impact on capitalist development. At the most elementary level (Braudel's 'material life'), the relationship to state formation is less obvious; it can, however, be argued that the extraction of resources for state-building purposes allows for more or less explicit and effective projections of the criteria pertinent to material life into the political arena. This is the perspective summed up in Max Weber's concept of the *oikos*: the economic domain seen as an enlarged household, i.e. as a framework of material reproduction. State-centred and society-wide versions of the *oikos* model have appeared in various guises at different historical junctures, and in modern as well as premodern contexts; apart from the command economies of self-styled socialist regimes, economic nationalism draws on this source.

The above summary of Braudel's views can now serve to outline a problematic for comparative study. The historical analysis of capitalist formations, their common characteristics and their divergent destinies shows that multiple lines of differentiation must be taken into account. A survey of the 'varieties of capitalism' can begin with the diverse forms and degrees of mercantile capitalist inputs into the sphere of production. Relationships between capitalist sectors and the rest of economic life differ from case to case, not least because of varying patterns of interaction with state structures and their inbuilt dynamics. But the distinctive effects of cultural traditions also contribute to the differentiating process;

Braudel's approach underlines the composite character of the spirit of capitalism in all its versions, and more particularly the interaction between elementary and superstructural layers. Both cultural and political conditions of – and obstacles to – capitalist development must be analyzed in the broader context of different civilizational complexes; the enduring but sometimes innovative impact of civilizations on economic history is one of Braudel's main themes. One reason why this factor has often been underestimated by analysts of modern economies is the more visible presence of another diversifying force. Nation-states and their internal social configurations have been central to the debate on varieties of capitalism. This last topic takes us beyond Braudel's field of inquiry and back to the issues raised at the beginning of the chapter; but Braudel's references to the gradual divergence of European paths to higher growth point the same way.

The Japanese transition: From containment to development

Braudel's work makes a twofold contribution to the historical sociology of capitalism: it redefines a general category, and it throws new light on the pattern of differentiation within that framework. In both regards, it represents a major step beyond the Weberian frame of reference. Braudel's general concept of capitalism is more specific and open to historical variation than the Weberian one; his concrete analyses of capitalist dynamics in premodern and early modern settings correct Weber's overdrawn contrast between traditional and modern capitalism. In view of these path-breaking insights, it seems appropriate to begin the discussion of the Japanese case with Braudel's own reflections on the subject.

For obvious reasons, Japan does not figure as prominently as other major non-European civilizations – China, India and the Islamic world – in the survey of global economic history in the early modern era: it was, although far from completely isolated, much less directly integrated into international trading networks. It was, as Braudel puts it, a very special case. But when it comes to the question of modern capitalist development, in the sense of a generalized dynamic transforming both the material basis and the social framework of economic life, Japan appears in a different light. The capitalist transition was successful in Europe, began to take shape (Braudel's term is 's'esquisse') in Japan, but failed to materialize in the other relevant cases.[13] Braudel thus goes beyond the familiar view that Japan proved uniquely capable of adopting and adapting modern capitalist forms of economic life when they were brought to global presence by the expanding West; he suggests that the turn was adumbrated within Japan before the nineteenth-century opening to the West. His defence of this claim leaves much to be desired, but may provide some useful pointers to the problem at issue.

Braudel's argument begins with an extensive reference to Norman Jacobs's work on capitalism in East Asia. Jacobs developed his ideas at a time when the Japanese case seemed more atypical in the context of the East Asian region than most analysts came to think after the take-off to high growth in neighbouring countries, and his account of Japanese exceptionalism must be read with that background in mind, but it represents a significant chapter in the history of Western attempts to make sense of the Japanese experience; the main points are therefore worth recapitulating. Jacobs saw the divergent paths of China and Japan – and their respective ways of responding to the capitalist challenge – as a conclusive example of the primacy of social structures, rather than cultural patterns. Obvious cultural affinities between the two countries had obscured basic differences on the institutional level. Jacobs used the distinction between patrimonialism and feudalism to pinpoint the crucial contrasts. By redefining patrimonialism in a way which broadened the conventional Weberian meaning and drew on Marxian conceptions of Asiatic societies, he found a formula for the supposedly invariant core structure of Chinese society (as well as of other societies on the Asian mainland): 'a symbiosis between a small group of center-controlled officials and the populace, who lives autonomously in communities, left to their own devices so long as they meet their tax and corvée obligations and do not overtly rise up against the center. The link between the two orbits is provided by local notables.'[14] This patrimonial order is flexible enough to accommodate a more or less sustained growth of commercial capitalism and it can – under pressure from a changing global environment – adapt its inherited structures effectively enough to embark on the path of modernization, but not development. For Jacobs, this distinction is fundamental: modernization is the 'introduction of novel means in order to improve a society's performance, but with the aim that those changes not challenge, and in fact reinforce, certain cherished goals and organizational procedures', whereas development is 'the maximization of the potential of a society, regardless of the society's existing goals and organizational procedures'.[15]

Development in general and capitalist development in particular is more compatible with the legacy of feudal societies, whose superior dynamism is based on the 'constant and effective competition which was the rule in Japan and Europe', and on 'generalized values concerning rights and privileges'[16] which proved congenial to capitalist enterprise. The two societal types are thus linked to long-term trajectories of social change, even if concrete cases often contain an admixture of both (Jacobs saw the Tokugawa regime as an attempt to impose a patrimonial superstructure on Japanese feudalism).

Braudel accepts much of Jacobs's analysis, but lays a stronger emphasis on commercial growth in China (he does not speak of commercial capitalism in general). In that context, the Japanese advantage over China – with regard to capitalism in Braudel's specific sense, not the market economy as such – seems paradoxical. On the one hand, the Tokugawa regime limited contacts with the external world, imposed strict controls on foreign trade and barred Japanese merchants from active involvement. There was thus no scope for a European-style fusion of imperial and capitalist expansion. On the other hand, Braudel argues that limited but not insignificant compensations for this blockage were built into the social and political structure of Tokugawa Japan. His explanation for this unusual constellation stresses both geographical and historical factors. On the geographical level, the Japanese archipelago could – if other conditions were fulfilled – facilitate the formation of commercial networks which in certain respects resembled those of long-distance trade elsewhere (Braudel refers to the Inland Sea as a Japanese Mediterranean). As for the historical context, its long-term dynamic is oversimplified: the fifteenth and sixteenth-century phase of fragmentation appears as a natural outcome of trends comparable to those of medieval Europe (and there is no mention of the long-drawn-out decomposition of the *ritsuryō* state), but for our purposes, Braudel's description of the constellation taking shape after 1600 is more important. His uncertain grasp of details (he refers to the founder of the Tokugawa shogunate as Iedoshyi!) should not distract attention from the genuine and relevant questions posed by his interpretation of the overall picture.

As Braudel sees it, the most crucial aspect of the Tokugawa settlement was the formation of two mega-cities, vastly more important than any other urban centres. Osaka was to production what Edo was to consumption; he also refers to the former as the silver and the latter as the gold pole of the Japanese economy. The social and economic impact of this dual urban core was to some extent comparable to the role of 'capitalist cities' – such as Venice, Antwerpen, Amsterdam or London – in creating and maintaining international trading networks. On the more local Japanese scale, the merchants based in Osaka gained control of the economic surplus; they developed complex financial techniques and institutions and merchant capital stimulated the development of manufacture from within a traditional economy of handicrafts. 'Everything thus converges towards a primary capitalism which is not grounded in imitation of foreign models nor in any religious framework'.[17] Braudel also refers to the metropolitan culture of Tokugawa Japan as a 'veritable bourgeois civilization'[18] and argues that it resembled the European pattern more than any other non-European region in the early modern world. The prior experience of a capitalist 'world within walls' (to borrow the term which Donald Keene used to describe Edo culture) must have been of major importance to the later development of industrial capitalism in a more outward-looking Japan. The specifics of that connection are beyond the scope of Braudel's work. His analysis may nevertheless be a useful guide to issues which have been debated at great length, but too often in isolation from more general questions. As we have seen, the argument centres on two main claims. A capitalist layer of the market economy which developed within the Tokugawa order is seen as a local analogy to processes unfolding in the global context of European expansion, and the reference to a 'bourgeois civilization' suggests – in a less explicit way – that a lasting cultural legacy counted for something in the rapid reorientation of economic life after the opening of the country. There is, in other words, a prima facie case for linking the spirit of Japanese capitalism to Tokugawa beginnings.

Before going on to discuss the question of the Tokugawa backdrops to Meiji and post-Meiji Japan, we should briefly note the demise of one particularly ambitious and influential answer. The idea of an incomplete and anomalous 'bourgeois revolution', accomplished by a merchant class in alliance with the more adaptable part of a feudal elite, is no longer a matter of serious debate. Analyses of the Meiji Restoration, its background and its aftermath have shown beyond any doubt that this model is fundamentally misguided. It might be objected that new perspectives on the modern Japanese transformation are less important than the 'revisionist' historiography which has challenged Marxist theories of revolution in their original Western context. But there is a crucial difference between Western and Japanese patterns of radical change. The ongoing reinterpretation of European revolutions still leaves room for strong claims as to the role of 'bourgeois' social forces, defined in a broad sense and without the Marxian presupposition of an invariant link to the capitalist mode of production. There is much less to be said for such views on the Japanese experience. Here the main revolutionary episode, seen by key participants and authorized interpreters as a restoration, was more directly and completely shaped by the dynamics of state formation than any comparable European case. The momentous turn taken in 1868 was a response to new problems posed by interstate competition in a global arena; it resulted in a rapid and comprehensive remodeling of state structures; and its transformative force was due to a complex combination of regional, social and ideological conflicts within the samurai stratum which had been the main social basis of the Tokugawa state. The transition was, in other words, centred on the political forms of social power, but innovations in this domain changed the conditions and orientation of economic life. The state-contained proto-capitalism of the Tokugawa period gave way to a systematic coordination of state-building and capitalist growth.

This basic discontinuity of economic development does not exclude significant links between the two phases in question. Tokugawa antecedents and contributions to the modern transformation must be reconstructed across a political divide, but this is not to say that the *longue durée* loses all relevance. A new order could still build on older foundations and draw on inherited sources. More precisely and with particular reference to the historical and comparative analysis of Japanese capitalism, there are two questions to consider, corresponding to the two abovementioned themes of Braudel's work: the structures and dynamics of economic life under the Tokugawa order, and the cultural developments that may have helped to prepare the ground for later economic growth in a less restrictive environment. The first issue should now be discussed in connection with major recent reassessments of comparative economic history; Japan has so far not been central to this debate, but some implications are obvious. Although it would be premature to speak of a new consensus, a few key points of agreement stand out against the background of a changing global picture.[19]

Most importantly, more stress is now laid on the discontinuity between industrial and pre-industrial growth. The concept of 'Smithian growth', often applied to the pre-industrial phase, reflects a clearer grasp of the historical distance between the models of classical political economy and the world of industrial capitalism (this point was systematically obscured by classical theories designed to minimize the most revolutionary aspects of modern capitalism, and the same trend accounts for underlying affinities between Marxist and neo-classical views). Doubts have also been cast on the idea of 'proto-industrialization', previously introduced to emphasize the long-term pre-history of the late eighteenth-century breakthrough; as one historian puts it, 'a lot of proto-industry was a dead end and not "proto" at all'.[20] Rationalizing innovations did occur, but they are – on this view – best understood as results of a Smithian dynamic, and growth of that kind took place in the more advanced regions of various premodern civilizations. The Chinese experience of intensive agriculture and commercial development is an obvious and much-discussed case in point. Against the background of such parallels, the Western European (and more specifically British) transition to industrial capitalism seems all the more unique. Some analysts are therefore inclined to stress the role of contingent factors at critical junctures; for example, Kenneth Pomeranz singles out the availability and convenient location of coal in Britain. But he also has much to say about advantages derived from overseas expansion, especially the creation of a new periphery across the Atlantic. In that context the question of plantation slavery and its contribution to the 'rise of the West' is crucial. At the same time, the reference to colonies and overseas trade suggests a connection with Braudel's analysis. If the discontinuity between industrial and pre-industrial economies has been reaffirmed, it remains to be seen whether this historical divide can be linked to the discontinuity which Braudel posits within the pre-industrial world: the difference between a dynamic but not *ipso facto* radically innovative market economy and a more expansive but still relatively marginal capitalist superstructure. Pomeranz explicitly acknowledges a debt to Braudel when he underlines the role of state-supported overseas trading companies in paving the way for the 'great transformation' in Western Europe.

If the issues and alternatives of this unfinished debate are to be related to the Japanese case, it seems appropriate to begin with salient contrasts between Japan and China. It seems clear that pre-industrial growth continued well into the late imperial phase of Chinese economic history (R. Bin Wong refers to Smithian dynamics across much of China between the sixteenth and the nineteenth centuries).[21] But a long-established and widely shared view of Japanese economic history suggests that an early Tokugawa period of growth, coming to an end around 1700, was succeeded by a much less dynamic phase; and although traditional interpretations of this watershed between progress and stasis have – as we shall see – come under telling criticism, a fundamental change to underlying conditions and visible results is undeniable. If we are to speak of economic miracles, the early Tokugawa transformation of the Japanese economy would seem to merit this label at least as well as any other episode. At the beginning of the eighteenth century, Japan had 'a countrywide economy, well-developed transportation and communication webs, a large and complex urban society and an elaborate entrepreneurial system of commerce'.[22] The achievements – accompanied by rapid population growth – were exceptional by any standards, and there is no comparable case of internal mutation in conjunction with an all-round minimization and surveillance of contacts with the outside world. Braudel's description of Tokugawa Japan, quoted above, seems in line with the early phase even if it is short on details (among other things, Kyoto should have been included among the major urban centres), and his general concept of capitalism is clearly applicable. But then his argument is, by the same token, less illuminating when it comes to the eighteenth-century part of the story.

As I will try to show, the developmental landmarks that have been seen as miracles (or bear comparison with such cases) are inseparable from imaginary projections of broader meanings and frameworks. These accompanying constructs might also be described as operative myths or mirages. In the case of Tokugawa Japan, the wealth and power accumulated after 1600 were associated with a vision of Japan as a separate world, abstention from conquest and a far-reaching withdrawal from interstate relations. This self-contained Tokugawa order drew strength and legitimacy from the century of sustained growth; but the very achievements that had helped to consolidate the regime militated against any basic reorientation. The policy of closure was perpetuated as an unquestioned frame of reference during the later part of the Tokugawa period. Eighteenth-century reforms imposed further limits on foreign trade, and efforts to acquire more knowledge of foreign countries were – from the viewpoint of the rulers – aimed at a more complete self-sufficiency, rather than any preparation for closer contacts; new policies implemented – with mixed results – by the central authorities never affected the essentials of Tokugawa geopolitics.

The most clear-cut and influential explanation of the contrast between seventeenth and eighteenth-century trends was based on Marxist assumptions. From this point of view, the insoluble problems emerging during the latter phase of Tokugawa rule were due to a maturing crisis of the feudal economic system. A self-perpetuating class structure had become an obstacle to development. Geopolitical isolationism was an integral part of the grand strategy of a ruling class, but its effects were double-edged: although it helped to maintain a high level of social control, it was – in the long run – bound to aggravate the systemic crisis. Fundamentally similar versions of this model spread far beyond Marxist circles, but in the course of the last two or three decades, its premises have been contested in various ways. As a result, a new picture of the period in question is taking shape, and the ongoing reassessment of Tokugawa Japan has been extended to new fields of inquiry; here I can only touch upon a few points of particular relevance to the present topic. A massive counter-attack on Marxist or crypto-Marxist orthodoxy was launched by Susan B.Hanley and Kozo Yamamura, but their over-simplification of Marxist positions seems to have tempted them to propose an equally streamlined alternative.[23] Their interpretive framework (based on empirical studies and presented as a comprehensive hypothesis to be tested through further research) links continued economic growth and rising living standards in the later Tokugawa period to the all-round energizing effects of expanding commerce. The programmatic antithesis to mainstream Marxism is obvious: the growth of trade is envisaged as a cumulative process with transformative consequences for the economy as a whole, beneficial to all social groups drawn into its orbit, and ultimately conducive to a modernizing take-off. On this view, the interaction between urban centres and rural periphery took a mutually upgrading turn, and on the rural side, a more enterprising and economically rational peasantry moved to exploit new openings. According to Hanley and Yamamura, new techniques of population control were crucial to this success story. In contrast to many other cases of pre-industrial development, they ensured that the gain of economic growth were not offset by population growth. Although the two authors make only tentative suggestions about the implications of their thesis for our understanding of the Meiji transformation, the general thrust of the argument is clear: pre-industrial Japan is presented as a case of market-driven change on a scale and in a direction which make it much easier to explain rapid industrialization under the Meiji regime.

It is now beyond dispute that the later Tokugawa period saw significant developments in many areas. The idea of a stagnating system suppressing all challenges for a century and a half has been laid to rest. But many aspects of the record are still under debate and the set of claims advanced or adumbrated by Hanley and Yamamura is not the only alternative to the erstwhile consensus. Among the noteworthy analyses of late Tokugawa economic history, ideas put forward by Thomas C. Smith deserve mention because of their bearing on the questions to be discussed here. Smith's starting-point was the observation that a certain spread of preindustrial manufacture in the countryside was common to Europe and Japan, but it took place in markedly different contexts. In Europe, foreign trade and population continued to grow, whereas in Japan, the former had been marginalized and the latter stabilized. The Japanese pattern did not preclude growth, but when demand for non-agricultural products rose, this led to intensification and diversification of labour in the countryside and reduced migration to the towns. 'The expansion of the economy in the absence of foreign trade and population growth induces the decline of towns'.[24] Japan thus differs from Europe in that a de-urbanizing trend – all the more striking because of the earlier rapid progress of urbanization, unequaled anywhere at the time – set in during the last phase of pre-industrial growth. This de-centring of economic development – unparalleled anywhere in the West – had major consequences for the Japanese pattern of industrialization. It explains the dominance of light industry in general and textile industry in particular during the early industrial phase, as well as the prominent role of rural entrepreneurs in the economic transformation after 1868 (Smith singled this out as a strikingly under-researched part of Meiji history); the latter factor can also be seen as a distinctive cultural force and a contributor to the 'spirit of capitalism' that crystallized through a synthesis of several currents in a new historical context.

However, the most interesting corrective to one-sided views of later Tokugawa history is an ecological approach which leads to a redefinition of the eighteenth-century crisis, rather than to visions of continuous progress. Conrad Totman has developed this line of argument in a particularly incisive way. As he sees it, 'the years around 1700 witnessed the end of four centuries or more of sustained socioeconomic growth that Japan had experienced as intensive agriculture spread across the realm. During the early 1700s Japan entered a difficult period of stasis that persisted for a century and a half until the exogenous force of European imperialism ruptured the established political order'.[25] This perspective differs markedly from the Marxist one: the root cause of the crisis is not a supposedly obsolete feudal system (that model is in any case a misrepresentation of the Tokugawa order), but a growing tension between the power structure created around 1600 and a resource basis which set limits to development. After a phase of remarkably vigorous growth, scarcity of key resources – not only agricultural ones – began to affect economic life and policy. But the other aspect of Totman's argument is no less important: the organizational and order-building capacities reflected in the Tokugawa order were still evident in measures taken to cope with new problems. An uncompromising stance on strategic essentials did not prevent the ruling elite from initiating, encouraging or accommodating various attempts to maximize yields and optimize uses within the given limits. Such efforts resulted in a more complete appropriation of territorial margins (the progressive incorporation of Hokkaido into the Tokugawa realm was the main achievement of that kind), as well as in significant innovations in the use of natural resources (coal mining and regenerative forestry developed during the eighteenth century). But the most important response to the crisis was an overall rationalizing turn: 'the development of a rationing system, perhaps the most elaborate in human history, which constituted a major societal adaptation to the limits of an essentially fixed resource base'.[26] 'Rationing system' is Totman's term for a whole complex of policies, practices and adaptive techniques which served to mitigate the crisis and counterbalance the constraints. Population control was an integral part of this pattern. More generally speaking, Totman's interpretation does justice to the developments which others have seen as evidence of growth after 1700, without obscuring the difference between the earlier and the later Tokugawa period.

It is tempting to link the rationalizing drive behind these strategies of crisis management to the progress of economic thought in the eighteenth and early nineteenth century. Here the question of the 'spirit of capitalism' reappears with a new twist: to insist on the structural discontinuity between Tokugawa and Meiji institutions is not to deny the possibility that pre-revolutionary reflection on the problems of economic life might have taken a turn which pointed beyond existing barriers and prepared the ground for a more far-reaching practical reorientation. If we adopt Braudel's conceptual scheme, we can at best speak of a severely controlled and confined capitalism during the Tokugawa period; but it can be argued that the Tokugawa pattern of permanent dynamism within an inflexible framework was also at work on the level of economic thought, and that the results were radical enough to foreshadow a breakthrough. Recent work on Tokugawa intellectual history has done much to substantiate this view. Tetsuo Najita's analysis of the merchant academy in Osaka drew attention to an ideological current which earlier scholars in the field had overlooked or underestimated. The 'shaping of a merchant ideology that endorsed active engagement in trade as essential to the public order'[27] was linked to innovative reflection on a much wider range of theoretical and practical issues. The autonomous use of Confucian ideas for these purposes shows that a tradition often seen as alien to commerce could lend itself to more constructive involvement. Merchant visions of virtue should not be mistaken for purely manipulative versions of Confucianism and thus for evidence of its ultimate irrelevance to economic life); rather, the reference to Confucian ideas gave a distinctive bent to economic reflection and imagination, even when the results went beyond traditional boundaries. But both the Confucian connection and the advocacy of new approaches reflected what Najita calls the 'ideological proximity between wealth and power',[28] and this fundamental premise was rooted in structural principles of the Tokugawa order.

There is no doubt that eighteenth- and early nineteenth-century thought broke new ground in the domain of economic analysis, but this was not so much a matter of breaking with orthodoxy as of shifting the balance between Confucian sources and more context-dependent perspectives.[29] The power structure that permitted only a qualified alignment with Confucianism was at the same time conducive to ongoing reflection on the relationship between power and wealth. This led to new conceptions of prosperity and the proper ways to pursue it, summed up in the concept of *kokueki*. The most interesting Western-language work on this subject is Luke Roberts's recent analysis of 'mercantilist economic thought'[30] in late Tokugawa Japan and its role as a precursor of economic nationalism. As Roberts shows, *kokueki* thought – the term was first used in the early eighteenth century – represented a new framework for the definition, rationalization and justification of economic policies; it did not entail a radical break with traditional views, but the conceptual and rhetorical innovations opened up new horizons and made it possible to discuss alternative strategies. To understand the origins of this ideological current, a focus on the large and relatively self-contained domains of the south-west is essential (Roberts deals mainly with Tosa). Here the role of merchants – especially those involved in export to the central regions – is most evident. They were, as Roberts argues, the 'primary exponents and developers'[31] of *kokueki* thought in its early phases, and by comparison with the merchant culture of Osaka, their mode of discourse reflects a greater distance from the dominant ideological models. Although Roberts does not refer to Braudel, his line of argument suggests that the relationship of the export-oriented domainal merchants to their respective rulers might be seen as a Braudelian capitalist constellation on a smaller scale.

But *kokueki* thought was no mere window-dressing for merchant interests. The reference to the 'prosperity of the country' amounted to a double redefinition: economic activity was reoriented from household-centred service towards the creation of wealth, and the concomitant emphasis on the domain as a polity led to a 'shift from lord-centered toward a country-centered political imagination'.[32] Merchants were well placed to pioneer this turn, but their interpretive constructs could be appropriated by other social groups, most importantly by samurai bureaucrats involved in domain government and policy-making. The dialogue between merchants and bureaucrats was central to the development of *kokueki* thought. Controversies could thus be articulated within a common frame of reference: for example, *kokueki* arguments were used to justify both domain monopolies and demands for free trade. Within some of the most important domains, economic ideas, and strategies thus developed in a direction which prefigured transformations on a national scale after 1868. The Meiji vision of national prosperity, essential to the building of a strong state and dependent on expanding trade, drew on the tradition of domain mercantilism. This is one of the most striking examples of a more general pattern: the transfer of models and projects from the domainal to the national context. More precisely, the very crystallization of a modern national identity in the wake of the Meiji transformation was based on the double legacy of domains and central rule. But since the domains were operative parts of a more comprehensive order the mercantilist current may be seen as an integral part of the Tokugawa legacy. As Najita puts it, 'the late Tokugawa had generated two comprehensive and overlapping visions for national independence: political centralization and economic transformation through trade'.[33] The Meiji transformation resulted in a more effective fusion and a more dynamic combination of these two incipient projects.

Expansion and accumulation

The late Tokugawa constellation of political and economic structures, together with ideological trends which reflected underlying problems, was a crucial background factor in the making of a new order after 1868. Although a political revolution brought the old regime to an abrupt end and changed Japan's position in the global arena, the Meiji state had to build on foundations and could draw on potentials inherited from its predecessor. A close connection between the exercise of power and the management of resources was taken for granted; ideas developed in response to growing problems in both fields could serve to legitimize a more activist turn in the political as well as the economic domain. But the specific direction of change in both regards was determined by confrontation with a new international environment. The conversion to industrial capitalism was a geopolitical imperative, and as such inseparable from other changes needed to meet the demands of interstate competition. In borrowing economic, political and cultural models from the ascendant Western powers, Meiji Japan was entering a field where further adjustments to ongoing transformations would be required.

Both the structures of capitalist development and their national as well as international contexts underwent changes which called for new strategies of upgrading; the initial course taken by late but high-speed developers – such as the Meiji regime – could have lasting effects on their long-term trajectories. Moreover, the intercultural translation involved in the transfer of models from central to peripheral societies has a practical impact of its own. With regard to the case to be discussed here, perceptions and interpretations of capitalism in action elsewhere may be more or less shaped by indigenous premises, as well as by the accompanying set of strategic goals; they also differ as to their capacity for crystallizing into durable patterns of economic culture. These considerations are, as we shall see, relevant to key aspects of the Japanese experience.

The mid-nineteenth-century crisis resulted in a rapid transition to a particularly strong, dynamic and durably embedded nation-state. This institutional innovation became the principal framework for interaction between imported models and internal trends. In the global context, the Meiji state combined openness to lessons from Western achievements with a strategy aimed not only at preserving national independence, but at building a power basis for competition on more equal terms. In relation to the domestic legacy, a radical solution to structural problems of the old regime went hand in hand with a reaffirmation and ideologization of cultural continuity. The national aspect of the new order became effective on several levels. National identity, constituted through a fusion of multiple sources in response to a transformative historical experience, centred on imaginary significations of a particularly totalizing and cohesive kind; this interpretive core was closely linked to institutions which embodied the founding symbolism of the political system (the imperial institution, as it – somewhat misleadingly – became known in Western parlance, was central to this pattern). Ideological expressions of nationalism, often divergent in details but drawing on a common imaginary, demonstrated an unusual capacity to neutralize or absorb rival ideas, whether the challenge came from liberal or socialist quarters. But nationalism was also an operative ideology and a principle of orientation in all domains of social life, diffused and inculcated by a wide range of agencies.[34] Although the nationalism of the Meiji epoch should be distinguished from the ultra-nationalism of a later phase (analyzed in seminal works by Masao Maruyama), a powerful version of integral nationalism was on the rise from 1868 onwards, and it differed from European variants of the same type in that it had a stronger grip on state structures and faced less effective competition from other currents.

To insist on the centrality of the nation-state, its self-image and its strategic as well as ideological projects, is not to deny the relevance of broader historical perspectives. A civilizational viewpoint is – as I have argued elsewhere in this book – essential to the understanding of Japanese history, but its specific focus varies from one epoch to another; in the context of the Meiji transformation and its sequel, the main conduit of civilizational dynamics was a new pattern of state formation, with ramifications in the economic as well as the cultural dimension. With regard to the question of Japanese capitalism and its specific features, approach locates the civilizational aspects within historical settings and changing constellations, rather than on the level of invariant structures.[35] The connection is most explicit in definitions of national identity and their programmatic claims. If the concept of the 'civilizational nation' makes sense, modern Japan is surely one of the most obvious cases in point. But the civilizational side to Japanese nationhood and nationalism is made up of multiple components. A tradition of emphatic particularism, backed up by more or less elaborate images of Japan as a uniquely self-contained world, was inherited from the premodern epoch and developed into a particularly vigorous branch of nationalist ideology; it could use the language of Western civilizational theories for its own purposes. The long history of formative involvement in an East Asian China-centred civilizational sphere was never ignored and could be elevated to a more defining role when circumstances seemed to call for that. The Meiji experience, unique in the late nineteenth- and early twentieth-century world, was easily translatable into a civilizational mission. Japan's success in appropriating Western civilization while resisting Western domination seemed to mark it out as a model for others; this idea was, however, open to different interpretations. In the early phase of the Meiji transformation, some advocates of radical change identified their projects with progress and universal civilization, and this stance gave an iconoclastic twist to their nationalism (although it is worth noting that a reformer who at one stage even wanted to abolish the Japanese language did not question the imperial institution). But from the 1880s onwards, the dominant version of nationalism tried to link an unrelenting modernizing offensive to the maintenance of national identity and its reconstructed traditional symbols. From this point of view, Japan's distinctive achievement could be presented as a felicitous balance between the particularist and universalist meanings of the idea of civilization. Finally, the most paradoxical interpretation of Japan's special relationship to modernity was developed during the last phase of empire-building: for those who saw an 'overcoming of modernity' as the cultural meaning of the Pacific War, Japan's trailblazing effort to master modern techniques had empowered it to create and propagate a cultural alternative to the inseparably modern and Western civilization of its adversaries.

The above summary of antecedents and directions can serve to contextualize the question of the 'spirit of capitalism' and the specific characteristics of its Japanese variant. As we have seen, the cultural orientations of economic actors – and especially of those involved in capitalist development – are made up of diverse components (including correctives borrowed from anti-capitalist movements or traditions), and one such combination gives way to another as the broader historical context changes. On closer examination, the 'spirit of capitalism' thus appears as a sequence of composite patterns. With regard to the Japanese case, a convergence of multiple currents is already evident in the Tokugawa prelude. The analyses quoted above suggest that the main legacy to later strategists of growth was a rationalized and trade-oriented recipe for economic nationalism, practiced on a limited scale within the Tokugawa order but transferable to the larger arena of interstate competition after 1868. The Tokugawa power structure was, of course, an essential background to progress – and to visions of further progress – in the economic domain. And as for the imports from ideological traditions, their role is also best understood as an indirectly supportive one: no specific tradition can be credited with a pre-adaptive economic ethic, but available ideological frameworks – most obviously Confucian ones – were used to reinforce the new modes of practical reasoning which emerged at the interface of economics and politics, and the ongoing revision has thrown new light on this connection.

Before going on to discuss the Meiji beginnings and post-Meiji destinies of developmentalism, there is another general point to be noted. The successive 'spirits of capitalism' are superimposed on a shared layer of meaning. The combinations and recombinations analyzed by Boltanski and Chiapello presuppose an enduring focus of vision; as I have suggested, Castoriadis's concept of imaginary significations is the best key to this underlying unity. According to Castoriadis the capitalist imaginary is oriented towards an infinite expansion of mastery, but the same implicit, collective and anonymous project is also at work in other fields of modern social life (from permanent technological innovation to phantasms of total social control). From the Braudelian point of view, modern capitalism would thus appear as a partial fusion of old and new orientations: the invariant historical core of capitalism, i.e. the pursuit of accumulation beyond the routine patterns of the market combines with a new cultural – and in the last instance imaginary – dynamic which takes a variety of other forms beside the capitalist one. Following Christoph Deutschmann, the specific capitalist twist to the phantasm of rational mastery may be described as the 'promise of absolute wealth.'[36] This is the distinctively religious aspect of capitalism, more internal to its economic logic than any input from religious traditions, and inseparable from the symbolism of money: 'Money embodies a general power potential beyond the capacity to purchase particular goods. Individual command over *absolute wealth, over the totality of human possibilities*: this promise, which money contains, is perhaps the strongest utopian message that ever existed in history, stronger than historical religions and stronger even than socialism, as we know today.'[37] The concept of a secular religion, more frequently used with critical reference to anti-capitalist ideologies, seems applicable to the very driving force of capitalism. But as Deutschmann argues, there is no standard unchanging version of this religious message. Rather, it is periodically translated and retranslated into myths or phantasms which seem to concretize the capitalist promise in terms appropriate to changing historical situations, and may be more or less open to unorthodox interpretations. Taylorism and Fordism are classic cases in point; the contemporary cult of flexibility, deregulation and totally mobile capital belongs in the same category.

This analysis of capitalism draws on Marx, Simmel and Schumpeter. It raises a wide range of theoretical questions which cannot be discussed here. Our main concern is with its bearing on some aspects of the Japanese experience. Problems at that level will be easier to tackle if we first note a connection which is marginal to Deutschmann's argument, but implicit in his overall perspective. If the inbuilt – and ultimately religious – utopia of modern capitalism becomes operative through context-dependent and transient myths, this concretizing process must also bring it into contact with analogous formations in the political field. The interaction between these two types of myths and mirages could be seen as the other side of structural connections between state formation and economic development. Interrelated imaginary significations give rise to mobilizing visions of power as well as of wealth. To anticipate the following line of analysis, modern Japan is a particularly instructive case of both institutional and ideological linkages between the two domains.

The discussion must begin with the Tokugawa background. However significant the early modern seedbeds of Japanese capitalism may have been, there is no denying a basic contrast with the West: the isolated and closely supervised miniature version of a world system could not develop the same kind of internal dynamism as the expanding Western European world. There was, in other words, no Japanese parallel to the widening horizons and maturing self-images of early modern capitalism in the West. If we can – as Deutschmann argues – reconstruct a cyclical process of rising and declining myths, accompanying the dynamic of creative destruction, the story must include a pre-industrial chapter: visions of commerce transforming man and world preceded the technological and organizational myths of advanced capitalism.[38] But in Tokugawa Japan, the economic imagination was overshadowed by the political myth of a self-contained Japanese order. This ideological construct was maintained with astonishing consistency until it collapsed as a result of Western expansion into the region. It could not be adapted to the new global configuration of power. But less official interpretations of Japanese identity, tradition and culture had developed behind its protective walls, and they were to play a major role in the formation of nationalist ideologies and policies after the geopolitical turnaround.

Industry and empire: The Japanese pattern

As Bertrand Bernier argues, the development of an industrial economy (he dates the crucial phase from 1885 to 1919) was the real Japanese miracle: it was the first case of a non-Western country becoming an industrial power, and an unprecedented breakthrough by a latecomer.[39] There is no doubt that it was widely perceived as an exemplary achievement, notably by aspiring modernizers or revolutionaries in other parts of the non-European world. But we can at least speculate about less explicit responses. Victory over Russia in 1905 was the most spectacular outcome of Japan's rise to regional power, and it threw the Russian empire into a crisis whose aftereffects were still unfolding when a global military conflict destroyed the old imperial regime and cleared the way for a new one. Those who advocated a revolution within the revolution in 1905 and prevailed in 1917 based their project on a particularly extreme interpretation of the 'advantages of backwardness' and the possibilities of accelerated progress; their theoretical language was borrowed from the Western revolutionary tradition, but their aspirations were surely not unrelated to a broader context of efforts to redress uneven development. From that point of view, Japan was already a prominent part of the global landscape.

In short, we have reasons to believe that the ideological impact of Meiji Japan's achievements went far beyond the obvious cases of emulation. But irrespective of differences on the level of theoretical or practical conclusions, basic perceptions seem to have been uniform in that the success story of Japanese industrialization – and modernization in general – appeared as a singular example of general or universal principles in action. The particular context of the transformation seemed less relevant, and the other side of the Japanese phenomenon – the persistence of ostensibly archaic traditions – was regarded as external to the modernizing process (depending on the ideological perspective, emphasis could be placed on oppressive survivals or exotic treasures). But as I have suggested, the context is crucial to a comparative perspective; more precisely, the focus should be on successive contexts of changing developmental patterns, and the following discussion will approach Japanese capitalism from that angle. A contextual view will relativize the distinction between traditional and modern aspects. But for present purposes, it seems best to begin with a less controversial part of the historical setting: the connections between different components of the modernization strategy implemented after 1868.

The creation of an industrial capitalist economy was an integral part of the *fukoku kyōhei* (rich country, strong army) programme adopted by the Meiji leadership, and the interdependence of state strength and economic growth became a basic axiom of otherwise varying policies throughout the imperial and post-imperial phases. In that sense, the developmentalist stance of the Japanese state has never wavered, although the strategic premises and priorities changed in response to global transformations. By the same token, techno-nationalism, i.e. the assumption that 'technological innovation and the national welfare are indissolubly linked'[40] has been an invariant defining principle of the Japanese political economy. More generally speaking, economic rationalism was essential to the spirit of Japanese capitalism – from the self-images and ideological orientations of Meiji entrepreneurs to what Murakami Yasusuke calls the 'national "catch-up growth" consensus'[41] of the postwar period. National variations and nationalist admixtures were, on the whole, more characteristic of the 'first spirit of capitalism' than Boltanski and Chiapello's retrospective sketch would suggest; the Meiji constellation can thus be seen as a particularly distinctive and durable version of widespread trends. The subsequent turn to closer integration of empire-building and economic development went hand in hand with a more radical version of nationalism, but at the same time, it affected economic culture and ideology in ways more akin to the 'second spirit of capitalism'. Although this shift reflected radical changes to the international environment, it was also related to trends and problems inherent in the original Meiji framework of modernization.

After a phase of indecision the victors of 1868 opted for a strategy of state-building through controlled and selective application of Western models. In the late nineteenth-century context, colonial possessions appeared as an integral and indispensable part of political modernity: at the great power level to which Japan aspired, there could be no interstate competition without imperial expansion. Industrialization, nation-building, administrative reform and imperialism were, from this point of view, interdependent aspects of a grand strategy. The latecomers among the Western colonial powers – Germany and Italy – also embarked on imperial projects in the wake of national unification but the Japanese conversion to imperialism was part and parcel of a civilizational turn which had no parallel in the West. The unintended consequences of this choice were of major importance to the twentieth-century mutations of Japanese modernity; more specifically, four paradoxes of Japanese imperialism affected the path of capitalist development in particularly significant ways.

The first – and most fundamental – paradox has to do with the historical relationship between geopolitical and economic visions of empire. On the one hand, it seems clear that strategic security and territorial consolidation – defined, of course, as the security and consolidation of a prospective great power – were the main concerns of the Meiji empire-builders: 'No colonial empire of modern times was as clearly shaped by strategic considerations'.[42] Expansion within the neighbouring region was both the only available option for a latecomer with limited resources and the most rational course of action for a state preparing for a long-term involvement in global competition. On the other hand, the imperial domain acquired for these purposes – more thoroughly geopolitical than those of Western role models – could later serve as a framework for economic policies equally distinct from other modern cases. Economic interests found various outlets at successive stages of Japanese expansion, but the most momentous reorientation of imperial strategy took place at the beginning of the 1930s: a convergence of military and economic imperatives led to plans for a self-sufficient zone of development, centred on and controlled from Japan but organized with a view to maximizing industrial potential in the colonies. A contiguous regional empire was more adaptable to such goals than the far-flung possessions of Western powers. This translation of a geopolitical rationale into an economic one was prompted by crises and upheavals in the global arena, but here we must also allow for distinctive Japanese perceptions of developments which began elsewhere. From the Japanese point of view, World War I was not – as in the West – an irreversible breakdown of a whole international order; rather, the successful use of the situation to strengthen Japanese positions in the region seemed to foreshadow further progress along the path opened up by the victories over China and Russia. The disruptive impact of the war on relations between the great powers involved in East Asia, became clearer during the 1920s, and this upset was soon compounded by global depression, growing international tensions and a worldwide resurgence of economic nationalism. In the Japanese context, the ideological fusion of nation and empire affected both perceptions of the problem and the proposed solutions to it: the response was an imperial version of developmentalism, in some ways – as we shall see – reminiscent of Western alternatives to the liberal capitalist order but too distinctive to be subsumed under any general model.

The shift to a developmentalist conception of empire was, however, only one aspect of a complex process. It was first reinforced and then thwarted by another trend: an unstoppable drift towards strategic overstretch. This is perhaps the most widely noted of the paradoxes in question. The apparent advantages of a compact regional empire gave rise to uncontrollable complications and insurmountable difficulties. When Meiji Japan set out to colonize parts of East Asia and maximize its influence elsewhere in the region, the clearly delimited geopolitical arena was at first conducive to balanced policies. But expansion within East Asia led inevitably to growing involvement in the Chinese crisis, and the resultant problems were beyond the strength of the Japanese state. The informal empire in China was drawn into the greatest civilizational convulsion in modern history (the century-long transformation of China, triggered by Western intrusion and reoriented by adapted Western ideologies), and in the end, this set Japan on collision course with the United States. Historians of the Japanese empire see the beginning of full-scale war in China in 1937 as a point of no return, but in retrospect, it is hard to find an earlier date where the trend could have been reversed without radical changes to the whole framework of Japanese strategy. The 1931 foundation of a satellite regime in Manchuria, with ambitions to become at least one of the successor states of the Chinese empire, was a very major landmark. Louise Young's analysis of the 'total empire' which Japan began to build in Manchuria shows how crucial this episode was to the course of events in Japan as well as on the mainland. Informal empire, now based on complete control over a puppet government rather than on manoeuvring in a power vacuum, became a vehicle for far-reaching radicalization of the imperial project. As Young argues the empire was 'total' in roughly the same sense as total war. It entailed the 'mass and multidimensional mobilization of domestic society: cultural military, political and economic'; it also brought together – in unprecedented fashion – the strategic, economic and cultural ingredients of imperialism; finally, it can be described as 'total' because of its 'widespread, even comprehensive…impact on Japanese society'.[43] Developmentalism was a key component of this project. There is no doubt that the Manchurian venture was a catalyst of the overall redefinition of imperial goals as described above. But it should also be seen in the context of the Chinese struggle for succession to the defunct empire. At that level, the ambition to create a superior model and Japanese-controlled centre for the transformation of China – less obviously implausible in the 1930s than the wisdom of hindsight might suggest – reinforced the developmentalist current which sought solutions to structural and conjunctural problems at home. But the Manchurian crucible of imperial modernity became a quagmire of delusions: the pursuit of total empire led to total war in China, and ultimately to a global conflict which Japan was bound to lose.

After the Manchurian breakthrough, Japanese imperialism thus took a self-destructive turn: the 'images of empire soon came to override strategic logic; empire became an end in itself, not a means to achieving autarky.'[44] An aberrant version of geopolitics triumphed over all other considerations, but faced rapid and final defeat on its own ground. This brings us to the third paradox: the very excesses of the imperial imagination, i.e. the visions which led the strategists of the 1930s to embark on an unsustainable course, seem to have aided the elaboration of an ideology which proved capable of adjustment to new situations and translation into eminently effective policies. But this ideology drew on many sources and underwent major revisions. Its formative phase was marked by the fourth and last of the paradoxes: although Japanese imperialism was particularly closely connected with nationalist priorities and policies, it proved unusually capable of coopting an internationalist current which had emerged (and was to re-emerge) as the main outlet for principled oppositional thought. The relationship between Marxism and nationalism in interwar Japan was more complex than the polarizing retrospects of the postwar era could admit, and the importance of Marxist contributions to evolving nationalist ideologies was not fully recognized until much later.[45] The nationalist turns repeatedly taken by Marxist intellectuals, were often related to (or at least rationalized in terms of) unorthodox interpretations of Japanese imperialism. From Takahashi Kamekichi's theory of 'petty imperialism', put forward in the 1920s, to important Marxist figures associated with the wartime project of a 'new order', attempts to theorize a progressive role for the empire may be seen as a distinctive branch of the Japanese Marxist tradition. This trend cannot be dismissed as intellectual capitulation to the dominant ideology. The Marxist inputs into a developmentalist project based on nationalist premises were substantial and of some importance to practical outcomes. Here, too, the Manchurian venture marked a turning-point: Young's analysis, quoted above, shows that the 'total empire' attracted intellectuals and activists in search of new paths to radical reform, and that their ambitions – although vitiated by a fundamental refusal to face the facts of a colonial situation – were genuine enough to cause conflicts with the military authorities. But to understand the relationship between imperial practices and radical interpretations, the trajectory of Japanese developmentalism must be seen in a more long-term perspective. The implications of the two last paradoxes will, in other words, become clearer if we approach them from a broader historical and comparative angle.

Developmentalism in context: Ideologies, institutions and traditions

As Germaine Hoston's account shows, the indigenous Marxist debate on Japanese patterns of capitalist development was remarkably vigorous and many-sided. But it had no appreciable impact on Western interpretations of Japan. The Western debate on Japan as a paradigmatic case of developmentalism began much later and unfolded within a markedly non-Marxist frame of reference. Chalmers Johnson's book on MITI and the Japanese Miracle, published in 1982, set the stage for a prolonged controversy and focused attention on the *developmental state* as a central component of the Japanese model (it is worth noting that although Johnson referred explicitly to a 'capitalist developmental state', the first adjective has often been omitted by defenders as well as critics of the concept). The most constructive later contributions have proposed a broader definition of developmentalism as a sociopolitical pattern and objected to overestimations of state guidance; the state is, on this view, embedded in a framework of structures and strategies, and its role can change in response to more or less radical transformations of that context. The difference between the two stages of the debate should not be exaggerated. To quote Johnson's later summary of his argument, he 'never said or implied that the state was *solely* responsible for Japan's economic achievements or that it behaved like the state in command economies in assigning tasks and duties to the Japanese people'.[46] His primary purpose was to theorize a state whose mode of action differed from the American-style 'regulatory state' in that it set substantive developmental goals, but also from the Soviet model (then still functioning) in that it used market mechanisms for developmental purposes. This did not imply that the state's capacity for autonomous action could be treated as an independent variable. Conversely, those who argue for a broader definition of developmentalism do not deny that the transformative capacities of the state are always essential to developmentalist projects. But they insist that the 'embedded autonomy'[47] evident in the exercise of such capacities depends on a social field of forces, institutions and operative ideas.

With these qualifications in mind, it can nevertheless be argued that an enlarged conception of developmentalism is in the making, and that the Japanese experience is as crucial as ever to further discussion of the topic. The following comments will focus on three different lines of argument which have been explored in recent contributions to the debate. They have to do with the respective roles of ideological projects, institutional settings and civilizational legacies in the formation of developmentalist patterns. For present purposes, the analysis will be limited to the Japanese case. But before going on to specifics, a few words should be said about the contemporary context of the problem. Developmentalism – in the general sense of political intervention and coordination for developmental purposes – is now widely seen as outdated or at least on the defensive.

Even those who criticize the 'myth of the powerless state',[48] on the grounds that no really existing state will or can conform to the prescriptions of neo-liberal doctrine, are very explicitly going against the current of a dominant ideology. The present state of play between alternative models of capitalism is beyond the scope of this paper, but one fundamental point should at least be noted. Neo-liberal ideology presents the anti-statist turn as natural and unequivocal triumph of economic rationality; a less preprogrammed approach would have to begin with the observation that the dividing line is drawn between two different constellations of political and economic power, and that the political factor (including the global presence of American imperial power) plays an important role in the ostensibly de-politicizing push. There is no doubt that during the last decades, a significant retreat of the state has taken place: in the 1950s and 1960s, 'state policy varied between national capitalisms…, but it did so around a recognizably common agenda of extensive state involvement in economic life. Now it seems to vary around a much more restricted agenda…'.[49] The neo-liberal reading of recent history equates this reconfiguration of social power with a rationalizing breakthrough.

Whatever view we take of current ideological issues, the verdict on developmentalism should be backed up by an adequate account of its historical record, and as suggested above, research in this field is now opening up new perspectives. With regard to the Japanese case, the first aspect to consider is the ideological context; it was relatively marginal to earlier analyses of the developmental state, but Bai Gao's analysis of economic ideology in wartime and postwar Japan shows that it was of major importance to practical policies.[50] The following summary is – with some reservations on one major point – based on Gao's work.

A new ideology of development began to take shape in the early 1930s. It was constructed in response to the apparent disintegration of the world economy; from the Japanese vantage point, the crisis was more acutely perceived as a demise of established rules but also more readily countered with a nationalist strategy than in the West. The turn towards an autarkic imperial project was the most basic precondition for further changes of policy. But if the strategic shift began with an autonomous decision, the elaboration of a more concrete programme was anything but self-contained: the Japanese theorists and architects of a managed economy drew on European alternatives to the liberal capitalist order. In that context, however, Gao's argument is open to criticism. He sees the wartime Japanese regime as a version of Fascism, and concludes that its economic policies were in fundamental respects modelled on European paradigm. The German theory of total war was 'the theoretical foundation for the ideology of the managed economy'.[51] The main objections to this interpretation of Japanese history between 1931 and 1945 are well known, and there is no need to recapitulate them here. But if we take the view that the differences between Fascism and Japanese ultra-nationalism were significant enough to put the latter in a category of its own, the question of foreign models for the managed economy must also be answered in more nuanced terms. The Japanese regime borrowed ideas and organizational techniques from the rival totalitarianisms of the 1930s (Gao discusses the Soviet connection at some length, although he regards it as subordinate to the Fascist blueprint), and its very ultra-nationalism explains the ideological distance which enabled it to follow this eclectic course. This is not to deny that the affinities with Fascism were much more important, but they did not amount to wholesale ideological alignment. As for the other source, the influence of the Soviet model was to some extent separate from domestic Marxist inputs. As Gao shows, Japanese economic planners – especially those active in Manchuria – were willing to learn from the Soviet experience, even when they judged it from a purely technocratic point of view; on the other hand, some of the intellectuals involved in policy making had a non-party Marxist background. In addition to these different currents, New Deal policies were studied with a view to practical lessons.[52]

In short, a radical nationalist stance was combined with a strategy of selective borrowing; the specific choices and outcomes differed from those of the Meiji period, but the basic similarity of underlying attitudes seems undeniable. To stress nationalism as a common denominator (rather than any trans-national model) is not to suggest that there were no ideological conflicts. In the late 1930s and 1940s, reform bureaucrats put forward projects which met with strong resistance from the business elite and were therefore rejected by the political leadership. In some cases, Marxist connections or continuing interest in Marxist theory caused serious trouble. The nationalist consensus was not immune to controversy. But more importantly, it was capable of political adaptation and ideological innovation. Gao identifies 'three distinctive policy paradigms: the managed economy, which lasted from the beginning of the 1930s to the end of World War II in 1945, and then from 1946 to 1949; promoting exports, which dominated in the 1950s, and high growth and liberalization, which occupied the center of Japanese economic policy in the 1960s'.[53] Economic nationalism was a permanent premise of these successive models of industrial policy, but the specifics of economic ideology differed from one stage to another. Receptivity to economic theory was, however, a noteworthy feature of the whole process. As Gao shows, policy makers associated with the paradigm of promoting exports and technological innovation studied and applied Schumpeter's theory of capitalist development. Other theories came to the fore – within a pluralistic but strategically oriented frame of reference – when the relationship between state guidance and market mechanisms had to be redefined during the phase of high growth.

A persistent economic nationalism, a mutable framework of economic ideology and a pragmatic openness to economic inquiry thus combined to produce a very distinctive pattern of developmentalism. Its trajectory covers about half a century (it is only in the 1980s that one can speak of a rupture). The ideological dimension of this adaptable project was obscured by the self-limiting stance which Japan had to adopt when it became a subaltern ally of the United States. A retrospective survey of the whole process – seen as a radical and systematic reorientation of economic nationalism – corrects this misapprehension. The long-term perspective also helps to link the analysis of Japanese developmentalism to the debate on the 'spirit of capitalism', outlined at the beginning of the paper. There are obvious and important affinities between the developmentalist pattern, especially in its successive postwar versions, and the second spirit of capitalism, as described by Boltanski and Chiapello, but the features which set the Japanese variant apart from Western ones should also be noted. If the spirit of capitalism is understood as an operative ideology, it seems clear that economic nationalism in wartime and postwar Japan became more effective on that level than it had been during the Meiji phase. The change was twofold: economic concerns were – especially after the collapse of the empire – more central to the nationalist agenda than before, and nationalism was translated into more specific frameworks for economic action. This is not to suggest that the all too well-known 'Japan, Inc.' model might be applicable. Conflicting interpretations, interests and strategies were characteristic of the whole developmentalist phase (Gao's analysis is instructive on this point). But the framework within which they were articulated was – in decisive ways – shaped by economic nationalism. Another contrast has to do with historical antecedents and legacies: notwithstanding the common cultural and institutional characteristics of organized capitalism in Japan and the West, the Japanese model at work during the postwar phase of high growth had a more direct prewar ancestry than any Western version. Finally, the partial incorporation of a critique of capitalism, which Boltanski and Chiapello see as an integral aspect of the 'second spirit', has a parallel in Japan, but with a noteworthy difference: The Marxist critique of capitalism had influenced the imperial version of developmentalism, and this contribution counted for something in the postwar changes.

In the postwar phase the institutional setting became more important than it had been for the mobilized economy between 1931 and 1945. Although Gao stresses the 'institutional environment of economic reasoning,'[54] this level is less central to his argument than the ideological one. The most interesting institutional approach to developmentalism is T.J.Pempel's analysis of the 'developmental regime', explicitly proposed as an alternative to the models which have over-emphasized the role of governmental bureaucracy. The concept of 'regime' has been used in other contexts to describe relatively stable patterns of a somewhat elusive kind: they are irreducible to formal rules, normative frameworks or systemic mechanisms. Pempel refers to writers on international politics who have defined regimes as more or less explicitly recognized frameworks of interstate relations, but with some scope for disagreement on the relative weight of institutions and expectations. Castoriadis (whom Pempel does not mention) referred to democracy and totalitarianism as 'social regimes', thus stressing the need to go beyond the conventional notions of political systems or forms of government. More generally speaking the concept of regime seems congenial to Castoriadis's emphasis on the complex relations between significations and institutions. As for Pempel's use of the concept, it refers to 'a middle level of cohesion in the political economy of a nation-state'; in that capacity, it is more comprehensive than a particular economic policy, but less so than 'a 'political system', 'constitutional order', or 'economic system'.[55] The most succinct positive definition of a regime is that it 'involves a sustained fusion among the institutions of the state, particular segments of the socioeconomic order, and a particular bias in public policy orientation. Together, this mixture provides a pattern of elements so unified as a whole that its properties cannot be fully appreciated by a simple summation of its parts. "Regime" in this sense equates with such terms as "gestalt", "system" or "weltanschauung..."'[56] The last comparison, however metaphorical, may be taken as a reference to the interpretive or ideological components of regimes.

The concept of regime is obviously meant to open up a new field for comparative and historical studies. It focuses on connections which have often been neglected because of preoccupation with more formal or more visible patterns. Pempel is cautious when it comes to defining the scope of regime analysis: it is not to be taken for granted that the interaction of social forces and institutional frameworks will give rise to stable regimes. But he claims that such patterns have – to a great extent – been characteristic of postwar industrial democracies, as well as of some non-democratic states. Here I can only briefly outline three problematics to which he applies the concept of regime. First, it serves to clarify what Japan has in common with the other two East Asian cases of successful developmentalism, South Korea and Taiwan (the question of post-Communist China and its search for a viable developmental regime is not raised). A brief glance at the postwar history of the three countries is enough to raise doubts about any generalized concept of the developmental state. Forms of government, economic strategies and relations between state and society vary widely from one case to another. Pempel tries to show that they can nevertheless be categorized as variants of a distinctively developmental regime; the details of his analysis are too complex to be recapitulated here, but a few salient points will suffice to indicate the thrust of the argument. 'All three have "strong states"', i.e. states which concentrate power in the hands of technocrats and bureaucrats, but without a 'sharp dichotomy between state and society'; the power centre is backed up by 'semi-permanent socioeconomic coalitions'. The regimes in question reject the cult of the market and opt for 'active market manipulation'.[57] But at the same time they could take advantage of relatively open markets worldwide as a means by which to advance their own domestic transformations'.[58] The combination of market manipulation at home with efforts to compete in more open markets abroad was, of course, dependent on global constellations including the close alliance with America. A final point worth noting is that relatively high levels of social equality have been characteristic of all three regimes, despite the weakness of the political left and of organized labour. This can at least in part be explained as a result of economic nationalism and its strategies of mobilization.

Second, the Japanese regime can be compared to other 'prototypical ways in which capitalism and democracy assumed discrete patterns in the first three or four decades after the end of World War II'.[59] As the definition quoted above suggests, the key variables are alliances and cleavages between socio-economic sectors or forces, the structure of governmental institutions (they may be more or less conducive to the concentration or dispersal of power and authority), and the established paradigms of public policy. Pempel lists four Western cases which seem particularly illustrative of the range of regime variation. Swedish corporatism began with an alliance of organized labour and agriculture and went on to institutionalize a high level of cooperation between business and labour. In the United States, socio-economic pluralism made it more difficult to stabilize social alliances, but the New Deal regime was nevertheless based on a partly political and partly market-driven labor-capital accord. In Britain, a 'party-driven collectivism', grounded in bipartisan agreement on some fundamentals of social and economic policy, prevailed from 1945 until the Thatcher revolution of 1979. Finally, the Italian regime, regarded by some observers as similar to the Japanese one because of the enduring dominance of a conservative party, was characterized by extensive party patronage, state control of important enterprises without any coherent economic policies, and muted confrontation rather than cooperation between business and labour.

When the Japanese postwar regime is compared to these Western models, several distinctive features stand out in relief. Pempel stresses the importance of an anti-labour alliance between business and agriculture; this was the original and essential power basis of the ruling conservative party but it did not prevent the developmental state from making arrangements and concessions which disarmed opposition to the regime. The economic policies pursued by the conservative bloc were more unusual than its social background. Pempel coins the term 'embedded mercantilism': the mercantilist thrust was evident in the combination of export promotion with insulation of the domestic market, whereas the embedding strategies had to do with formal and informal co-ordination of key economic actors. LDP control of the state apparatus and a strong national bureaucracy were the key stabilizing factors of the governmental level.[60]

Third, Pempel's analysis links the achievements of the developmental regime in its heyday – the phase of 'creative conservatism'[61] – to the problems encountered during the 1980s and the crisis of the 1990s. All the regimes mentioned above unravelled in the 1980s, some of them more spectacularly than others, and as Pempel sees it, stable alternatives have yet to take shape. But in the Japanese transition differs from Western ones in significant respects. On the one hand, key components of the regime proved more resistant to change than elsewhere: there was (apart from a brief episode) no transfer of governmental power, no disintegration of the party system, and no neo-liberal wave. On the other hand, the structural crisis – due to a combination of internal and external factors – unfolded in a particularly dramatic fashion. Institutions and practices central to the regime became increasingly dysfunctional, and at the same time, growing exposure to a changing international economy posed problems which could not be solved within the established framework. Here I will only briefly mention some of the internal developments which Pempel discusses at length. New socio-economic divisions undermined the power basis of the LDP, even if they did not disrupt the whole system. Factional rivalries within the bureaucracy weakened a key component of the regime. Traditional techniques of market manipulation became obsolete or less effective. In short, a regime shift is in progress, but the long-term outcome is likely to reflect the legacy of the developmental regime. The wholesale conversion envisaged by some neo-liberal ideologists is a utopian fiction.

To conclude this discussion, the civilizational level of analysis should be revisited. More precisely, it remains to be seen whether the emerging enlarged model of developmentalism can still be usefully related to a civilizational perspective. The original theory of the developmental state was explicitly critical of culturalist approaches: the focus was on situational constraints, cumulative learning and strategic rationality. The same applies to the two abovementioned attempts to contextualize the developmental state. For Gao, Japanese developmentalism is 'a distinctive set of economic ideas and ideologies on how to create wealth for a late-developed nation',[62] and his narrative is meant to show how this mode of economic reasoning grew out of Japan's interaction with a changing economic, political and ideological environment. There is nothing to suggest a constitutive link to culture or tradition. According to Pempel, the construction of developmental regimes refutes the 'pessimistic predictions of culturally based modernization theory'[63]: their achievements show that pre-existing cultural patterns do not shape the course of history. In view of this consistently anti-culturalist stance it seems appropriate to begin with some conceptual preliminaries. The civilizational perspective, as understood here, does involve assumptions about culture, but cannot be subsumed under a generic culturalist model. Before going on to put the case in positive terms, the most common misconceptions should be put out of the way.

The argument is not about civilizations as self-perpetuating *deep structures*: if there is a civilizational background to strategies based on long-term learning processes (developmentalist projects are among the most obvious cases of that kind), it must be a matter of premises and orientations guiding the actions of historical protagonists, but also subject to adaptation and reinterpretation in practical contexts. It is equally misleading to think of a civilization as a *super-system*, encompassing – among other subsystems – a whole form of economic life and giving it a distinctive meaning. This view would simply shift the over-integrated image of society to the civilizational level. The above discussion of capitalism in general and developmentalism in particular should have made it clear that the economic dynamics in question do not fit in with that frame of reference. The only plausible approach is to see civilizational patterns as aspects of historical constellations where other factors – infra- and inter-civilizational ones – are also at work. Finally, a civilization is not a *self-contained core* of collective identity, unaffected by adaptive changes at the level of organizations and apparatuses (this is the stated or unstated assumption of current speculations about a 'clash of civilizations'). The civilizational perspective to be defended here concerns the institutional and organizational domains of social life, as well as the cultural ones, but not in the sense of a totalizing and self-sufficient framework.

Two examples of the civilizational approach to Japanese capitalism will show how these various pitfalls can be avoided, S.N. Eisenstadt refers to a Japanese 'mode of capitalism',[64] integral to the more general Japanese pattern of modernity; this term suggests a distinctive variant of the institutional complex commonly taken to define a capitalist economy, and the specific features are – at least in part – linked to the civilizational context, but only concrete historical analyses can clarify the scope of the civilizational factor (it may vary from phase to phase). More precisely, the civilizational aspects have to do with inbuilt and enduring conceptions of political economy. They have, throughout successive epochs of Japanese history, resulted in a strong tendency to embed the economic sphere in broader contexts of collective goals and networks, and thus to limit the scope of institutional and functional differentiation. In the modern setting, this traditional trend took a new turn: a more autonomous dynamic of the economic sphere had to be accepted as given, but it was still counterbalanced by the operative principle that it 'should be in the service of the nation – its development, its growth, its ability to withstand the force of Western powers – and not an autonomous arena propelled mainly by the utilitarian goals of individuals'.[65] After the collapse of the empire, the economic arena became more central to state strategy. The embedding or 'interlocking' logic was now translated into mechanisms of coordination at different levels: between bureaucracy and business, between economic units, and within the enterprises. Eisenstadt draws on a wide range of empirical analyses of the Japanese economy, but his model is perhaps closest to Michael Gerlach's account of 'alliance capitalism'.[66] His more general thesis is that a civilizational trend

– in this case a contextualizing vision of the economic sphere, emphasizing its intertwining with other activities within a broader societal framework – becomes effective through the strategies of social actors who respond to changing situations.

The other interpretation, proposed by Murakami Yasusuke, lays a much stronger emphasis on specific models of organization, supposedly typical of the Japanese tradition and applicable under modern conditions but not uniformly dominant throughout the modernizing process. Murakami distinguishes two 'cultural prototypes' of this kind. In contrast to the *ie* model which has already been mentioned, the *mura* ('village') variant is more loosely structured, based on more egalitarian principles and more adaptable to multiple functions. The *ie* emerged later than the *mura* (during the colonization of eastern Honshū in the late Heian and Kamakura periods), but had a much stronger impact on social development during the following centuries. In the twentieth century, it became – as Murakami argues – the mainstay of a Japanese version of organized capitalism. But the postwar economic regime is best understood as a combination of the two models: the *ie* pattern is still evident in the management practices of Japanese firms, whereas the various levels of informal organization – administrative guidance, the *keiretsu* groupings of companies, and the subcontracting system – reflect the *mura* tradition. These claims should not be mistaken for an exhaustive civilizational analysis of developmentalism. For Murakami, the developmental regime is still a variant of economic liberalism, inasmuch as it presupposes the mobilization of economic man, and it involves a mode of economic reasoning which he describes as a political economy of industrialization, in contrast to the political economy of capitalism which had prevailed in pioneering industrial societies: the promotion of technological progress becomes an integral part of economic policy. But as Murakami insists, liberalism is 'polymorphic', and civilizational legacies affect its forms in various ways.[67]

The details of Murakami's argument will not be discussed here. For our purposes, it is enough to note that it exemplifies a certain kind of civilizational analysis: one which avoids both holistic and reductionistic fallacies. The same applies to Eisenstadt's approach. But some concluding remarks on both examples are in order. Notwithstanding their differences, they seem to share a line of interpretation which leads them to pose the question of civilizational imprints on modernity in a specific way. Patterns characteristic of the Japanese tradition are reproduced within the institutional framework of Japanese capitalism, alongside similar continuities in other sectors of modern Japanese society. Parallels between contemporary institutional formations are thus subsumed under an over-arching and enduring civilizational framework. But this leaves open the question of a less direct connection: could the civilizational pedigree be traced through a specific overall direction of modern transformations, which would in turn affect the structures and dynamics of particular socio-cultural spheres? Here I can only outline a possible way to tackle this problem. As has been suggested in various contexts in the preceding papers, the civilizational dimension of nation formation and nationalism in modern Japan is particularly central to the whole pattern of modernity. More precisely, the interrelations of state, nation and society may be seen as a framework for sets and sequences of developments in various fields. The nation-state constructed after 1868 became the prime mover and main guide of efforts to translate the close association of wealth and power – established during the Tokugawa epoch – into a more activist and innovative project. This prior coordination of political and economic goals was the historical infrastructure of the developmental state. The concomitant development of nationalism gave rise to a whole complex of ideological currents, including the extreme visions of the nation as 'a measure of all things' that prevailed during the late imperial phase. But a resilient nationalism was also essential to the post-imperial redefinition of strategic goals and foreign policy priorities. The nationalist hegemony was consolidated through containment or absorption of radical protest and its ideological expressions; in that context, the metamorphoses of the Japanese Marxist tradition and the Japanese Communist movement merit more attention than they have so far received from Western scholars. In short, the civilizational approach to Japanese modernity should focus more systematically on the Japanese version of the 'civilizational nation.'

Notes

1 Introduction: The Peripheral Centre and Its Transformations

1. E. Shils, 'Center and periphery: An idea and its career', in L. Greenfeld and M. Martin (eds.), *Center: Ideas and Institutions*, Chicago: Chicago University Press, 1988, pp. 250–82, here p. 251. It should be noted that I follow the English convention and write 'centre' rather than 'center'.
2. Ibid., p. 252.
3. Ibid., p. 253.
4. Ibid., p. 256.
5. E. Shils, *Center and Periphery: Essays in Macrosociology*, Chicago: University of Chicago Press, 1975, p. 3
6. I have developed this interpretation of Weber elsewhere; see J.P. Arnason, *Praxis und Interpretation: Sozialphilosophische Studien*, Frankfurt: Suhrkamp Verlag, 1988.
7. Sheldon Pollock has raised this issue in various writings on the Indian tradition.
8. The writings of Clifford Geertz and Lucian Pye are among the most representative examples of this approach.
9. Shils, 'Center and periphery', p. 262.
10. Ibid., p. 262.
11. S. N. Eisenstadt, *Political Sociology: A Reader*, New York: Basic Books, 1971, p. 16.
12. Ibid., p. 252.
13. S. N. Eisenstadt, *Japanese Civilization: A Comparative View*, Chicago: Chicago University Press, 1996, p. 420.
14. Ibid., p. 421.
15. Ibid., pp. 318–44.
16. See J. P. Arnason, *Social Theory and Japanese Experience*, London: Kegan Paul International, 1997, pp. 82–138.
17. J. Piggott, *The Emergence of Japanese Kingship*, Stanford:

Stanford University Press, 1997, p. 177; Ishimoda Shō is quoted as an early proponent of this view. Piggott's lucid and convincing analysis highlights the extreme complexity of the process and the very unusual character of the polity that grew out of it; it is therefore hard to understand why she tones down her own argument by describing *ritsuryō* Japan as a 'typical early state' (ibid., p. 278; the term is attributed to Lawrence Krader), and as a 'theatre state' in the sense defined by Clifford Geertz. None of the Bali states for which Geertz coined this concept could have been described as an insular version of all under heaven.

18 Ibid., p. 276.
19 On the question of Confucianism in seventh-and eighth-century Japan, see C. Holcombe, '*Ritsuryō* Confucianism', *Harvard Journal of Asiatic Studies*, 57:2(1997), pp. 543–74.
20 Piggott, op.cit., p 283.
21 P. F. Souyri, *Le monde a l'envers: La dynamique de la société médiévale*, Paris: Maisonneuve et Larose, 1998, pp. 255–56.
22 Ibid., p. 287.
23 See Souyri, op. cit., and Mary E. Berry, *The Culture of Civil War in Kyoto*, Berkeley: University of California Press, 1994. Berry's book is a particularly convincing account of the cultural impact of the 'convulsion' which separates traditional and early modern Japan.
24 See the discussion in M. J. Hudson, *Ruins of Identity: Ethnogenesis in the Japanese Islands*, Honolulu: University of Hawai'i Press, 1999, pp. 233–44. Hudson describes 'ancient Japan' as a lateral ethnie, but expresses scepticism about the belief in divine origins of land, nation and dynasty: 'until the modern era only a tiny minority of the Japanese people would have even been aware of such concepts' (p. 238). He goes on to dismiss the claims made on behalf of the imperial house by Kitabatake Chikafusa, the chief ideologist of the Kenmu restoration, as an isolated anachronism. But apart from the question whether the restorationist project was wholly anachronistic, ideas similar to those of Chikafusa (but less centred on dynastic supremacy) were invoked in other contexts during the Muromachi period.
25 Amino Yoshihiko, 'Deconstructing Japan', *East Asian History* 3(1992), pp. 121–42.
26 M. S. Adolphson, *The Gates of Power: Monks, Courtiers, and*

Warriors in Premodern Japan, Honolulu: University of Hawai'i Press, 2000, p 353. This is the most systematic Western-language work on the triangular power structure (known as *kenmon taisei*) which prevailed from the twelfth to the fourteenth century.
27 See Kuroda Toshio, 'The discourse on the "land of kami" (*shinkoku*) in Medieval Japan', *Japanese Journal of Religious Studies* 23: 3–4 (1996), pp. 353, as well as other papers by Kuroda and comments on his work in the same issue, especially F. Rambelli, 'Religion, ideology of domination and nationalism', pp. 387–426.
28 On early modern constructions of imperial genealogies for commoners, see B. Tadashi Wakabayashi, 'In name only: Imperial sovereignty in early modern Japan', *Journal of Japanese Studies* 17:1 (1991), pp. 25–58.

2 East Asian Approaches: Region, History and Civilization

1 Although it is relatively easy to define the core and the periphery of the East Asian region, it should be noted that its outer boundaries are less clear-cut. Because of its traditional cultural and institutional dependence on the Chinese model, Vietnam is sometimes seen as a part of East Asia, but it is better understood as a composite of East Asian and Southeast Asian elements. Its cultural traditions contain strong indigenous currents which had some effect on the institutional structure created after separation from China; as an independent state, it became a part of the Southeast Asian geopolitical constellation, and together with most of the rest of Southeast Asia, it came under Western colonial rule. All things considered, the Southeast Asian connection would seem to have been more decisive for Vietnam's modern history than the Chinese one. Another demarcation problem – which will not be discussed here – has to do with the Central Asian conquests of eighteenth-century imperial China, inherited but still not fully assimilated by the communist successor regime.
2 See Bruce Cumings, 'The origin and development of the Northeast Asian Political economy', *International Organization* 38:1, 1984, pp. 1–40.

3   See Th. Cohen, *Remaking Japan*, New York: Free Press, 1987.
4   S. Lone and G. McCormack, *Korea Since 1850*, Melbourne: Longman, 1993, p. 93.
5   See J.-P. Beja, 'Naissance d'un national-Confucianisme', *Esprit* 218 (1996), 77–88.
6   A. Dirlik, 'Confucius in the Borderlands. Global Capitalism and the reinvention of Confucianism', *Boundary 2*, 22:3 (1992), pp. 228–73, here p. 230–31.
7   For the two approaches, see respectively Th. A. Metzger, *Escape from Predicament*, Chicago: Chicago University Press, 1977, and S. N. Eisenstadt, 'Innerweltliche Transzendenz und die Strukturierung der Welt', in W. Schluchter (ed.), *Max Webers Studie über Konfuzianismus und Taoismus*, Frankfurt, Suhrkamp Verlag, 1983,
8   On this problematic, see L. Vandermeersch, 'Le nouveau Confucianisme', *Le Débat* 66(1991), 5–16.
9   See Carsun Chang, *The Development of Neo-Confucian Thought*, vol. 2, New York: Bookman Associates, 1962, pp. 455–83.
10 It seems clear that the changing roles of Confucianism in the two other countries can only be understood in the light of both prior and parallel developments in China. Obvious deviations stand out against the imperial Chinese pattern. Attempts to identify a distinctive Japanese brand of Confucianism and credit it with a key role in the making of modern Japan (e.g. M. Morishima, *Why has Japan 'Succeeded'?*, Cambridge: Cambridge University Press, 1982) have not withstood criticism; in the Japanese combination of religious traditions, Confucian elements always played a less self-contained and less central role than in China (although their relative strength grew in the early modern phase), and after the transition to advanced modernity, they were adapted to the language and ideology of integral nationalism. Moreover, the Japanese variants of Confucianism were – as all other aspects of the Japanese tradition – from the outset shaped by interaction with a more dynamic and innovative process of state formation than in China. As for Korea, a sweeping attempt to implement and institutionalize a Confucian programme – which had no parallel in Japan – began at a relatively late date and could therefore draw on the systematizing efforts of

Chinese neo-Confucianism, but was in practice forced to compromise with an indigenous power structure; as a result, the early modern Korean mixture of monarchy, bureaucracy and aristocracy proved particularly resistant to change and unresponsive to Western interventions in the region, but the critical and reformist impetus of Confucian thought remained strong enough to sustain a less official current whose relevance to later developments remains a matter of debate (see J. Palais, *Confucian Statecraft and Korean Institutions*, Seattle, Washington University Press, 1997). After the destruction of the old order, fragments of the Confucian tradition survived in a context dominated by the Japanese colonial regime and the nationalist response to it.

11 Tai Hung-chao (ed.), *Confucianism and Economic Development. An Oriental Alternative*, Washington: Washington Institute, 1989, p. 3, 7.
12 S.N. Eisenstadt (ed.), *The Protestant Ethic and Modernization*, New York, Basic Books, 1968.
13 L. Vandermeersch, *Le nouveau monde sinisé*, Paris, Presses Universitaires de France, 1985, pp. 186–203.
14 Th.A. Metzger, 'Confucian culture and economic modernization: An historical approach', in *Conference on Confucianism and Economic Development in East Asia*. Taipei: Chung-hua Institute, 1989.
15 E. Shils, 'Reflections on civil society and civility in the Chinese intellectual tradition', in Tu Wei-ming (ed.), *Confucian Traditions in East Asian Modernity*, Cambridge/Mass., Harvard University Press, 1996, p. 71.
16 Metzger, op.cit., p. 186.
17 J.-Y. Chevrier, 'L'empire distendu: esquisse du politique in Chine, des Qing à Deng Xiaoping', in J-F. Bayart (ed.), *La greffe de l'état*, Paris: Karthala, 1996.
18 P. Huang, 'Public sphere/Civil society in China? The third realm between state and society', *Modern China*, 19:2 (1993), 216–40.
19 See B. A. Elman, *Classicism, Politics and Kinship*, Berkeley: University of California Press, 1990, and F. Wakeman, 'Boundaries of the public sphere in Ming and Qing China', *Daedalus* 127:3 (2000), 167–89.
20 M. Elvin, *Another History. Essays on China from a European Perspective*, Sydney: Wild Peony, 1996, p. 352.

21 L. Vandermeersch, *Le nouveau monde*..., p. 156.
22 See Tu Wei-ming, *Centrality and Commonality*, Albany: State University of New York Press, 1989, and *Way, Learning and Politics*, Albany, State University of new York Press, 1993.
23 S.N. Eisenstadt, 'Innerweltliche Transzendenz...', p. 388.
24 See M. Elvin, 'Was there a transcendental breakthrough in China?', in S. N. Eisenstadt (ed.), *The Origins and Diversity of Axial Age Civilizations*, Albany: State University of New York Press, 1986, and Th.A. Metzger, 'Eisenstadt's analysis of the relations between tradition and modernization in China', *Li-shih Hsüeh-pao* 12(1984), 345–418.

3 Comparing Japan: The Return to Asia

1 See L. Vandermeeersch, *Le nouveau monde sinisé*, Paris: Presses Universitaires de France, 1985.
2 See especially S. P. Huntington, *The Clash of Civilizations and the Remaking of World Order*, New York: Simon and Schuster, 1996.
3 H.Z. Schiffrin, 'The responses and reactions of East Asia to its scholarly study by the West', in B. Lewis, E. Leites and M. Case (eds.), *As Others See Us – Mutual Perceptions, East and West*, New York: International Society for the Comparative Study of Civilizations, 1985, pp. 253–65
4 F. Maraini, 'Japan, the essential modernizer', in S. Henny and J-P. Lehmann (eds.), *Themes and Theories in Modern Japanese History*, London: Athlone Press, 1987, pp. 44–63.
5 For a seminal example, significantly different from the then predominant paradigm of modernization theory, see N. Jacobs, *The Origin of Modern Capitalism and East Asia*, Hong Kong: Hong Kong University Press 1958; here the common cultural otherness of China and Japan is noted in passing, only to underline its irrelevance to a social bifurcation which sets Japanese feudalism – accompanied by a more general fragmentation and localization of power – apart from the Oriental patrimonialism of the mainland.
6 See especially T. Parsons, *The System of Modern Societies*, Englewood Cliffs NJ: The Free Press, 1971.
7 See Th. Barfield, *The Perilous Frontier*, New York: Blackwell, 1989.
8 L. Vandermeersch, op.cit. pp. 127–51

9 C. Gluck, 'The fine folly of the encyclopedists', in A.V. Heinrich (ed.), *Currents in Japanese Culture. Translations and Transformations*, New York, Columbia University Press, 1997, pp. 223–52, here p. 229.
10 For an interesting discussion, see D. Pollack, *The Fracture of Meaning: Japan's Synthesis of China from the Eighth to the Eighteenth Centuries*, Princeton: Princeton University Press, 1986.
11 S.A. M. Adshead, *China in World History*, London: Macmillan, 1995, p. 309.
12 M. Jansen, *Japan and its World: Two Centuries of Change*, Princeton: Princeton University Press, 1989, p. 11.
13 See S. C. Chu and Liu Kwang-ching, *Li Hung-chang and China's Early Modernization*, New York: M.E. Sharpe, 1994.
14 See especially G. Hoston, *The State, Identity and the National Question in China and Japan*, Princeton: Princeton University Press, 1984.
15 See N. Jacobs, *The Korean Road to Modernization and Development*, Urbana: University of Illinois Press, 1985.
16 J.B. Palais, 'Confucianism and the aristocratic-bureaucratic balance in Korea', *Harvard Journal of Asiatic Studies* 44:2 (1984), pp. 427–68; 'A search for Korean uniqueness', *Harvard Journal of Asiatic Studies* 55:2 (1995), pp. 409–25.
17 G. Rozman, 'Comparisons of modern Confucian values in China and Japan', in id. (ed.), *The East Asian Region: Confucian Heritage and its Modern Adaptation*, Princeton: Princeton University Press, 1991, pp. 157–203.
18 G. Rozman, 'The East Asian region in comparative perspective', ibid., pp. 3–42, here p. 32.
19 G. Rozman, 'Comparisons…', p. 164.
20 Ibid., p. 166.
21 Ibid., p. 167.
22 See E. Ikegami, *The Taming of the Samurai*, Cambridge/MA: Harvard University Press, 1995.
23 See, e.g., B. Cumings, 'The origin and development of the Northeast Asian political economy: Industrial sectors, product cycles and political consequences', *International Organization* 38:1 (1984), pp. 1–40.
24 R. Brague, *Europe: La voie romaine*, Paris: Criterion, 1993.
25 D. Obolensky, *The Byzantine Commonwealth: Eastern Europe, 500–1453*, London: Weidenfeld & Nicholson, 1971;

G. Fowden, *From Empire to Commonwealth: Consequences of Monotheism in Late Antiquity*, Princeton: Princeton University Press, 1993.
26 Fowden, op.cit., p. 170.
27 D. N. Levine, 'Ethiopia and Japan in comparative civilizational perspective', *Passages: Interdisciplinary Journal of Global Studies*, 3: 1 (2001), pp. 1–32.

4 Is Japan a Civilization *Sui Generis*?

1 I have discussed the relevant work of Durkheim and Mauss elsewhere: J.P. Arnason, 'Social theory and the concept of civilization', *Thesis Eleven* 20 (1988), pp.87–105, esp. 88–95. Cf. also their 'Note on the notion of civilization', translated and introduced by B. Nelson, *Social Research* 38:9 (1971), pp.808–13. For a condensed but very informative history of the concepts of culture and civilization cf. Jörg Fisch, 'Zivilisation, Kultur', in *Geschichtliche Grundbegriffe*, vol.7, Stuttgart 1997, pp.679–774.
2 Cf. M. Mauss, 'Civilisations – éléments – formes', in id., *Oeuvres*, t.2 (ed. V. Karady), Paris: Ed. de Minuit, 1968, pp.456–523.
3 Eisenstadt has not published a systematic exposition of his civilizational theory; his ideas on the subject have mostly been developed in conjunction with more specific themes, such as the comparative study of Axial civilizations. Brief but representative accounts can be found in the introduction to the second edition of his *Political Systems of Empires*, New Brunswick: Transaction Books, 1992 and the introduction to *The Origin and Diversity of Axial Civilizations*, Albany: State University of New York Press, 1986.
4 It should be noted that some significant attempts have been made to reconnect the problematic of this tradition to sociological inquiry. In this context, the work of Jaroslav Krejcí deserves more attention than it has so far received; cf. especially his essays 'Religion and civilization', *Religion* 12 (1987), p.29–47, and 'Civilisation and social formation', *History of European Ideas* 8:3 (1987), pp.349–60.
5 On the Japanese appropriation and ideological use of Western concepts of culture cf. Tessa Morris-Suzuki; 'The invention and reinvention of Japanese culture', *Journal of Asian Studies* 54:3 (1995), pp.759–80.

6 Cf. especially B. Schwartz, *China's Cultural Values*. Occasional Paper no. 18, Center for Asian Studies, Arizona State University, 1985, and *The World of Thought in Ancient China*, Cambridge/MA: Harvard University Press, 1982. For a critical discussion of Schwartz's views, as well as other approaches to the problem, cf. A. J. Nathan, 'Is Chinese culture distinctive?', *Journal of Asian Studies* 52:4 (1993), pp. 923–36.
7 Schwartz, *World of Thought*, p.412.
8 Cf. the discussion in Schwartz, *The World of Thought*; and the rejoinder by Th. A. Metzger, 'The definition of the self, the group, the cosmos, and knowledge in Chou thought: Some comments on Professor Schwartz's study', *American Asian Review* 4:2(1986), pp.68–116.
9 For a pioneering analysis of the beginnings of imperial Japan from this point of view (as an adaptation of Chinese notions of order), cf. P. Beonio-Brocchieri, 'La "tradizione del Tao" e l'idea della continuità nazionale nel pensiero politico giapponese,' in V. Beonio-Brocchieri (ed.), *Stato, popolo e nazione nelle culture extra-europee*, Milano 1965, pp. 31–67.
10 This is the term used by David Pollack, *The Fracture of Meaning: Japan's Synthesis of China from the Eighth to the Eighteenth Centuries*, Princeton: Princeton University Press, 1986.
11 Cf. Joan Piggott, *The Emergence of Japanese Kingship*, Stanford: Stanford University Press. 1996.
12 Beonio-Brocchieri, op.cit., p.47.
13 Ph. Pelletier, *La Japonésie: Géopolitique et géographie historique de la surinsularité au Japon*, Paris 1997.
14 On primary and secondary state formation, cf. J.P. Arnason, 'State formation in Japan and the West', *Theory, Culture and Society*, 13:3 (1996), pp. 53–76 (now in this volume).
15 Here I draw on the work of Andrew Goble: *Kenmu: Go-Daigo's Revolution*, Cambridge MA: Harvard University Press 1996, and 'Social change, knowledge, and history: Hanazono's *Admonitions to the Crown Prince*', *Harvard Journal of Asiatic Studies* 55:1 (1995), pp.61–128. Goble sums up Hanazono's reflections in the following terms (p.64–65): 'In addressing the ideas of history and rulership in the *Admonitions*, Hanazono does not give dominant emphasis to Buddhism or Shintō; he evinces a quite different conception of history than that put forward by Jien and Chikafusa; he more

or less rejects outright the tenet that somehow continuity through the Imperial institution is a notable and unique characteristic of Japan, and in addition he suggests that divine descent is a very poor ideology of political legitimation'. But these potentially explosive ideas did not reach beyond a marginal section of court society.

16 Cf. the introduction to S. Tönnesson and H. Antlöv (eds.), *Asian Forms of the Nation*, Richmond: Curzon Press, 1996.
17 J.W. Dower, *Embracing Defeat*, New York: W. W. Norton, 1999.
18 Cf. particularly H. Ooms, *Tokugawa Ideology*, Princeton: Princeton University Press, 1987.

5 State Formation in Japan and the West

An earlier version of this paper was presented to a session on figurational sociology at the ISA congress in Bielefeld in 1994. The revised version has benefited from the comments of various participants, especially Johan Goudsblom, Helmut Kuzmics and Stephen Mennell; the distinction between composite and unitary states, not included in the first version, grew out of conversations with them. It should be noted that the paper was finished before Eiko Ikegami's *The Taming of the Samurai: Honorific Individualism and the Making of Modern Japan* (Cambridge, MA: Harvard University Press, 1995) became available.

1 For a representative example of recent approaches to state formation, see Charles Tilly, *Coercion, Capital and European States, AD 990–1990*, Oxford: Blackwell, 1990. The only explicit reference to Elias in this book is a comment to the effect that the monopolies of taxation and violence form 'two voices of a trio', and that the missing link is credit (p. 85). But here Tilly misses Elias's point: credit is not a monopoly like the two other mechanisms. Elias was interested in monopolizing processes as the core dynamics of state formation, and it was obvious to him that various complementary factors are involved, including credit which is admittedly a very important one, especially – as Tilly notes – in relation to mercenary armies. As for the theoretical framework, Tilly constructs a typology of earlier – and as he sees it, one-sided – conceptions of state formation: they stress either the internal or the external origins of states, and either their dependence or

independence with regard to the economy. A combination of these two distinctions results in a fourfold classification: theories of the mode of production (internal and dependent), world system theories (external and dependent), statist theories (internal and independent) and geopolitical theories (external and independent). There is no attempt to fit Elias into this scheme. In fact, it could he argued that he had already relativized both distinctions: he analysed the growth of internal state structures in close connection with interstate competition, but did not attribute any systemic primacy to the patterns of the latter, and he treated state formation and economic (more particularly: commercial and capitalist) development as interconnected long-term processes whose relative weight could vary without making either of them purely dependent or wholly independent.

2 J. Fulcher ('The bureaucratisation of the state and the rise of Japan', *British Journal of Sociology* 39:2 (1988, pp. 228–54) stresses the importance of Japan for the comparative study of bureaucracy. But bureaucratization should he seen as one – albeit crucial – aspect of the more complex process of state formation.

3 N. Elias, *Über den Prozess der Zivilisation* Bd. 1, Frankfurt: Suhrkamp Verlag, 1977, p. 1, and *The Civilizing Process*, Oxford: Blackwell, 1994, p. 269.

4 N. Elias, *The Court Society*, Oxford: Blackwell, 1993.

5 On this problematic see Norman F. Cantor, *Inventing the Middle Ages*, New York: Morrow&Co., 1991. There is nothing to show that this author has taken note of Elias; and more generally speaking, his discussion of the sociological contribution to the 'invention' (this is a needlessly provocative term for an ongoing effort of interpretative reconstruction) leaves more than a little to he desired.

6 See P. Clastres, *Society Against the State*, Oxford: Blackwell, 1977, and M. Gauchet, *The Disenchantment of the World*, Princeton: Princeton University Press, 1997.

7 See S. N. Eisenstadt, M. Abitbol and N. Chazan, 'Les origines de l'État: une nouvelle approche', *Annales: Économies, Sociétés, Civilisations*, 38:6 (1983), pp. 1232–55.

8 Elias, *The Civilizing Process*, p. 273–86.

9 See T. N. Bisson, 'The "feudal revolution"', *Past and Present*, 142 (1994), pp. 6–42.

10 See C. Morris, *The Papal Monarchy*, Oxford: Clarendon Press, 1989.
11 On conquest and expansion during the High Middle Ages, see R. Bartlett, *The Making of Europe: Conquest, Colonization and Cultural Change 950–1350*, Princeton: Princeton University Press, 1993.
12 See D. Abulafia, *Frederick II. A Medieval Emperor*, London: Allen Lane, 1988.
13 See T. Barfield, *The Perilous Frontier: Nomadic Empires and China*, Oxford: Blackwell, 1989.
14 See C. J. Halperin, 'The ideology of silence: Prejudice and pragmatism on the medieval religious frontier', *Comparative Studies in Society and History* 26:3 (1984), pp. 442–66.
15 H. Koenigsberger, *Medieval Europe, 400–1500*, London: Longman, 1987, p. 341.
16 One connection worth noting is the Byzantine source of the heresies that began to spread in the West in the early 11th century (see J. P. Poly and E Bournazel, *La mutation féodale*, Paris: PUF, 1991, pp. 421–36). This challenge was one of the reasons for structural reforms within the Church, which in turn influenced the progress of state formation.
17 See H. G. Creel, *The Origins of Statecraft in China*, vol. 1, Chicago: Chicago University Press, 1970, pp. 12–24.
18 See M. Raeff, *The Well-Ordered Police State*, New Haven and London: Yale University Press, 1983.
19 See H. Koenigsberger, '*Dominium regale* or *Dominium politicum et regale*: Monarchies and parliaments in early modern Europe', in id. , *Politicians and Virtuosi: Essays in Early Modern History*, London: Hambledon Press, 1986, pp. 1–26.
20 I have discussed this question at length in other papers (J.P. Arnason, 'Figurational sociology as a counter-paradigm', *Theory, Culture and Society* 4:2–3 (1987), pp. 427–56, and 'Civilization, culture and power: Reflections on Norbert Elias's genealogy of the West', *Thesis Eleven* 24 (1989), pp. 44–70.). Briefly, the underdeveloped character of Elias's theory of culture affects his argument on three different levels. With regard to basic concepts, the description of the human condition as a set of basic controls – i.e. a network of power – tends to reduce cultural patterns and orientations to one form of power among others. The historical reconstruction of the

Western process of state formation neglects its cultural dimension; more specifically, the role of changing and often conflicting images and interpretations of power is not discussed. Finally, Elias's emphasis on continuity between modernity and its medieval prehistory leads him to disregard the cultural rupture inherent in the transition to modernity.

21 Se G. Barnes, *China, Korea and Japan. The Rise of Civilisation in East Asia*, London: Thames& Hudson, 1993. It should be noted that this author uses the term 'secondary state formation for what I call 'dependent' or 'derivative' processes.

22 See I. Mitsusada, 'The century of reform', in D. Brown (ed.), *The Cambridge History of Japan*, vol, 1, Cambridge: Cambridge University Press, 1993, pp. 163–220.

23 For different versions of this new approach, see J. P. Mass, *Antiquity and Anachronism in Japanese History*, Stanford: Stanford University Press, 1992, and W. W. Farris, *Heavenly Warriors. The Evolution of Japan's Military 500–1300*, Cambridge, MA: Harvard University Press, 1992.

24 J.P. Mass, 'The emergence of the Kamakura *bakufu*', in J. W Hall and J. P. Mass (eds.), *Medieval Japan – Essays in Institutional History*, New Haven and London: Yale University Press, 1974, pp. 127–56, here p. 127.

25 J.P. Mass, 'The Kamakura *bakufu*', in K. Yamamura (ed.), *The Cambridge History of Japan*, vol. 3, Cambridge: Cambridge University Press, 1990, pp. 46–88, here p. 46.

26 J. W. Hall, 'The Muromachi *bakufu*', ibid., pp. 175–230, here p. 175.

27 See K. A. Grossberg, *Japan's Renaissance: The Politics of the Muromachi Bakufu*, Cambridge/MA: Harvard University Press.

28 For a seminal discussion of the changing role and character of the *daimyō*, see J. W. Hall, 'Foundations of the modern Japanese daimyo', *Journal of Asian Studies* 20:4 (1961), pp. 317–29; this text has been of decisive importance for all later discussions of the subject.

29 On various aspects of state formation in Tokugawa Japan, see H. Ooms, *Tokugawa Ideology*, Princeton: Princeton University Press, 1989; H. Bolitho, 'The *Han*', in K. Yamamura (ed.), *The Cambridge History of Japan*,vol. 4: *Early Modern Japan*, Cambridge: Cambridge University Press, 1991, pp. 183–234; M.E. Berry, 'Public peace and private attachment: The goals

and conduct of power in early modern Japan', *Journal of Japanese Studies* 12: 2 (1986), pp. 237–72; P. C. Brown, *Central Authority and Local Autonomy in the Formation of Early Modern Japan*, Stanford: Stanford University Press, 1993; J. H. White, 'State growth and popular protest in Japan', *Journal of Japanese Studies* 14: 1 (1988), pp. 1–26; C. Totman, *Early Modern Japan*, Berkeley: University of California Press, 1993.

30 See C. Johnson, *MITI and the Japanese Miracle*, Stanford: Stanford University Press, 1982.
31 See especially R. P. Toby, *State and Diplomacy in Early Modern Japan. Asia in the Development of the Tokugawa Bakufu*, Stanford: Stanford University Press, 1991.
32 See H. Conroy, *The Japanese Seizure of Korea, 1868–1910*. Philadelphia: University of Pennsylvania Press, 1960.
33 For critical – and sometimes overly polemical – reflections on post-war Japan as an incomplete state see K. van Wolferen, *The Enigma of Japanese Power: People and Politics in a Stateless Nation*, London: Macmillan, 1989, and M. Tamamoto, 'Reflections on Japan's postwar state', *Daedalus* 124:2 (1995), pp. 1–22.

6 Elias in Japan: State Power, Military Elites and Organized Violence

1 N. Elias, *The Civilizing Process: The History of Manners* and *State Formation and Civilization,* Oxford: Blackwell, 1994, pp. 526–27, n. 22
2 See N. Elias, *The Court Society,* Oxford: Blackwell, 1993. For a more recent discussion, see J. Duindam, *Myths of Power,* Amsterdam: Amsterdam University Press, 1995.
3 M. E. Berry, 'Public peace and private attachment: The goals and conduct of power in early modern Japan', *Journal of Japanese Studies* 12:2 (1986), pp. 237–72, here p. 242.
4 The most radical recent challenge to traditional conceptions of feudalism is Susan Reynolds, *Fiefs and Vassals: The Medieval Evidence Reinterpreted*, Oxford: Oxford University Press, 1994. Reynolds argues that the idea of feudalism grew out of misconstructions of the medieval evidence by later lawyers and scholars. Although her argument cannot be discussed here, it may be suggested that a more nuanced reading of it would

converge with the above interpretation of Elias's work: if feudalism is to be understood as an integral part of a process of state formation, rather than a self-contained system, it seems likely that it was misunderstood by those who considered it from the viewpoint of a more advanced phase of the process. A historical analysis of the feudal phenomenon would, in other words, involve a twofold relativization: it must be seen in the context of a more complex power structure, and distinguished form the over-rationalized constructs of later interpreters. That said, it still seems useful to retain the concept of feudalism to describe certain aspects of the socio-political structure of medieval Western Christendom: it denotes a peculiar pattern of fragmented authority, counterbalanced by specific forms of hierarchy.

5 Elias, *The Civilizing Process,* p. 402.
6 See the review article by M. Collcutt, 'The "emergence of the samurai" and the military history of early Japan', *Harvard Journal of Asiatic Studies* 56:`1(1996), pp. 151–64. Collcutt rightly stresses the divergences between recent accounts of the origins of the samurai. What is being suggested here is that a clearer focus on state formation might help to integrate different perspectives into a coherent picture.
7 E. Ikegami, *The Taming of the Samurai: Honorific Individualism and the Making of Modern Japan,* Cambridge, MA: Harvard University Press, 1995, p. 34.
8 See ibid., pp. 47–77.
9 Ibid., pp. 29–31.
10 For a recent discussion of the origins and character of medieval Western knighthood, see F. Erkens, 'Militia und Ritterschaft: Reflexionen über die Entstehung des Rittertums', *Historische Zeitschrift* 258:3 (1994), pp. 623–59.
11 E. J. Shultz, *Generals and Scholars: Military Rule in Medieval Korea,* Honolulu: University of Hawai'i Press, 2000, p. 85.
12 See H. Ooms, *Tokugawa Ideology,* Princeton: Princeton University Press, 1989, pp. 3–62.

7 Multiple Modernities and Civilizational Contexts: Reflections on the Japanese Experience

1 See especially C. Black et al. (eds), *The Modernization of Japan and Russia*, NewYork1976; R.E. Ward and D. Rustow (eds.),

Political Modernization in Japan and Turkey, Princeton: Princeton University Press, 1964.
2 Cf. B. Anderson, 'Studies of the Thai state: The state of Thai studies', in E.B. Ayal (ed.), *The Study of Thailand,* Ohio University 1978, pp. 193–247.
3 A. Giddens, *The Nation-State and Violence,* Cambridge: Polity Press, 1985, p. 473–4.
4 For a succinct introductory discussion of these issues, cf. Akira Iriye, 'Japan's drive to great power status', in *The Cambridge History of Japan ,*vol. 5*: The Nineteenth Century,* Cambridge: Cambridge University Press, 1985, pp. 473–4.
5 Cf. particularly M. Maruyama, *Thought and Behaviour in Japanese Politics,* 2.ed., London: Oxford University Press, 1963.
6 Cf. particularly J.L. McLain et al. (eds.), *Edo and Paris: Urban Life and the State in the Early Modern Era,* Ithaca: Cornell University Press, 1994; and A. Macfarlane, 'Japan in an English mirror', *Modern Asian Studies* 31:4 (1997), pp. 763–806.
7 Cf. the contributions in *Modern Asian Studies* 31:3 (1997), edited and introduced by V. Lieberman.
8 G. Rozman et al. (eds.), *The East Asian Region: Confucian Heritage and its Modern Adaptation,* Princeton: Princeton University Press, 1991.
9 This point is made by M. Geyer and Ch. Bright in 'Global violence and nationalizing wars in Eurasia and America: The geopolitics of war in the mid-nineteenth century', *Comparative Studies in Society and History* 38:4 (1996), pp. 619–57.
10 Cf. B. Cumings, 'The origins and development of the Northeast Asian political economy', *International Organization* 38:1 (1984), pp. 1–40.
11 Cf. M. Maruyama, *Denken in Japan,* Frankfurt/M: Suhrkamp Verlag, 1988.
12 T. Parsons, *The System of Modern Societies,* Englewood Cliffs: Tree Press, 1971, pp. 134–7.
13 Cf. S.N. Eisenstadt, *Japanese Civilization: A Comparative View,* Chicago: Chicago University Press 1996, p. 23–49.
14 Cf. Murakami Yasusuke, 'Modernization in terms of integration: The case of Japan', in S.N. Eisenstadt (ed.), *Patterns of Modernity,* vol.2*: Beyond the West,* London: Pinter, 1987, pp. 65–88.
15 Cf. S.N. Eisenstadt and B. Giesen, 'The construction of

collective identity', *Archives Europeennes de Sociologie* 36 (1995), pp. 72–102.
16 Cf. C. Gluck, *Japan's Modern Myths*, Princeton: Princeton University Press, 1985.
17 Cf. K. Doak, 'Ethnic nationalism and romanticism in early twentieth-century Japan', *Journal of Japanese Studies* 22:1(1996), pp. 77–103.
18 L. Vandermeersch, *Le nouveau monde sinisé*, Paris: PUF, 1985, pp. 152–3.
19 Cf. L. Vandermeersch, *Wangdao ou la voie royale: Recherches sur l'esprit des institutions de la Chine archaique,* vol. 1–2, Paris: EFEO, 1977 and 1980; id., *Le nouveau monde sinisé*; J.F. Billeter, 'La civilisation chinoise', in J. Poirier et al. (eds.), *Histoire des moeurs*, vol. 3, Paris: Gallimard, 1993, pp. 865–931. Billeter also draws attention to the interesting but neglected work of L. E. Stover, *The Cultural Ecology of Chinese Civilization*, New York: Pica Press, 1974.
20 Cf. Vandermeersch, *Le nouveau monde sinisé*, pp. 152–203.
21 Cf. Eisenstadt, *Japanese Civilization*.
22 Ibid., p. 321.
23 Ibid., p. 421.
24 Cf. Eisenstadt and Giesen, 'The construction of collective identity'.

8 Miracles and Mirages: Comparative Perspectives on Japanese Capitalism

1 For an interesting version of this argument, see Fosco Maraini, 'Japan, the essential modernizer', in S. Henny and J.P. Lehmann, *Themes and Theories in Modern Japanese History,* London: The Athlone Press, 1988, pp.44–63. Maraini's thesis is that the pre-adaptive capacities of Japanese culture are grounded in the most enduring characteristics of its religious heritage.
2 Such predictions were made by high-profile social scientists; for example, Immanuel Wallerstein ('Japan and the future trajectory of the world system: lessons from history', in id., *Geopolitics and Geoculture*, Cambridge: Cambridge University Press, 1991, pp.36–48; first published in 1987) saw Japan and Western Europe as two possible successors to US hegemony, and thought that Japan was more likely to win.

3   See Pierre-Antoine Donnet and Anne Garrique, *Le Japon: la fin d' une économie*, Paris: Folio-Actuel, 2000.
4   A prime example of the early polarizing approach is Michel Albert, *Capitalism vs Capitalism*, New York: Four Walls Eight Windows, 1993 (first published in French in 1991). Here the main contrast is between 'Anglo-Saxon' and 'Rhenan' models, and Japanese capitalism appears as an offshoot of the Rhenan type. For representative examples of the later discussion, see J.F. Bayart (ed.), *La réinvention du capitalisme*, Paris: Karthala, 1994.
5   L. Boltanski – E. Chiapello, *Le nouvel esprit du capitalisme*, Paris: Gallimard, 1999.
6   F. Braudel, *Civilisation matérielle,économie et capitalisme, XV–XVIIIe siècle, t.3: Le temps du monde*, Paris: Armand Colin, 1979, p.540.
7   C. Castoriadis, "La 'rationalité' du capitalisme", in id., *Figures du pensable*, Paris: Editions du Seuil, 1999, pp.65–92.
8   See Boltanski and Chiapello, op. cit., pp.48–50.
9   This seems a better translation of Braudel's 'économie-monde' than 'world economy'; the latter has hitherto been preferred by English translators, but should be reserved for the more literally worldwide formations.
10 Braudel, op. cit., t.2, p.534.
11 See C. Castoriadis, *The Imaginary Institution of Society*, Cambridge: Polity Press, 1987, pp. 135–56. To sum up, imaginary significations may be described as constellations of meaning which transcend experiential sources, rational structures and functional imperatives.
12 See especially K. Pomeranz, *The Great Divergence: China, Europe and the Making of the Modern World Economy*, Princeton: Princeton University Press, 2000.
13 Braudel, op. cit., t.2, p.529.
14 N. Jacobs, *The Origin of Modern Capitalism and Eastern Asia*, New York: Octagon Books, 1981 (first published in 1958), p.xi.
15 N. Jacobs, *The Korean Road to Modernization and Development*, Urbana and Chicago: University of Illinois Press, 1985, p.6.
16 Jacobs, *Origin...*, pp.21, 215.
17 Braudel, op. cit., t.2, p. 528.
18 Ibid., t.1, p.382.
19 See especially R. Bin Wong, *China Transformed*, Ithaca:

Cornell University Press, 1997. Pomeranz, op. cit.; S.R. Epstein, *Freedom and Growth: Markets and States in Modern Europe,* London and New York: Routledge, 2000; G. Deng, *The Premodern Chinese Economy,* London and New York: Routledge, 1999; P.H.H. Vries, 'Are coal and colonies really crucial?', *Journal of World History*, 12:2 (2001), pp.407–446.
20 Vries, op. cit., p.421.
21 Wong, op. cit., p.17.
22 C. Totman, *Early Modern Japan*, Berkeley: University of California Press, 1993, p.159.
23 See S. B. Hanley and K. Yamamura, *Economic and Demographic Change in Preindustrial Japan 1600–1868,* Princeton: Princeton University Press, 1977. For a discussion which stresses both the diversity of Marxist approaches (some of which had already challenged conventional wisdom about the eighteenth century) and the complexity of rural society in late Tokugawa Japan, see B. Bernier, *Capitalisme, société et culture au Japon,* Montréal: Presses de l'Université de Montréal, 1988, pp.105.44.
24 T. C. Smith, *Native Sources of Japanese Industrialization, 1750–1920*, Berkeley: University of California Press, 1988, p.35.
25 C. Totman, *A History of Japan*, Oxford: Blackwell, 2000, p.246.
26 Ibid., p.257.
27 T. Najita, *Visions of Virtue in Tokugawa Japan*, Chicago: The University of Chicago Press, 1987, p.59.
28 Ibid., p.287.
29 For an interpretation of *kokueki* thought as a radical antithesis to Confucian 'physiocratism', see G. Distelrath, *Die Japanische Produktionsweise,* München: iudicium verlag, 1996, pp.63–80. The section on *kokueki* is useful, but the notion of a closed Confucian orthodoxy seems incompatible with the results of recent scholarship on Tokugawa thought. But this is only one aspect of a more general problem. Distelrath's main aim is to demolish a set of misconceptions about Japanese economy and society, supposedly common to Marxists who draw more or less directly on the notion of an Asiatic mode of production, Weberians who applied and expanded the concept of patrimonialism, modernization theorists who stress the Confucian legacy, and economists

who take a state-centred view of the Japanese system. The following formulation is typical of the whole argument: 'In Marx's work, the 'Asiatic theory' (Wittfogel) refers to a neglected and deviant case, but for Max Weber, it became a necessary basis for his whole theoretical construct' (p.40). A vaguely defined but vehemently rejected 'Asiatic theory' seems to have migrated across a whole spectrum of intellectual traditions. And to cap it all, this unwieldy amalgam is subsumed under the stereotype of 'Orientalism'.

30 L.S. Roberts, *Mercantilism in a Japanese Domain: The Merchant Origins of Economic Nationalism in 18th Century Tosa*, Cambridge: Cambridge University Press, 1998.
31 Ibid., p.2.
32 Ibid., p.10.
33 Najita, op. cit., p.9.
34 The most thorough Western-language analysis of Meiji nationalism is C. Gluck, *Japan's Modern Myths: Ideology in the Late Meiji Period*, Princeton, Princeton University Press, 1885.
35 The model of *ie* society, developed by Murakami Yasusuke and his associates, is a prime example of the search for civilizational invariants. On this view, a specific cultural model of organization is encoded in the Japanese tradition; it can appear in tightly structured as well as attenuated versions, which Murakami defines respectively as the *ie* and the *mura* prototype. For a succinct presentation of these ideas in the context of political economy, see Y. Murakami, 'The Japanese model of political economy', in K. Yamamura and Y. Yasuba (eds.), *The Political Economy of Japan*, vol.1, Stanford: Stanford University Press, 1987, pp.33–90.
36 C. Deutschmann, *Die Verheissung des absoluten Reichtums*, Frankfurt: Campus Verlag, 1999; 'The promise of absolute wealth: Capitalism as a religion', *Thesis Eleven* 66 (2001), pp.32–56.
37 Deutschmann, 'The promise…, p.41.
38 See the classic discussion by A. Hirschman, *The Passions and the Interests: Political Arguments for Capitalism Before its Triumph,* Princeton: Princeton University Press, 1977.
39 Bernier, op.cit., p. 4.
40 R.J. Samuels, *Rich Nation, Strong Army: National Security*

and the Technological Transformation of Japan, Ithaca: Cornell University Press, 1994, p.31.
41 Y. Murakami, op. cit., p. 48. On business ideology in imperial Japan, see B.K. Marshall, *Capitalism and Nationalism in Prewar Japan*, Stanford: Stanford University Press, 1967.
42 M.R. Peattie, 'The Japanese colonial empire, 1895–1945', in P. Duus (ed.), *The Cambridge History of Japan*, vol.6: *The Twentieth Century*, Cambridge: Cambridge University Press, 1988, pp.217–70, here p.218.
43 L. Young, *Japan's Total Empire: Manchuria and the Culture of Wartime Imperialism,* Berkeley: University of California Press, 1998, p.18.
44 C. Kupchan, *The Vulnerability of Empire,* Ithaca: Cornell University Press, 1994, p. 299.
45 The most systematic analysis of this problematic is G. S. Hoston, *Marxism and the Crisis of Development in Prewar Japan* Princeton: Princeton University Press, 1986, and *The State, Identity and the National Question in China and Japan,* Princeton: Princeton University Press, 1984. As Hoston shows, the *tenkō* episode (the public conversion of some Japanese Communist leaders) was only one aspect (admittedly a very important one) of a more complex process. On Takahashi, see *Marxism and the Crisis*, pp. 76–94.
46 C. Johnson, 'The developmental state: Odyssey of a concept' in M. Woo-Cumings (ed.), *The Developmental State*, Ithaca: Cornell University Press, 32–60, here p.34.
47 See P. Evans, *Embedded Autonomy: States and Industrial Transformations*, Princeton: Princeton University Press, 1995.
48 L. Weiss, *The Myth of the Powerless State,* Cambridge: Polity Press, 1998.
49 D. Coates, *Models of Capitalism: Growth and Stagnation in the Modern Era*, Cambridge: Polity Press, 2000, p. 228
50 B. Gao, *Economic Ideology and Japanese Industrial Policy,* Cambridge: Cambridge University Press, 1997.
51 Ibid., p.99.
52 See ibid., pp.109–10, on Japanese interest in the Tennessee Valley Authority.
53 Ibid., p.22.
54 This is the title of the last chapter of the book: ibid., pp.225–79.

55 T.J. Pempel, *Regime Shift: Comparative Dynamics of the Japanese Political Economy*, Ithaca Cornell University Press, p.20.
56 T.J. Pempel, 'The developmental regime in a changing world economy', in Woo-Cumings, op.cit., pp.137–81, here p.157.
57 Ibid., p.160.
58 Ibid., p.176.
59 Pempel, *Regime Shift,* p.29.
60 Ibid., p. 42–80. On the changing relationship between state, business and labour in the later phase of the regime, see W. Seifert, *Gewerkschaften in der japanischen Politik von 1910 bis 1990,* Opladen:Westdeutscher Verlag, 1998.
61 This is the title of an earlier work; T.J. Pempel, *Policy and Politics in Japan: Creative Conservatism,* Philadelphia: Temple University Press, 1982.
62 Gao, op. cit., p.2.
63 Pempel, 'The developmental regime', p.142.
64 S.N. Eisenstadt, *Japanese Civilization: A Comparative View*, Chicago: Chicago University Press, 1996, pp.54–64; see also ibid., pp.292–93.
65 Ibid., p.292.
66 M. Gerlach, *Alliance Capitalism: The Social Organization of Japanese Business,* Berkeley: University of California Press, 1992.
67 See Murakami, op. cit., pp. 41–56, and id., *An Anticlassical Political-Economic Analysis,* Stanford: Stanford University Press, 1996, especially pp. 144–228.

Index

Abitbol, Michel 213 n
absolutism/absolutist state 93–94, 99–100, 118–122
Abulafia, David 214 n
Adolphson, Michael 21, 214n
Adshead, S.A.M. 209n
Aksumite state 65
Albert, Michel 220n
America s. United States
Amino, Yoshihiko 20, 83, 204n
Amsterdam 171
Anderson, Benedict 218n
Antlöv, Hans 212n
Antwerpen 171
Arnason, Johann P. 203n, 210–211n
Asakawa, Kan'ichi 16
Ashikaga, Yoshimitsu 113
Asiatic societies 169, 221–222n
axial and non-axial civilizations s. civilizations

bakufu s. shogunate
bakuhan system 110–111
Bali 204n
Barfield, Thomas 208n, 219n
Barnes, Gina 215n
Bartlett, Robert 214n
Bayart, Jean-Francois 207n, 219n
Beja, Jean-Pierre 206n

Beonio-Brocchieri, Paolo 82, 211n
Bernier, Bertrand 185, 221–222n
Berry, Mary Elizabeth 120, 204n, 215–216n
Billeter, Jean-Francois 148, 219n
Bisson, T. N. 213n
Black, Cyril 217n
Bloch, Marc 62, 105
Bohemia 101
Bolitho, Harold 215n
Boltanski, Luc 161–164, 183, 187, 195, 220n
Bonwit, Ralf 117
bourgeoisie 121–122, 172
bourgeois revolution 171–172
Bournazel, Eric 214n
Brague, Rémi 62, 209n
Brandenburg 96
Braudel, Fernand 164–174, 178–179, 184, 220n
Bright, Charles 218n
Britain 135, 173, 197
Brown, Philip C. 216n
Buddhism/Buddhist establishment 15–16, 21–22, 44, 53–54, 65, 77, 80–81, 85, 105–106, 147, 153, 211n
    Kamakura 128
    kenmitsu system 21–22

225

Zen 128
bunmei kaika 139
Byzantium 64–65, 99
 Byzantine commonwealth 64–65

Cantor, Norman F. 213n
capitalism/capitalist
 development 27–28, 32–34, 120, 137, 158
 critique of 161–164, 195
 East Asian 150
 genealogy of 164–168
 Japanese 92–93, 142–143, 155, 158–202
 operative myths of 174–175, 184–185
 reinventions of 160
 spirit of 32–34, 161–164, 178–180, 183–185, 187, 195
 varieties of 160–161, 167–168, 192
Carolingians 94–95, 105
Case, Margaret 208n
Castoriadis, Cornelius 74, 145, 165–166, 184, 196, 220n
Catholic Church 95, 128–129
Central Asia 45, 204n
centre and periphery
 in geopolitics 1–2
 in Japanese history 1–5, 10–23
 in social theory 5–12
 urban and rural 175–176
Chang, Carsun 206n
Chazan, Naomi 213n
Chevrier, Yves 37, 207n
Chiapello, Eve 161–164, 185, 187, 195, 220n
China 2–3, 14, 18, 22, 24–29, 31–40, 45–59, 61–65, 68, 73–78, 97, 113–116, 136–138, 146–147, 169–170, 188–190
Chinese bureaucracy 99, 108
Chinese/Sinic civilization s. civilization
Chinese economic development 173–174
Chinese empire 2–3, 12–17, 37, 47–50, 62–65, 74, 77–78, 128, 204n
Chinese writing system 46–47, 149
Ch'oe family 129
Christianity/Christendom 64–65, 95, 109
 Western 96, 99
civilization
 Buddhist 54
 Chinese/Sinic 12–15, 39, 52, 53–55, 68, 73–78, 143, 148–152, 168
 Christian 53, 75
 civilizational nation 182, 202
 concept and theories of 66–73, 117, 145–146, 199–200
 Confucian 29, 53–55, 148
 Hindu 53, 74–75
 Indian 68
 intercivilizational encounters 72–73, 146–147
 Islamic 53, 68, 74–75, 168
 Japanese 10–14, 45, 61–63, 66, 68, 78–91, 141, 151–154; as a dual constellation, 154–157
 plurality of civilizations 5, 9–12, 61–63, 67–73
 Western 54, 62, 74, 93, 182
civil society 35–37

Clastres, Pierre 94, 213n
Coates, David 223n
Cohen, Theodore 206n
Cold War 24, 29–30
Collcutt, Martin 217n
collective identity 10, 89, 112, 143
Communism 147, 160
  Chinese 26, 28, 31–32, 50, 115, 137
  Japanese 202, 223n
  Soviet 26, 114–115, 136, 191, 193
Confucianism/Confucian tradition 3, 12, 15, 29–39, 53–60, 111, 136–138, 145
Confucian civilization s. civilization
  in China 54–59, 75–78, 80, 148–150, 206–207n
  in Japan 54–59, 86, 153–154, 156, 178–179, 183, 204n, 206–207n, 221n
  in Korea 52–53, 55, 206–207n
  neo-Confucianism 81, 89, 137, 207n
Conroy, Hilary 216n
court, imperial 16, 21–22, 105–107, 119, 157
court society 100
  Japanese and Western, compared 118–119
Creel, Herrlee G. 214n
crusader states 97
Cumings, Bruce 204n, 209n, 218n

daimyō 108–110, 215n
dao 15
Daoism 76–77, 80

Deng, Gang 221n
Deutschmann, Christoph 184–185, 222n
developmentalism 28, 188–203
developmental regime 195–199
developmental state 27, 34–35, 50–51, 59–61, 112, 151, 155, 191–203
democracy/democratization 35–36, 195
Dirlik, Arif 206n
Distelrath, Günter 221–222n
Doak, Kevin 219n
Donnet, Pierre-Antoine 220n
Dower, John W. 212n
Duby, Georges 128
Duindam, Jeroen 216n
Durkheim, Emile 14, 44, 67–69, 71, 73–74, 145, 162, 209n
Duus, Peter 223n

East Asia 2–3, 17, 22, 24–30, 32, 34–35, 41–42, 45–54, 58, 60, 62–64, 68, 113–116, 136–138, 115, 196, 204n
  as a civilizational constellation 144–148, 149–151, 163, 182, 188–189
Edo 11, 122, 171
Eisenstadt, Shmuel N. 5, 9–13, 34, 39, 45, 69–71, 80, 94, 141–144, 151–154, 200–201, 203n, 206–208n, 210n, 213n, 218–219n, 224n
Elias, Norbert 61, 67, 70–71, 92–97, 100–104, 106,

108, 110, 117–123, 125, 130–131, 212–217n
Elliott, John H. 100
Elman, Benjamin A. 207n
Elvin, Mark 38, 207–208
empires 9–10, 64–65
England 96, 101
Epstein, S. R. 221n
Erkens, Franz-Rainer 217n
Ethiopia 64–65, 133
ethnicity 19–20
Europe 2, 42–43, 62–63, 97, 119, 166, 170, 176
 East Central 27
 European expansion s. Western expansion
 European revolutions 172
 Western 22, 92–102, 121, 123
Evans, Peter 223n

Farris, William W. 215n
Fascism 147, 193
Feudalism
 in Europe 43, 62, 92–96, 105, 109–110, 117, 120–121, 169–170
 ideology of 128–129
 in Japan 43, 62, 92–93, 105–106, 109–110, 117, 120–121, 124, 169–170, 175, 177
Fisch, Jörg 209n
Fordism 163, 184
Fowden, Garth 64, 210n
France 50, 101, 110, 113, 135–136
Frederick II, Emperor 97
Fujiwara family 127
fukoku kyōhei 186
Fulcher, James 213n

Gao, Bai 193–195, 199, 223–224n
Garrique, Anne 220n
Gauchet, Marcel 213n
Geertz, Clifford 203n
gekokujō 18
Gerlach, Michael 200, 224n
Germany 29, 110, 113, 135, 187
Geyer, Michael 218n
Giddens, Anthony 7, 133, 218
Giesen, Bernhard 143, 153, 218–219n
Gluck, Carol 209n, 219n, 222n
Goble, Andrew 211n
Go-Daigo, Emperor 107–108
Goudsblom, Johan 212n
Greece
 Ancient 39, 62–63, 152
 Homeric 117
Greenfeld, Liah 203n
Grossberg, Kenneth 215n
Guomindang regime 115

Habsburg Empire 101–102
Hall, John W. 16, 215n
Halperin, Charles 214n
Han dynasty 14
Hanazono, Emperor 86, 211n
Hanley, Susan B. 175–176, 221n
Heian period 16, 20–21, 81, 103, 105, 201
Heinrich, Amy V. 209n
Henny, Sue 208n, 219n
Hermeneutics 6–7
Hideyoshi s. Toyotomi
Hintze, Otto 62, 117
Hirschman, Albert 222n

Hokkaido 177
Holcombe, Charles 204n
Hong Kong 31, 45
Honshū 20, 201
Hoston, Germaine 191, 209n, 223n
Huang, Philip 37, 207n
Hudson, Mark J. 204n
Huntington, Samuel J. 208n

ie/ie society 126–127, 201, 222n
Ieyasu s. Tokugawa
Ikegami, Eiko 124–125, 127, 131, 209, 212n, 217n
imperial institution 3–4, 11–12, 15–23, 51, 57, 79–91, 105–109, 110–112, 127, 181
India 9, 12, 22, 39, 88, 152
Inner Asia 2, 24, 46
Inoue, Mitsusada 215n
Iriye, Akira 219n
Ishimoda, Shō 204
Islam 47, 97, 99
Israel, ancient 39, 152
Italy 50, 187, 197
Itō, Hirobumi 88

Jacobs, Norman 169–170, 208–209n, 220
Jansen, Marius 209n
Japanese civilization s. civilization
  empire/imperialism 26, 46, 114–115, 135, 138, 185–191; and developmentalism, 188–189, 193–194
  hegemony 159
  miracle 27, 159, 174

Jien 211
Johnson, Chalmers 112, 142, 191, 216n, 223n

Kamakura period 21–22, 81, 201
  regime s. shogunate
Keene, Donald 171
keiretsu groupings 201
kenmitsu s. Buddhism
Kenmu restoration 16–17, 86, 107–108, 157, 204n
kingship, Japanese 15–16, 79–80, 82, 104–105
Kitabatake, Chikafusa 204n, 211n
Koenigsberger, Helmut 99–100, 214n
kokueki thought 179–180, 221n
kokugaku (School of Native Learning) 90
Korea 2–3, 24, 26, 27–29, 35, 41, 45, 48–49, 51–53, 55, 81, 83–84, 87, 98, 113–114, 116, 129, 136–138, 146–147, 196
  aristocracy and bureaucracy 52–53
  military rule 129
  slavery 52–53
  yangban class 52–53
Korean War 28
Krader, Lawrence 204n
Krejcí, Jaroslav 210n
kuni and *shima*, duality of 83
Kupchan, Charles 223n
Kuroda, Toshio 21–22, 204n
Kuzmics, Helmut 212n
Kyoto 16, 174
Kyushu 109

229

LDP (Liberal Democratic Party) 198–199
Legalism 11, 150
Lehmann, Jean-Pierre 208n, 219n
Leites, Edmund 208n
Leninism s. Marxism-Leninism
Levine, Donald N. 64–65, 210
Lewis, Bernard 208n
liberalism/liberal democracy 147, 159–160, 201
Lieberman, Victor 218n
Liu, Kwang-ching 209n
London 171
Lone, Stewart 206n
Luhmann, Niklas 141

McCormack, Gavan 206n
Macfarlane, Alan 136, 218n
McClain, James L. 218n
Manchuria 26–27, 138, 189–190, 193
Mann, Michael 7
Maoism 29, 35
Mao Zedong 76
Maraini, Fosco 208n, 219n
market economy, Braudel's conception of 165–167
Marshall, Byron K. 223n
Martin, M. 203n
Maruyama, Masao 139, 143, 181, 218n
Marx, Karl 42, 184
Marxism 44, 92, 117, 122, 124–125, 169, 172–173, 175, 177, 195, 221–222n
  Chinese 50–51
  Japanese 50–51, 139, 158, 190, 193–158, 190, 193–194, 202

Marxism-Leninism 29, 158
Mass, Jeffrey P. 215n
material life, Braudel's conception of 165, 167
Mauss, Marcel 14, 67–69, 71, 74, 78, 145, 209n
Meiji period 4, 44, 133, 143, 171, 194–195
Meiji restoration/state/transformation 4, 28, 59–60, 112–114, 133–135, 137, 139, 142–143, 172, 176, 178, 180–183, 186–189
Mennell, Stephen 212n
merchant/commercial elites 121–122, 171–172, 179–180
Metzger, Thomas 35–36, 204n, 207–208n, 210n
Middle Ages, European 92–94, 96–99, 128–129
military counter-state/society 11, 17–18, 85, 90, 106–111, 130, 157
Ming dynasty 31
MITI 19
modernity 32, 50, 138–148
  Japanese 19, 44, 87–90
  compared to other patterns 138–148
  in civilizational perspective 148–151, 182, 187, 199–202
  multiple 141
  non-European 159
modernization 25–28, 32, 42–44, 60–61, 87, 169–170
  cognitivist conception of 138–141

Japanese, compared to other cases 132–138, 185–186
reflexive 140
Mongols 2, 47
Morishima, Michio 206n
Morris, Colin 214n
Morris-Suzuki, Tessa 210n
mura organization 201
Murakami, Yasusuke 126, 142, 187, 201, 219n, 222–224n
Muromachi period 204n
Muromachi regime s. shogunate

Naitō, Konan 19
Najita, Tetsuo 178, 180, 221–222n
Nara period 81, 103
Nathan, Andrew J. 211n
national identity/community 111–113, 155, 181–182
nationalism 147
  Japanese 19–23, 89, 143–144, 153, 158, 181–183, 185, 187, 190, 193–195, 202
  ultra-nationalism 114–115, 143–44, 193, 197
nation-state 160, 168
  in modern Japan 143–144, 181–183
  Japanese and Western origins 119–120
Nelson, Benjamin 72, 146, 209n
Netherlands 101
New Deal policies 194
Nobunaga s. Oda
Normans 96, 99, 101

Obolensky, Dimitri 64, 209n

Oda, Nobunaga 86, 109
Ōnin war 19
Ooms, Herman 212n, 215n, 217n
Opium war 25
Orientalism 222n
Osaka 122, 171, 178–179

Pacific War 26, 114, 183
Palais, James B. 52, 207n, 209n
Parsons, Talcott 7, 140–141, 208n, 219n
Peattie, Mark R. 223n
Pelletier, Philippe 83, 211n
Pempel, T.J. 195–199, 224n
Piggott, Joan 15–16, 82, 203–204n, 211n
Pollack, David 63, 209n, 211n
Pollock, Sheldon 203n
Poly, Jean-Pierre 214n
Pomeranz, Kenneth 173, 220–221n
Portugal 101
Protestantism/Protestant ethic 33–34, 44
Pye, Lucian 74, 203n
Qin dynasty 14
Raeff, Marc 214n
Rambelli, Fabio 204n
rangaku (Western learning) 90
Reformation 44
regime/regime analysis 195–199
Reynolds, Susan 216n
ritsuryō regime 16, 125–128, 170, 204n
Roberts, Luke S. 179, 222n
Roman Empire 50, 62–65, 94–95
  Holy 97

Roman law 95, 99
Rozman, Gilbert 55–59, 209n, 218n
Russia 26, 64, 100, 114, 133–134, 186, 188
Rustow, Dankwart 217n
Ryukyu Islands 45–46

sakoku (closed country) 113
Samuels, Richard J. 222n
samurai/warrior class 106–112, 124–131, 172
  bureaucrats 179
  compared to military elites in the West 118–119, 128–129, 131
  in Korea 129
  honour culture of 128–129
Sansom, George 16
Schifrin, Harold Z. 208n
Schluchter, Wolfgang 206n
Schwartz, Benjamin 74, 211n
Scotland 101
Schumpeter, Joseph 184, 194
Seifert, Wolfgang 224n
sengoku period 18–19, 108, 131
seventh-century transformation of Japan 2, 13–16, 79–83, 86, 104–105, 112, 118–119, 125, 157
Shang dynasty 76, 149
Shils, Edward 5–10, 36, 203n, 207n
shinkoku discourse 21–22
Shintō 22, 51, 211n
shi-nō-kō-shō system 111
shogunate 17–18, 21
  Kamakura 11, 21, 103, 106–107, 128–130
  Muromachi (Ashikaga) 17–18, 21, 86, 103, 108, 130, 156
  Tokugawa 60–61, 103, 119–124, 131–135, 156–157, 170–172, 174–180, 183, 185
Shōmu, Emperor 15
Shultz., Edward J. 129, 217n
Sicily 96–97, 99
Simmel, Georg 184
Singapore 29, 45
Smith, Anthony 20
Smith, Thomas C. 176, 221n
Smithian growth/Smithian dynamic 173–174
Soga family 104
Sombart, Werner 162
Song dynasty 31, 78, 86, 107
Southeast Asia 29, 41, 45, 115, 133, 204n
Souyri, Pierre 18–19, 204n
Soviet model s. Communism
Spain 97, 101
Spengler, Oswald 72
state and economy in modern Japan 142
state and society in modern Japan 142–143
state formation 92, 94, 102, 117–118, 130–131, 212–213
  autonomous and dependent 96–97, 102–104, 107–108, 110
  culture and 102
  endogenous and derivative 97–99, 102, 104, 107–111
  immanent and transformative 99–100, 102, 104–105, 107–112

in China 97, 107
in East Asia 98
in France and Germany, compared to Japan 110
in Inner Asia 98
in Japan 3, 15–19, 56, 103–113, 117–131, 182
in Korea 98, 129
in the West 93–102, 117–124, 130–131
primary and secondary 85, 94–96, 102–108, 110, 112
unitary and composite 100–102, 105–107, 110–111
state system
in East Asia 2, 81, 103, 113–116, 123–124
in Europe 95–96, 109, 123–124
within Japan 109–111, 123–124
Stover, Leon E. 219n
Sui dynasty 2, 15, 77
Sweden/Swedish corporatism 197
Switzerland 101
Systems theory 140–141

Tai, Hung-chao 207n
Taika reform 28
Taiping rebellion 26, 137, 146
Taira, Masakado 20
Taishō period 143, 160
Taiwan 24, 26–29, 31, 35, 36, 41, 136–138, 196
Takahashi, Kamekichi 190, 223n
Tamamoto, M. 216n
Taylorism 184
T'ang dynasty 2, 77, 80

Tanuma, Okitsugu 122
tenkō 223n
tennō system 3, 112
Thailand 133
Thatcher revolution 197
Tilly, Charles 212n
Toby, Ronald P. 216n
Tokugawa, Ieyasu 109
Tokugawa period 85, 89, 155, 174–180, 202.
regime s. shogunate
thought 89–90, 178–179, 221n
Tönnesson, Stein 212n
Tosa domain 79
totalitarianism 193, 195
Totman, Conrad 177, 216n, 221n
Touraine, Alain 7, 9
Toynbee, Arnold 72–73
Toyotomi, Hideyoshi 109
Tu, Wei-ming 38, 207–208n

United Kingdom 101
United States 135, 189, 194, 197, 219n
Uno school 158

Vandermeersch, Léon 35, 38, 148–152, 206–208n, 219n
Venice 171
Vietnam 29, 45–46, 204n
Vries P. H. H. 221n

Wakabayashi, Bob Tadashi 204n
Wakeman, Frederic 207n
Wallerstein, Immanuel 219n
Ward, Robert E. 217n
Washington consensus 159

Weber, Max 7–8, 31, 33–34, 39, 44, 54, 69–71, 120, 160–162, 166, 168, 221–222n
Weiss, Linda 223n
Western expansion 25–26, 30, 42, 48, 132–138, 146–147, 155, 171, 185
Westernization 25, 41, 88–89, 115, 132–138n, 148
White, James C. 216n
Wittfogel, Karl A. 222n
Wolferen, Karel van 216n
Wong, R. Bin 173, 220n
World War I 188
World War II 28, 159, 162, 194, 197

Yamamura, Kozo 175–176
Yamato state 15, 78, 103–104
Yin period 149
Young, Louise 189–190, 223n

Zhou dynasty 76